CROSSING PATHS

CROSSING PATHS

A Pacific Crest Trailside Reader

PATHS

Edited by Rees Hughes and Howard Shapiro

Illustrations by Amy Uyeki

MOUNTAINEERS
BOOKS

MOUNTAINEERS BOOKS is dedicated
to the exploration, preservation, and enjoyment
of outdoor and wilderness areas.

1001 SW Klickitat Way, Suite 201 • Seattle, WA 98134
800.553.4453 • www.mountaineersbooks.org

Printed in the United States of America
Distributed in the United Kingdom by Cordee, www.cordee.co.uk
25 24 23 22   1 2 3 4 5

Copyeditor: Chris Dodge
Design and layout: Heidi Smets
Cartographer: Martha Bostwick
Cover art and illustrations by Amy Uyeki

Library of Congress Cataloging-in-Publication data is on file for this title
at https://lccn.loc.gov/2021039974 and ebook record is available at
https://lccn.loc.gov/2021039975.

Mountaineers Books titles may be purchased for corporate, educational, or
other promotional sales, and our authors are available for a wide range of events.
For information on special discounts or booking an author, contact our customer
service at 800-553-4453 or mbooks@mountaineersbooks.org.

♻ Printed on recycled paper

ISBN (paperback): 978-1-68051-570-1
ISBN (ebook): 978-1-68051-571-8

An independent nonprofit publisher since 1960

To Jim "Salt Lick" Peacock, who for forty years has been as integral a part of my PCT experience as the trail itself. His willingness to continue to share our grand adventure despite living 3,000 miles away is a demonstration of friendship that very few would be willing to make. Thank you, brother.

—Rees Hughes

I would like to dedicate my small part of this book to my wife, Kathy, whose unwavering support makes all the difference in the world. From the very first spark of intention to develop this collection, she intimately understood the draw these stories and project had on me. Her many years of urging me on to complete the trail and her consistent encouragement to make this book a reality have been priceless gifts. I am, and will always be, eternally grateful for her love.

—Howard Shapiro

CONTENTS

SOUTHERN CALIFORNIA
LAND OF LITTLE RAIN

Covering California Section A—Section F
Campo · Warner Springs · San Gorgonio Pass · Cajon Pass ·
Agua Dulce · Tehachapi Pass · Walker Pass

SOUTHERN SIERRA
RANGE OF LIGHT

Covering California Section G—Section I
Walker Pass · Mount Whitney · John Muir Trail · Tuolumne Meadows ·
Sonora Pass

NORTHERN SIERRA
MOUNTAINS AND RIVERS WITHOUT END

Covering California Section J—Section M
Sonora Pass · Echo Lake · Donner Pass · Yuba River · Feather River Canyon · Belden

CASCADES AND THE KLAMATH KNOT
THE REALM OF FIRE

Covering California Section N—Section R
Belden · Feather River Canyon · Lassen Peak · Burney Falls · Castle Crags · Etna Summit · Seiad Valley · California Border

THE OREGON CASCADES
FORESTS FOREVER

Covering Oregon Section A—Section G

California Border · Fish Lake · Crater Lake · Cascade Crest · Willamette Pass · McKenzie Pass · Barlow Pass · Columbia River

THE COLUMBIA AND VOLCANIC WASHINGTON
LAVA, MOSS, AND LICHENS

Covering Washington Section H—Section I

Columbia River · Bridge of the Gods · White Pass · Mount Rainier · Snoqualmie Pass

THE NORTH CASCADES
THE GREAT WHITE NORTH

Covering Washington Section J—Section L
Snoqualmie Pass · Stevens Pass · Glacier Peak · Rainy Pass ·
Manning Provincial Pass

THE PACIFIC CREST TRAIL

Bellingham

Manning Park

CANADA

Harts Pass
Rainy Pass
Glacier Peak

Seattle

Stevens Pass

Snoqualmie Pass

WASHINGTON

Mount Rainier
Goat Rocks

IDAHO

Trout Lake

Mount Adams

Portland

Columbia River

Bridge of the Gods
Mount Hood

Three-Fingered Jack
Mount Jefferson

The Three Sisters

Bend

OREGON

Mount Thielsen
Crater Lake
Devil's Peak

Ashland

P a c i f i c   O c e a n

Seiad Valley

Etna
Mount Shasta

Castle Crags

Old Station

Lassen Peak
Feather River

halfway point

Sierra City

Donner Pass

Lake Tahoe

NEVADA

Echo Lake

Sonora Pass

Tuolumne Meadows

San Francisco

Mammoth Lakes

CALIFORNIA

Muir Pass
Forester Pass
Mount Whitney

Kennedy Meadows

Tehachapi Mountains

Walker Pass

Agua Dulce

Wrightwood

Mojave Desert

Big Bear City

Los Angeles

Warner Springs

Mount San Jacinto

Mount Laguna

San Diego

Campo

0   100 kilometers
0   100 miles

MEXICO

THE NEVER-ENDING STORY OF THE PACIFIC CREST TRAIL

When I was hired to lead the Pacific Crest Trail Association (PCTA) in 2001, I had no idea where the job would take me or whether it would last. The organization was small back then. I was one of three employees, and I shared a phone line in our small office with a fax machine and a credit card reader. We've certainly come a long way.

Even as I reflect on that modest beginning, I'm not surprised to be in my twentieth year leading the organization. I've walked much of the trail and have come to know it intimately, so I'm not surprised that it's kept my interest or that I still enjoy getting out there. I still feel like there are so many places to see, people to meet, and much to learn.

Knowing the people who care for the trail—volunteers, government employees, donors, trail lovers, and our dedicated PCTA staff—I'm not surprised by how much energy I get from the work we do together. There's so much passion behind this effort. That's why the last two decades often seem like a blur.

What do surprise me continually are the stories. This amazing trail that winds through three states, across sparse deserts, through dense forests, and up and down rugged mountains intersects with us in many different ways. The trail is certainly about place, but it's about us, the people who love and use the trail, even more. It's about our times in those places and what they mean to us. We find solace or build bonds of love and friendship. We discover humility, our physical limits, and what's most important to us. We connect with nature in meaningful ways. We rise above our troubles and differences and discover what matters most.

Each of us who has experienced the Pacific Crest Trail (PCT) or has a passion for the outdoors is a part of this ongoing story. The tales unfold season after season and generation after generation. We're all on the same path, traveling separately and together at the same time. We are writing our individual stories and building on the collective. The PCT connects us all.

Ten years after the original publication of the two volumes of *The Pacific Crest Trailside Reader*, this new anthology incorporates dozens of stories, many collected over the last decade and many written for this edition. A look at the long list of stories reminds me of how special our vast and diverse community is, how it continues to grow and change, and how it is shaping the trail and its future.

There are stories about place and about the trail community and the relationships forged along the path. There are stories about the wildlife one encounters, about the unselfish gifts of trail angels and the simple hard work of climbing a mountain pass or fording a rapidly running stream. The book includes the sad account of an accidental death of a young hiker, stories about the reality of the trail experience for Black and Indigenous people and other people of color, and stories about the increasing effect wildfires and our changing climate are having on the trail experience.

Love. Happiness. Humor. Hardship. Daring. Fear. Racism. Rescue. Music. Passion. Peace. They are all here, in these pages, in deeply personal accounts. That's what the trail is really about. Life and death. Especially life.

On it goes, inexplicably, twisting along a dirt path. Each of us intersects the trail in our own way. The trail's amazing power to connect us is inspiring. It breaks us down to the essentials and helps us see that we're all the same at heart as we celebrate the wild places, the intense experiences, and our glorious differences—creating stories for the ages that will never end.

—*Liz Bergeron, executive director,*
Pacific Crest Trail Association

INTRODUCTION

WHY THIS BOOK

In late 2011, Mountaineers Books published two anthologies, *The Pacific Crest Trailside Reader: California* and *The Pacific Crest Trailside Reader: Oregon and Washington*. About half of the nearly one hundred stories included in those books were written by hiker-writers regarding their contemporary PCT experience. The remainder were split between classic environmental literature (by authors such as Wallace Stegner, Barry Lopez, and Gary Snyder) and historical accounts about the area traversed by the PCT (such as "Winter on Donner Pass," "The Battle of Castle Crags," and "Triumph and Tragedy at Stevens Pass"). Since those books were published, we have managed a companion website—pcttrailsidereader .com—where hundreds of additional stories, poems, photos, art, commentary, and trail news have been posted.

Crossing Paths: A Pacific Crest Trailside Reader continues the tradition of telling stories from the trail. As long as people walk the PCT, there will be new tales to be told. We have also tried to include contributions that document the changing trail and comment on the way forward. It is our hope that these three books, and those that may follow, will serve as essential companions for all who love the PCT like we do.

We carefully considered hundreds of stories in the process of selecting and soliciting the sixty or so that fill *Crossing Paths*. Our goal was a representative collection capturing diverse experiences and relying on a variety of voices to tell the PCT story. We also felt that it was important to address the impact of a changing climate, growing numbers of trail users, and the influence of technology. There is humor, reflection, joy, sadness, amazement, and wonder to be found in these pages. The opportunity to curate this collection was as daunting as it was an honor, and we are confident that we missed what would have been some very good choices.

OUR PCT

As detailed in "Breaking the PCT Speed Record" (in this collection), we have a long friendship that began prior to our first experience on the PCT in 1981. For over forty years we have shared an intense interest in the

PCT, walking much of the trail together, often with our good friend, Jim Peacock. Over these years our interest in the trail has only grown. When we return to the trail, as we regularly do, we do so as pilgrims, using the time for reflection and reconnection with each other and with nature. We hope that the respect we have for the trail permeates this book. Ownership and responsibility for the PCT belongs to all of us. Indeed, it is *our* Pacific Crest Trail.

All who spend any length of time on the PCT come to appreciate the generosity of so many along the way: those who envisioned the trail, who planned and built and now maintain the trail, who give rides or host total strangers or provide trail magic. We have often experienced the unconditional support that has helped to define trail culture. In that light, it seems fitting that, as was done with *The Pacific Crest Trailside Reader: California* and *The Pacific Crest Trailside Reader: Oregon and Washington*, the royalties generated by this book will all go to support the trail through the work of the Pacific Crest Trail Association. We feel that this is the best way to honor our love for the PCT.

Every author of every story in this collection feels the same way we do and donated the use of their contribution, which heartens us and validates our goal of supporting the trail.

THE CHANGING TRAIL

Curating this anthology has given us an excellent opportunity to reflect on some of the changes that have occurred since the first volumes were published. And it has challenged us to consider the future of the PCT.

We wish to highlight three major areas of change impacting the trail over the past decade. These interrelated changes also influence our vision of the future of the PCT.

1. **Number of people using the trail.** In 2019, the PCTA issued nearly eight thousand long-distance PCT permits, a fourfold increase from 2013. This increase is also reflected in the number of people who report finishing the PCT. In 2011, when the first volumes were published, there were 158 recorded finishers. In 2019, that number was 963 (a sixfold increase). In an attempt to spread out the impact on the trail, efforts have been made to limit the number of NOBO (northbound) hikers beginning at Campo, the southern terminus, to 50 daily. The ADZPCTKO (Annual Day Zero PCT Kick Off) has been discontinued. Trail angels who have long been a fixture of the trail experience have

retired. It is difficult to imagine operations on the scale of Hiker Heaven and Casa de Luna and Scout and Frodo re-emerging (see Eric Smith's "Farewell to Angels" in this volume). And, of course, the number of hikers changes the trail experience. There are reasons to be concerned about the impact on fragile alpine and desert ecosystems, the overuse of popular campsites, and the increasing problem of human waste disposal. All reinforce the continued emphasis on leaving no trace (LNT).

The numbers are growing, and the demographics are changing. The annual PCT survey reported in the *Halfway Anywhere* blog shows a change in the composition of long-distance hikers on the PCT. The increase in women and international hikers is most apparent. There remains a concerning under-representation of BIPOC hikers (see Crystal Gail Welcome's story "Cleansing Dirt" in this volume to gain insight into the special challenges facing a person of color on the PCT). Based on a more informal assessment, there are many more hikers who begin walking the trail with less outdoors experience than in years past. Many of these hikers rely more heavily on technology and less on firsthand backpacking knowledge to tackle the trail.

2. **Technology.** Nearly everything that we put in our backpacks has been affected by technology. There are new strong, lightweight fabrics used in clothing, tents, and the packs themselves. There are smartphones that serve as cameras, maps, guidebooks (using apps like Guthook), and mobile entertainment consoles, powered by uber-efficient solar chargers. Water purification technology, stoves, headlamps, and even food have all been transformed. Alice Tulloch's and Jack Haskel's contributions to this anthology explore this topic in some detail. Unfortunately, one of the consequences is that outfitting oneself can be very expensive, limiting trail access to those who can afford the high cost of equipment.

3. **Climate change.** Fire seasons have been starting earlier and ending later, the fires have been immense and intense, and the droughts have been more severe. Over the past decade, it has increasingly been a rare year when hikers have not been rerouted around a fire closure.

Here are two images that represent the impact of climate change on the trail. After walking the PCT through the beautiful forests along the Transverse Ranges about five months before the Station Fire (2009) decimated the landscape all of the way to Messenger Flats, we returned nine years later to find that these magnificent forests were returning as permanent chaparral. There is a similar pattern occurring west of

Big Bear and east of Deep Creek and elsewhere along the Southern California PCT.

The second image is of that of the forests south of Cottonwood Pass all of the way to Walker Pass. The severe drought of the past decade has weakened so many trees that pests and disease have ravaged the forest in that region. It was challenging to find a completely healthy tree.

We have included Mark Larabee's reflections on the expanding impact of fire along the trail and a glimpse into the trail six decades from now in "A Future Filled with Gratitude."

THE FUTURE OF THE PCT

There are many challenges facing the PCT. At a minimum, maintaining a fragile path that transits rugged terrain blasted by severe weather and used by tens of thousands of hikers is no small achievement. Factor in the vagaries of climate change, with greater extremes of heat, drought, rain, and snow. It is highly speculative to read the tea leaves, but our look forward suggests that there will be:

» **Increasing efforts to limit and spread out those using the PCT.** While the permit system is currently voluntary, we predict that there will be an increasing effort to give permits teeth. What we see now in Yosemite, near Mount Whitney, and along the John Muir Trail will be extended to other high-impact and sensitive areas. Oregon has instituted some restrictions in the Jefferson Park area. There also will be an increase in efforts to develop awareness of the "leave no trace" philosophy, discourage campfires, and reduce lakeside and streamside camping.

» **Increasing desertification, fires, and changes to the hiking season.** It is sad to see the current trend toward hotter and drier summers that start earlier and last longer. We anticipate that there will be more and more hikers beginning in March or even February. We also think that there will be more people who section-hike over several years, avoiding the peak of the fire season.

» **Encroaching development.** Despite the wonderful successes of the PCTA to secure some of the 10 percent of the PCT still in private hands (see Megan Wargo's sidebar "Protecting the PCT One Parcel at a Time"), there will be constant pressure on particular parts of the trail from development. Protected somewhat by the general recognition of the value of the PCT as a global treasure, the trail charts a path through a thin veneer of wilderness in places like Anza, Big Bear, the Tejon Pass area, Agua Dulce, Green Valley, the Burney area, and Snoqualmie Pass.

The threats take many forms—logging, urban sprawl, ski resort growth, and wind farms, to note a few. But there will be some good news too. The Tejon Ranch reroute should be completed in the next decade.

» **Changes in trail culture.** We believe that we can extend some aspects of Appalachian Trail culture to imagine what the Pacific Crest Trail culture will look like in the years to come. We think that the PCT will become increasingly social (although if you want the quiet experience of immersion in nature, you will still be able to find that). Trail angel endeavors like Hiker Heaven and Casa de Luna will be replaced by for-profit hostels. As there are more hikers, there will be more trail infrastructure development at particular nodes along the way. We also predict that there will be growth in the number of southbound thru hikers.

» **Even more pervasive influence of technology.** Although there will be a stalwart community of hikers committed to "the Old Way," there is no stopping technology. It will continue to impact all aspects of trail life. It will be easier and easier to communicate by phone from virtually anywhere along the trail. SPOT devices will go the way of the typewriter.

» **Increasingly large numbers of relatively inexperienced hikers.** Enabled by technology and supportive infrastructure, inexperienced hikers will continue to be attracted to the PCT in growing numbers. When that reality is combined with earlier starts and the increasing likelihood of extreme weather events ("global weirding" as Thomas Freidman characterizes global warming), there will be plenty of exhilarating survival stories for the twentieth anniversary edition of *The Pacific Crest Trailside Reader.*

Despite these changes and those we cannot foresee, the PCT and the trail experience will remain. As noted in the sidebar "A Short Interview with Barney "Scout" Mann," "We are tempted to lament the death of the PCT. 'Oh, if I had only hiked the trail twenty years ago.' But, the PCT will always be an iconic experience. It will still be a wilderness experience."

READING THIS BOOK

While basic knowledge of the Pacific Crest Trail may enhance the appreciation for some of the detail in many of these stories, it is not a prerequisite for enjoying this book. The stories are accessible to the armchair traveler and wonderfully familiar to the seasoned PCT veteran. Although these stories are organized parallel to the geographic sections of the PCT beginning near the southern border and moving north, each story stands alone and does not need to be read in order. Unlike a hiker, you can easily skip ahead, moving across regions. But like the trail itself, there is always something new just around the bend or over the next rise.

Among the stories in this book, interspersed with poems, are tales of survival, courage, and challenge as hikers confront rain, snow, lightning, river crossings, and more. Struggle with Philippe Gouvet as he navigates an early season snowstorm in Southern California's Lagunas, or feel the penetrating cold as Natalie Fisher races to the Canadian border on a wintry final stretch. Share David Smart's efforts to cope with long days of discouraging rain, or accompany Gail Storey as she battles her fears to cross raging Sierra rivers. Join Mark Collins as he desperately seeks shelter under meager whitebark pine krummholz near tree line, or hold your breath with Heather Anderson as she confronts a mountain lion at night. And feel the anguish of a father's loss as you read Doug Laher's heart-wrenching homage to his son who tragically fell to his death in the San Jacintos.

Read stories that explore trail culture, the changing trail experience, technology, and climate change. Enjoy Barney Mann's tutorial on trail names, Rachel Newkirk's perspective on trail angels' giving and receiving, Glenn William Jolley's sweet story about trail magic, and Claire Henley's account of meeting—and marrying—Caleb Miller. Vicariously experience the stories of the youngest hikers and some of the oldest hikers on the PCT, Shawn Forry's winter thru hike with Justin Lichter, and concert cellist Mark Votapek's twenty-seven performances along the trail. And read (or reread) an excerpt from Cheryl Strayed's *Wild*, a book with a profound impact on the PCT. These stories are so varied that you will soon find yourself pulled along the trail.

Crossing Paths reflects the connections we make on the Pacific Crest Trail. It represents the intermingling of thru hikers, section hikers, and day hikers on the trail and their diversity of perspective and backgrounds. It captures the connections contemporary hikers make with those instrumental in the creation and the preservation of the PCT. And it reminds us that we share the wilderness and the trail with the animals and plants we encounter along the way. This idea of crossing paths even touches on the way this book and its timeless stories link with those in the two-volume *Pacific Crest Trailside Reader* published in 2011.

Begin your journey on the next page.

PACIFIC CREST TRAIL PIONEERS

BILL ROBERTS AND PEGGY GOSHGARIAN

The year 2018 marked the fiftieth anniversary of the National Trails Act. Commemorating the legislation that birthed an expanding system of national scenic, historic, and recreation trails including the Pacific Crest Trail, Bill Roberts and Peggy Goshgarian wrote this poem acknowledging PCT pioneers. Bill and Peggy have an intimate knowledge of the PCT, and Bill has run pack trains near Seiad Valley since 1971 in support of the trail. In this poem honoring those whose dreams became reality through determination, perseverance, and imagination, they remind us that the trail from Mexico to Canada represents a collective spirit and was created piece by piece and step by step over many years.

> *It started as a vision*
> *In the minds of just a few,*
> *But over time it came alive*
> *And blossomed, then it grew.*
>
> *He was horseback-herding cattle*
> *On the valley floor*
> *As he gazed upon the distant peaks*
> *In eighteen eighty-four:*
>
> *Theodore Solomons, just thirteen,*
> *Saw the white Sierra Range.*
> *The mountaintops called out to him,*
> *And, though it may seem strange,*

It became his mission
To walk past every hill and dale
Near lakes and streams and meadowlands
Along a mountain trail.

He made three trips
Between eighteen ninety-two and ninety-five
And blazed a trail through the mountains.
It was good to be alive.

On his first trip he took Whitney,
His camera-packing mule,
To photograph the scenery
Where every lake's a jewel.

He made notes, drew maps, took photographs
Of everything he saw,
Naming lakes and peaks and valleys
Beautiful. He was in awe.

He'd found a route and laid it out.
His report had said it all.
He'd poured his heart and soul in it
Every spring, summer, and fall.

The state got behind the plan.
The money Gods were kind.
John Muir had passed, they named it fast
For the man with the mountain mind.

Fifty-four years since seeing those peaks
Shining in the sun,
The vision of a thirteen-year-old,
The John Muir Trail was done.

But that was just the start.
There were more lakes and streams
On the Pacific mountain crest
In other people's dreams.

Working for the Forest Service
Fred Cleator had begun
An influential career
In Oregon and Washington.

He was assigned to make a road
In nineteen twenty, lay out the route
Through the Oregon Cascades,
But he began to have some doubt.

To cut a road up on the crest
Through wilderness so rare
His team felt would be a shame
A thought they couldn't bear.

A diamond shape to mark the route,
Five hundred signs were made.
The Oregon Skyline Trail would rise,
Two hundred seventy miles of Oregon Cascade.

You can see those signs today
From Mount Hood to Crater Lake,
And be thankful it's a meandering trail
Winding slowly like a snake.

But Cleator had a vision
Of what else the trail could be
North through Canada to Alaska
South to Mexico for all to see.

Later in the summer
A grand idea was born.
To extend the Skyline Trail
Another West Coast trail was worn.

Four hundred fifty more miles,
In ten more years, no less,
Completed the Washington section
We call the Cascade Crest.

While up in Bellingham, Washington,
In nineteen twenty-six
Catherine Montgomery's love of tramping
The PCT she does predict.

Promoted by the mountain clubs
Of the Pacific Northwest
To mimic the Appalachian Trail
At Catherine's behest.

She said on a high, winding trail
Of our western mountains we'll go
From the border with Canada
Down below to Mexico.

The Father of the PCT
Is how he came to be known.
He arrived in California
To start a life of his own.

Clinton C. Clark had lots of energy
And maybe a buck or two.
He joined the Sierra Club
And became part of the crew.

He met the lofty mountain range
On some Sierra Club trips,
Was active in the Boy Scouts,
And took photographic pics.

He had a favorite typewriter
That he liked to use.
He wasn't sure who to write to
But he had some thoughtful clues.

He proposed to the National Park and Forest Service
The idea of a trail
From Canada to Mexico.
With his drive it couldn't fail.

The project was approved.
They wanted him to run the show
So he got out his trusty typewriter
And then they watched him go.

He hand-typed a thousand letters
To those he thought might care,
Compiled maps and information
Sent in from everywhere,

But there were no funds that came along.
The Great Depression was in force.
There was nothing else to do
So he used his own money, of course.

The PCT Conference
Was the organization of the day,
Also the predecessor
Of our own PCTA.

The Sierra Club got involved
To get the conference going,
And the idea of a relay
Got the interest really flowing.

Warren Rogers from the YMCA
Was the conference executive secretary,
But when the relay bogged down
He did just what was necessary.

He became the dedicated guide
To get the logbook through.
Four summers and forty teams,
That's what he would do.

I met Warren Rodgers
In nineteen seventy-one
At the café here in Seiad
My work had just begun.

A tall and friendly man,
Enthusiastic, I would say,
And passionate about the trail.
I also felt that way.

He talked about the relay
And the YMCA boys,
How he helped the lads along,
The hardships and the joys.

He spoke of how the trail was pieced together
From the other trails around
Where the Cascade Crest and Skyline
And the John Muir Trails were found.

I'd started building trails and bridges,
Blasting rock out of the way,
Packing mules and horses
Until my hair turned gray.

Warren Rogers kept the trail alive,
Inspiring countless youth along the way.
I am so glad he touched my life.
I still feel that way today.

SOUTHERN CALIFORNIA LAND OF LITTLE RAIN

COVERING CALIFORNIA
SECTION A–SECTION F

Campo • Warner Springs • San Gorgonio Pass •
Cajon Pass • Agua Dulce • Tehachapi Pass •
Walker Pass

I LOVED THE DESERT THE BEST

CARROT QUINN

How best to begin this anthology? Every memoir penned by north-bound (NOBO) thru hikers invariably spends a chapter beginning with the obligatory embrace of the monument marking the southern border and ending with the welcome descent twenty miles later to Lake Morena County Park. That day often feels like an epic introduction to the PCT, complete with views, snakes, thirst, and exhaustion. However, we liked Carrot Quinn's perspective on the six hundred miles of the arid south-ern quarter of the PCT written from near the north end of the trail. It was not written in the heat and filtered by the awe of those first days but with the wisdom that comes after experiencing the length of the trail.

I am sitting on the Stehekin shuttle bus in the early morning, bumping down the pitted road along Lake Chelan, when the question comes up behind me.

"What part of the trail was your favorite?" says a hiker in polar fleece.

"The Sierra," says his companion.

"And what was your least favorite?"

"The desert."

I bite into the bacon-and-cheddar-stuffed croissant that I am clutch-ing, and flakes of pastry fall into my lap. I also have two pieces of pizza, a chocolate cookie, and a giant cinnamon roll, all safe in a greasy paper bag stuffed into the top of my pack. We are eighty trail miles from the Canadian border, and we have just been to the bakery, the Stehekin Bakery, to be exact. I usually do not eat gluten, but I ran out of food in the last section in a major way—fifty miles on 1,500 calories—and I almost blacked out from hunger. One of the things that kept me going in those dark days was the knowledge of this bakery, where piping hot blackberry pies sit cooling on glass countertops and beautiful, rosy-cheeked young people pull golden trays of cinnamon rolls from the oven. Now I am eating this dense beast of a croissant as we bump our way back to the trail, thinking about what the hikers behind me have said.

"I loved the desert the best," I say, turning to face them. They glance at me, frowning, and continue their conversation.

It's true. I think about this while I stare out the window at the lake, the bacon-and-cheddar monstrosity slowly disappearing into my stomach, where it will become glue. I can feel the gluten fog descending already, like a ghost. I think of the desert, and I imagine the soft sand, the extravagant spread of the Milky Way, the thorny little plants, the temperamental nature of the wind. And the hot sun at midday, hot enough and bright enough that if you stayed out in it long enough it might vaporize you. Like Mars. Or Venus, as a hiker once corrected me.

The Kelso Valley Road cache, where there is no shade, just a mound of plastic water jugs glittering in the sun. Where MeHap and I sat against the wire fence, our sleeping pads pulled over our heads to make a sort of awning, and fed ourselves melted peanut M&Ms. And then Spark and Instigate and NoDay arrived, and we charged up the hill to the single, solitary Joshua tree, with its ever-shifting poles of shade. We sat half in and half out of this shade, sweating profusely in the bleary heat, until several hours had passed, at which time it was still hot. Thankfully there was another Joshua tree in a mile and we collapsed there again, until dusk.

Cowboy camping in the desert. The warm sand, releasing the heat of the day, and the night sky, in which every single star, every single other planet and possible far-away reality could be seen. All of it, all of space and time and possibility, the future, the past and the present, twinkling obligingly and singing its song of eternal, never-ending magic. Just up there, twinkling. All for me, in my sleeping bag on the warm sand, a little breeze crinkling my ground sheet, my shoes lined up next to my head. I'll check those for scorpions in the morning. Remembering the *Far Side* comics of my youth, which formed my most basic ideas about cowboy camping in the desert. Men in cowboy hats in neat square bed-rolls, big rattlesnakes curled up on their laps.

Rattlesnakes. Rattlesnakes everywhere. Rattlesnakes stretched across the trail, lounging. Almost tripping over big, fat rattlesnakes, catching myself at the last moment. Rattlesnakes slithering away. Always there were rattlesnakes, slithering away. Under every bush. After a while I was no longer afraid of them; they became like a reassurance to me. Rattlesnakes exist. Rattlesnakes exist, therefore I am.

Water. Water in hot gallon jugs, water in troughs that wriggled with little white worms. Water from campground spigots, from hotel bathrooms, from springs labeled "Danger! Uranium!" and with contradictory reviews in the water report. "Best water I ever had!" "DO NOT drink this water!" Before I started the trail I was the sort of person who carried a big steel water bottle everywhere I went and sipped on it nervously. *What if I'm dehydrated?* I would think. *What if I'm dehydrated, like, right now?* Then I ran out of water right before the fourteen-mile descent off the San Jacintos, and when I reached the maddening drinking fountain at the bottom I was still alive. Well, how about that? Soon stretching the distance between water sources became almost as thrilling as it was frightening— can I make it five more miles? Ten more? Fifteen? Even so, I was never as good at this game as my hiking partners, who were shocking in their disregard for hydration. After the desert, Spark never carried water at all. "It's heavy," he said.

The wind. The air was like a living thing that moved all around you. The smell of the chaparral, the dystopic burns that rang with the sounds of chewing insects and smeared your arms with charcoal. The windstorm before Mojave, where I was alone on the mountain, breathless, my nostrils smashed against my face, struggling to stay upright. *Just blow me off the mountain,* I thought. *Just blow me right off the mountain.* In the valley below they had rerouted the highway, and when I reached the Motel 6 in Mojave after dark I slammed the door against the wind and sat in the shower under the hot water for a very long time.

The Mojave. The Joshua trees against the stormy sky, the slowly churning windmills, the bleak plots of land with rusting trailers that reminded me of scenes from *Breaking Bad.* Hiker Town, with its strange shacks filled with cats, where I ate a giant salad and replenished my dwindling food stores with Trader Joe's oatmeal cookies from the hiker box.

And the people. There was all of this, and then there were the people. A gaggle of us gathered around the water trough in a bit of dappled shade, our shoes and clothing bright, staring at each other thinking, *Can we do this? Are we really going to do this? Walk this whole way, over all this convoluted earth, rise to meet all of these obstacles?* Passing around a ziplocked bag of melted gummy bears, saying "Touch it, touch it." Laughing until we could not breathe, gasping for air, our voices filling up the empty desert with its rattlesnakes and resident cougars, rising up to the night sky and the Milky Way, everything that is possible and not possible swirling around above us, forever and ever and ever.

From *Thru-Hiking Will Break Your Heart: An Adventure on the Pacific Crest Trail*, by Carrot Quinn (self-published, 2015). Reprinted with permission of the author.

TRAIL NAMES

BARNEY "SCOUT" MANN

Barney has done such a wonderful job of explaining the concept of "trail names" that we decided his story requires no additional introduction. We couldn't resist a postscript, however.

Whether they hike the 2,650-mile Pacific Crest Trail, the 2,180-mile Appalachian Trail, or the 3,100-mile Continental Divide Trail, nearly every thru hiker ends up with a trail name. It's emblematic of the separate reality of a long trail, and most hikers wear theirs like a badge. If Sandy [Barney's wife and frequent hiking companion] had picked one herself, she'd be Intrepid or Dauntless. But trail names are bestowed, not chosen, often for something unique, smart, or just plain dumb that a hiker does. Few of the hikers we met in those first miles had a trail name of their own, but it didn't take long for them to acquire one.

Mark had a shock of wavy brown hair and intense brown eyes, incongruous with his bantam-weightlifter's build. He was the first chair cellist for the Honolulu Symphony Orchestra. Early on, sitting with others during a trail break, he mused, "Wouldn't it be awful if you ended up with a trail name like . . . Cuddles?" The name stuck.

Lauren was a cross-country runner, fresh out of college. Every day on the trail, she had a moment when she felt, *This is the best day of my life.* Worried about hitching rides into small trail towns to pick up supplies, she concocted a plan with Coyote, a Canadian hiker closing in on sixty. He would lie down on the side of the road and pretend to be ill while she frantically waved down the first vehicle to approach, asking for help for her "grandfather." "You're Gazelle," Coyote offered up, "because you're speedy, agile, and thin of leg."

At six foot four, Max had a shaved head and a long, purple hiking shirt. On his thirteenth day on the PCT, he lost the trail at low-lying San Gorgonio Pass. After the seven-thousand-vertical-foot switchback descent from Mount San Jacinto's ponderosa pines to swirling sand and cacti, he reached Interstate 10. Knowing the trail had to be on the other side, he ran across all eight lanes of the busy artery between Los Angeles and Palm Springs. "Freeway" became his own legend.

Sandy loved the concept of trail names, but she got huffy about gender-confusing ones. "How can Cucumber Boy be a girl? How can Hot Sister be a guy?" Don't talk to her about Girl Scout. She had avidly read Girl Scout's online journal for weeks before discovering "she" was a "he."

Nine months ago, the idea of commissioning a custom ring for Sandy had popped into my head. Cast from platinum and gold, it would commemorate our planned PCT thru hike and our thirtieth wedding anniversary. Front and center would be the PCT trail emblem, with a single tree set against a mountain silhouette. A recessed channel would have four trail icons in bas-relief—the southern border monument, then California's Mount Shasta and Oregon's Mount Hood, and, last, the northern monument. I gave her the ring in Campo, weeks before our anniversary, to mark the start of our hike. Both of us cried.

Maybe I should have known. *The Lord of the Rings* movies were still popular, and I had given her "the one ring" at the start of a quest to far places with great unknowns. Within hours of arriving at Kickoff, some of the hikers we had hosted surrounded Sandy in what felt like a coronation. "We know your trail name!" they cried. The shouts echoed over her. "You are Frodo."

"Noooo," she protested, "Frodo's a GUY."

To this day she's Frodo.

My parents named me Bernard, but everyone has always called me Barney. To my trail community I am simply Scout.

From *Journeys North: The Pacific Crest Trail*, by Barney Scout Mann (Mountaineers Books, 2020). Reprinted by permission of the publisher.

As Scout (Barney Mann) notes, there are almost as many trail names as there are PCT hikers, and those names are generally given by others. I concluded that trail names should not be bestowed on others in the first five hundred miles of thru hiking because, all too often, those monikers have very little to do with the basic character of the hiker. This is how trail names like Short Shorts, Dog Piss, Boots, and Baby Lungs curse hikers.

I encountered a hiker several years ago who introduced himself as Ugliest Cheerleader. I groaned and began to launch into my diatribe about not being given a trail name for the first five hundred miles. Thinking that he would appreciate my commiseration, I was surprised when the hiker smiled and said that he liked the name and thought that it fit. He shared this backstory. Some years before, he had been leaving the Andersons and Casa de Luna and was lamenting about how slow a hiker he was. Kushy, a guy helping at the Andersons, would have none of this self-pity. "It is like," he observed, "being the ugliest Dallas Cowboys cheerleader. You are still a Dallas Cowboys cheerleader."

While I am not a big fan of the Dallas Cowboys or cheerleaders or the Dallas Cowboy cheerleaders, I loved his point. You may be the slowest hiker on the trail (someone has to be the slowest), but you are still out hiking the PCT. I now like his trail name too.

—RH

A SHORT INTERVIEW WITH BARNEY "SCOUT" MANN

Barney Mann has been a devoted and effective advocate on behalf of the PCT for many years. In addition to hiking the length of the trail, Barney was elected to the board of the PCTA and served in that role for nine years (including three as chair). At the time of this writing he was serving as the president of the Partnership for the National Trails System (an organization that supports all of the national scenic and historic trails). In addition Barney and his wife, Sandy, have been devoted trail angels, hosting some six thousand PCT hikers over the course of many years. We feel that he has an invaluable perspective on the changes impacting the trail we love and its future.

Rees Hughes (RH): The PCT has been discovered and risks being loved to death. Since your 2007 thru hike, the numbers of hikers have climbed exponentially. What does the future of the PCT look like? How do you see the sheer numbers of people on the trail impacting the PCT experience?

Barney Mann (BM): Let me first talk about the cause of the increase. I believe that the recession of 2008 resulted in a number of people deciding that spending a season walking the PCT was far better than being unemployed. I also feel that there was a very positive feedback loop about the PCT experience that was occurring. Hikers would tell others about their positive experience. So when *Wild* was published in 2012, the PCT was already primed to take off. The numbers accelerated from arithmetic growth to exponential growth post-*Wild*.

We are tempted to lament the death of the PCT. "Oh, if I had only hiked the trail 20 years ago." But, the PCT will always be an iconic experience. It will still be a wilderness experience. Although we don't really know what the carrying capacity of the PCT is, based upon a recent north-to-south section hike I took during the peak of thru-hiker traffic, it still did not feel overly crowded.

It seems to me that the permit system has largely worked. One day in 2014, I remember, two hundred started, and another hundred [started] the next [day]. That kind of bolus no longer happens.

RH: Are there other threats to the PCT that should be of concern?

BM: There are three issues I want to emphasize:

The trail can disappear overnight. A severe weather event like the storm that decimated the trail around Glacier Peak. A fire like the one that occurred in the San Jacintos. And sections of the trail easily become overgrown. We rely upon volunteers to maintain so much of the trail.

Still nearly one in every ten miles of the PCT is in private hands. The recent Great American Outdoors Act passed by Congress includes money for land and easement acquisition.

Development encroaches on the trail. Homes, power lines, ski resorts are a continuous challenge. Thank goodness the PCTA staff keeps a watchful eye on such issues and works to mitigate the impact of development.

Much of the magic of the PCT is that it is continuous. It can never be allowed to be broken.

RH: Is the PCT attracting a different kind of hiker these days?

BM: The typical PCT hiker these days starts with less outdoors and back-packing experience than thru hikers used to have. For example, I estimate that something like three quarters of those thru-hiking the CDT [Continental Divide Trail] finish it. And it used to be that perhaps half of the PCT thru hikers and a quarter of the AT [Appalachian Trail] thru hikers finished those trails. It is not because the CDT is an easier trail, it is because those that walk it tend to be seasoned hikers. I would guess these days 20 to 25 percent of the thru hikers that begin the PCT finish. They just have less experience.

There has been a big increase in international participation. Of the hundreds of people we have whose first stop is our home, I would estimate that 30 to 35 percent are from other countries. Germany sent over a TV crew and produced a special on the PCT shown in Germany, and we saw an impact after that show aired. Same with a special in South Korea. And there are more women and more couples on the trail. Regrettably, only a small increase in hikers of color.

RH: You and Sandy are calling it quits after hosting and helping thousands of hikers. The Andersons and the Saufleys have done the same. How is trail angeling changing?

BM: On the AT, when I hiked it in 2017, there were no trail angels similar to us or the Andersons or the Saufleys. If you felt passionately about helping people on the trail [the AT], you opened a hostel and ran it as a business. The numbers are big enough to justify that. There was a hostel at Big Bear for several years but no longer. Maybe that will be the future.

We have loved doing it, but we [recently] had our first grandkid, and it is time to focus on our own bucket list and health.

RH: What is the best way for hikers to give back to the trail?

BM: 1. Belong to the PCTA. Numbers matter!

2. Volunteer.

3. Belong to the Partnership for the National Trail System.

UNE PROMENADE DE SANTÉ

PHILIPPE GOUVET

As observed in the interview with Barney Mann, increasingly the PCT has attracted an international crowd. In 2019, long-distance hikers came from forty-seven countries and territories, and according to the 2019 annual PCT survey reported by Halfway Anywhere, of the 846 hikers who participated, one-third were from countries outside of the United States. PCT memoirs have been published in such languages as Korean, French, Dutch, and German. There is global recognition that the PCT offers an unparalleled wilderness experience that combines trail quality, spectacular scenery, relative safety balanced with challenge and unbroken length. It has no equal anywhere else in the world.

Frenchman Philippe Gouvet's introduction to inclement weather in the desert is not unique. The Lagunas rise to six thousand feet and are often buffeted by strong winds and capture moisture off the Pacific Ocean. In our own experience, we have been blasted by bone-chilling wind and rain once, and on a second passage were enveloped in a cold fog that rested along the mountaintop. As Philippe concludes, "Southern California desert, you said?"

I hate those American weather forecast guys. Their reliability and accuracy is mind-boggling. Their forecast called for warm weather until today. Well, this I can confirm: the first couple of days walking to Lake Morena were stiflingly hot, a blast furnace for this French thru hiker rookie not used to desert hiking. And a bad nighttime storm, with rain and snow, was predicted. Until 6:00 p.m. we had bright blue sunny skies and more sweltering temperatures at the Lake Morena campground. I was starting to speak about that forecast derisively, the way I would while watching French TV. But at the very instant the sun went overboard behind Morena Butte, the temperature abruptly fell, the wind rose, and a first cloud sailed in. I was shivering, and by six thirty I was already lying in my sleeping bag trying to fight away the cold.

And guess what happened? During the night a violent downpour drenched our camp. Yet I was lucky. At least I could keep dry under my tent. Some of my companions had less fortunate fates, with their sometimes sketchy tarps, hammocks, and bivy sacks. At dawn, in the cold rain, the main issue was to pack up while keeping my gear dry, in a tiny, very wet tent. I did my best and ran to the shower block to reorganize and attempt to dry my soaking tent.

In hindsight, I realize that was the moment when things started going wrong. I spent far too long carefully packing and I wasn't on my way until late. The accepted wisdom is to take it easy during the first weeks of a thru hike, not to push too hard, to avoid getting injured. Yet, at Lake Morena I was contemplating a very long hiking day to get to Mount Laguna, twenty-three wet, cold miles away. That is a lot on a third day. In Mount Laguna a motel beckoned, and a shower and laundry, and a hot dinner and warm bed. Mount Laguna is in the mountains, as the name suggests, far, far from Lake Morena's desert landscape. This is the reason most thru hikers split that stage in two and spend the night in Fred Canyon.

Yet some of the hikers were thinking of pushing it to Mount Laguna to get away from the nasty weather. In such appalling weather, with a soaking wet tent, you would be hard put to fantasize about a night in Fred Canyon.

I hadn't made up my mind yet. I was tired, and my pack was way too heavy, but thinking of a night under a wet tent in the rain was not particularly exciting. I gulped down a cereal bar and was on my way in heavy, cold rain.

For the first few hours, I felt good. I was able to hike efficiently on that pink quartz sand trail, between two blooming hedges. But then my GPS batteries started playing tricks on me. By midday, I realized they were dead, and the data my GPS had supposedly recorded were obviously wrong. Most importantly, the distance I had hiked. My morale collapsed. I was dumbfounded. I thought I had hiked a decent number of miles, but my GPS disagreed. Or did I try to convince myself the GPS was wrong? And the weather was so bad I didn't feel like getting Halfmile's maps out and doing the math.

Keep hiking, that was all I could do. The weather had deteriorated further. A polar wind was blowing rain across that steep ascent toward the Lagunas, and I was freezing. Okay, I can imagine that reading this in

a comfy armchair you will wonder why I didn't stop to put on more clothing. Well, because I was too cold, because it was raining, because I hadn't
much in the way of winter clothing, because I would have had to stop, take
off my backpack, and undress to put on new layers. You're apt to think you
will eventually get warm if you hike hard enough. No, you won't. I was
getting colder and colder.

In the afternoon I eventually reached Fred Canyon, where I could have
called it a day. Soaked, muddy, gloomy. Leaden skies in the persistent
mist. What should I do? I refilled my bladder, no shortage of water for
sure. I had one more look at my GPS. It told me Mount Laguna was 6.8
miles away. Now that was good news. I hadn't expected the lodge to be so
close. That was wrong—the GPS had gone berserk, as far as recording
distances was concerned—but I didn't realize it. Or my brain had frozen
and stopped me from reasoning soundly. I didn't feel like putting up a
wet tent. The thought of a warm motel bed suddenly felt heavenly to me.
Okay, let's go for it!

For the next few more hours, it was a roller coaster of emotions. My
attitude improved when the trail wasn't too steep, but then it collapsed
whenever the trail shot upward or I got a distant cloudy glimpse of a
tree-covered mountain that looked like the pictures I had seen of Mount
Laguna. No, it couldn't be! It was much too far away! But I had no choice.
Laguna or bust. Shrouded in the mist, I couldn't see much. Maybe that
was better for my morale. I began looking for boulders to lean on for a few
seconds' rest, shivering, trying to catch my breath. Once, twice, a dozen
times, but never for too long, because my muscles would tighten and the
diminishing light reminded me night was near.

Lo and behold, in spite of my pathetic struggle to keep moving, night
fell before I could confirm where I was. I had reached a mountain, I was
among trees, but the lodge was elusive. That wet, cold, muddy, foggy hike
seemed endless. My temperamental GPS seemed positive I was beyond
Mount Laguna Lodge, a somewhat puzzling and depressing thought. I was
in the midst of a dark forest (that was the good news: I must be getting
closer) and could hardly discern the thin ribbon of a trail.

Okay, time to get my headlamp out. I was about to lose the trail completely. I removed my pack, found the headlamp, turned it on. (Please,
please, I need the batteries to hold on!) I was shivering and shaking and
now surrounded by utter darkness. To further complicate matters, what
had been rain at lower elevations was snow here.

In sum, I was in snow, in an unfamiliar pitch-black forest, on a moon-less foggy night, and I had no idea whatsoever where I was. Where was that damned lodge, for heaven's sake?

What I didn't expect, because I hadn't looked at my maps—courtesy of the appalling weather—was that the PCT did not pass Mount Laguna Lodge. To get there, you had to leave the trail to reach a paved road and follow it. But when you are shivering in the dark on a foggy night, how on earth can you find that damned exit trail to the road? I was obviously somewhat hypothermic. I couldn't stop shaking.

I tried not to be overwhelmed by the situation. My body wouldn't get to be the one in charge. I had to make the right decisions. I asked the GPS for a bearing to get to the road. Great! I was supposed to climb cross-country up a steep snow-covered forested slope. In complete darkness. Another option, please? No, sorry, you are in serious trouble and no one will come to the rescue. I started climbing slowly and painfully through undergrowth and downed trees, unsure if there was a road up that steep slope. I could see no light in the fog, hear no engine noises, nothing. Maybe stumbling on a bear would make the disaster more complete.

After a long time, with numerous shivering pauses, bent double on my hiking poles to catch my breath, I looked up and caught a headlight glimmer in the fog above. The road was there, and I finally reached it. I could barely see the painted white stripe. A deserted road, of course, in such weather. Just a short distance away, I came to a fire station. Can you begin to imagine how happy and relieved I was? One of the firefighters drove me to the lodge. The lodge was dark and closed. We rang the night bell until Tom, the manager, abandoned his TV and came downstairs to open the store for me. He told me there was a microwave in the bungalow. I needed something warm, quick. I rushed to grab frozen food. Quite ironic, I know.

When I got to the room, among the swaying fir trees, I started shaking even more violently. Uncontrollably. My body was letting me know it didn't appreciate my very special walk in the park. I was shaking so hard I struggled to remove my clothes. My sore muscles rebelled, and I could hardly move. I had a quick look at my toes: two were black. I turned the room heating to maximum, filled the tub with hot water, and threw the food into the microwave. I knew I had been in the danger zone, serious hypothermia and exhaustion, and I was glad I had not decided to set up camp in the forest in my wet tent. I gulped down the food and painstakingly attempted to thaw in the hot bath. No way could I stop the shaking, though. I was almost paralyzed, yet my body was in spasms. I then swallowed nearly all the pills I had—ibuprofen, anti-inflammatory stuff, and even cortisone—and collapsed into bed.

It snowed all night.

The day before, as if in a dream, I had hiked between Campo and Lake Morena in searing heat. Southern California desert, you said?

JUST NORTH OF CAMPO AND DAY 32, MAY 3

BARBARA WIEDEMANN

Barbara Wiedemann and her sister, Anita, hiked about 230 miles of the PCT in the summer of 2013. Wiedemann returned in 2015 to hike another 2,000 miles. During both journeys, Wiedemann, a retired professor of English literature, penned poems that we have sprinkled through this anthology. In the original *Pacific Crest Trailside Reader* volumes we included hiking haiku, poems by Gary Snyder and Jim Dodge, and song lyrics by Walkin' Jim Stoltz. These poets' rhythmical composition and economy of words, with rich but simple descriptions, capture the PCT experience in a refreshing way that prose does not.

JUST NORTH OF CAMPO

Barrel cactus with chartreuse flowers and long pink spines
teddy bear cactus also with chartreuse flowers,
cholla with newly formed pale yellow thorns
prickly pear adorned with magenta blossoms
and ocotillo with long spiky stems blooming red—
all signal spring in this southern California desert,
a day's walk from the border wall with Mexico.

But all is not paradise
in this mountainous aridity.
Six feet long and thick like my forearm,
the rattlesnake stretches across the trail.

Disturbed, it coils instantly,
then eases into the grasses,
rattles when my dog and I sneak by,
and on this second day
of my five-month hike
I feel like a trespasser.

DAY 32, MAY 3

Sitting on a rock
drinking English Breakfast tea,
the favorite tea of Jewels
who hailed from New Zealand,
drinking the tea
remembering the windy, icy night
we spent shivering on San Jacinto,
remembering my frozen boots and socks—
I don't know if I'll see her again.

Sitting on a rock
watching the sun slip behind a mountain
listening to the calls of birds I don't recognize
watching a woodpecker on a tree
silhouetted against the reddening sky
listening to the wind move through the trees—
this is why I am here.

"WE HAVE TREVOR"

DOUG LAHER

As a parent and a PCT hiker, I can't imagine a more difficult but therapeutic testimonial for a father to write than the one that follows. Laher's son, Trevor, died on March 27, 2020, after slipping on ice and falling several hundred feet to his death near Apache Peak not far south of Idyllwild. This poignant reflection will help Trevor be remembered as a complex, passionate young man and not just a statistic. Given the impact of the COVID-19 pandemic, this account adds to the deep sadness felt by many for an abbreviated 2020 hiking season. Since 1983 there have been twenty recorded PCT thru hiker deaths. Six of these deaths were the result of falls. Two have occurred from drowning, two from heatstroke, two from cars, and one from a falling tree. In addition to these unfortunate deaths, there are numerous missing hikers who have not been located. This tribute is a reminder that despite our best planning we can be vulnerable to unexpected circumstances that can have serious, even fatal, consequences.

—HS

"We have Trevor."

Three relatively benign, innocuous words in the grand scheme of life.

When Trevor was five years old and missed the bus stop on his first day of kindergarten, we were relieved to hear those words when the bus driver called and said Trevor had fallen asleep on the bus and he would drive him home.

Or when Trevor was sixteen and the call was from the police who said Trevor had violated curfew while out "doorbell ditching" with friends at an overnight birthday party. "Boys being boys."

But when that call comes from the Riverside County coroner who verified that the death on the PCT earlier in the day involved your son, those words are life-changing.

THREE – SIMPLE – WORDS and my life was forever changed. My best friend, my hero, my gift to the world was taken from me on that fateful day, March 27, 2020.

Parents don't allow themselves to think of the unthinkable. Losing a child is too painful to comprehend. But, to be truthful, anything a parent conjures up in their mind about the death of a child pales in comparison to the reality of it happening. Most of us live our lives hoping and praying that our children will outlive us. That's how life is supposed to happen. But that's not the story of my life, my family's life, or that of Trevor "Microsoft" Laher.

Early in the summer of 2016, Trevor was invited to go to Yosemite with a friend for a family vacation. For three days, Trevor hiked in the Yosemite Valley. Those three days changed Trevor's life and sealed the fate of his impending death.

It was as if he had lived his life in black and white and suddenly saw the world in vibrant colors. He fell in love with hiking and wanted to do more of it. So much so that Trevor and I went on a thirty-mile section hike along the Appalachian Trail just prior to him leaving for his freshman year in college.

Neither of us had any backcountry experience, and so we packed for our fears (carried too much food and water, bear spray, a buck knife), and off we headed into the mountains in our cotton clothes, with forty-five-pound packs strapped to our backs. Those three days were some of the most grueling of my life. It mattered not whether I enjoyed hiking. I loved spending time with Trevor.

During the summer after his freshman year, he hiked the Presidential Traverse in the White Mountains of New Hampshire. And, whenever he came home to Texas, he and I would find a quick backcountry expedition we could go on. We hiked Big Bend and the Eagle Rock Loop in the Ouachita National Forest of Arkansas. Hiking was his thing, and if it was his thing, it became my thing, because it was my opportunity to spend quality time with my son.

It was sometime during his junior year that Trevor informed me of his intentions to graduate early so that he could hike the Pacific Crest Trail. While hiking the PCT was not what I had envisioned for my son, it's exactly what he envisioned for himself. Sadly, it took me many months before realizing that this was his life and I needed to let him live it.

After relenting and realizing that this adventure was going to happen, I spent nearly a year reading books and watching gear reviews and vlogs from hiking influencers like Darwin, Dixie, and IBTAT. For his graduation gift, my wife and I agreed to purchase all of the gear he would need for his trek. We spared no expense—it was ultralight all the way. As the days got closer, I think I wanted this trek for him as much as he wanted it for himself, although deep down I knew that wasn't possible.

Trevor was six foot three and 185 pounds. He was like a mountain goat who could accelerate up steep climbs. Trevor loved hiking. He loved hiking by himself. He loved hiking with others. He loved the endorphin rush of a punishing climb to the top of a mountain. Hiking was in his DNA.

Trevor graduated in December 2019, just three months prior to his permit date of March 16. He upped his level of fitness during those three months. He ran thirty miles per week and worked on his leg strength and core muscle development. Trevor continued to hike whenever possible, including a quick fifteen-mile training hike we did together in February, the last hike my son and I ever went on together.

It was Monday, March 9, 2020, and Trevor, his sister Olivia, and I hopped on a plane to Phoenix to visit my parents. Our plan was for Olivia and me to stay in Phoenix until Friday when we would head back to Texas. My parents were going to drive Trevor to the southern terminus the following Monday.

When we left for Phoenix, concerns about COVID-19 had been percolating, but, when we landed, the world had changed. The stock market had collapsed, and that night the NBA started cancelling games. Trevor and I discussed whether leaving for the trail was a smart idea, but it was a one-sided conversation. "I'm within spitting distance of the terminus, Dad. Nothing is going to stop me from getting on the trail."

It was on Friday the 13th that I last saw my son alive. Olivia and I were dropped off at the airport. A few tears were shed. There was a big hug, bigger than usual. The hug was tighter and longer, and after a long pause Trevor whispered into my ear, "I love you, Dad. Thanks so much for helping me make this dream a reality." To which I replied, "Go hike the shit out of that trail." And off we went, back to Texas, Olivia and me.

Trevor's grandparents dropped him off at the southern terminus on Monday morning, March 16, 2020. It was a cool, overcast day. Lots of smiles, big hugs, a few pics, and Trevor was off to start the adventure of a lifetime.

The first several hundred yards of the PCT wind in and out of the landscape parallel to the dirt road leading to the monument. My parents drove slowly, watching Trevor weave in and out of the flora that lined the trail. They honked their horn as if to say "We love you Trevor," and Trevor signaled back to them by clicking his trekking poles together as if to say "I love you too!"

Trevor made it to Lake Morena on day one and by day three had made it to Mount Laguna. By then, concerns over COVID-19 were rampant, and the governor of California had just issued a shelter in place order for all Californians. I spent the next three or four days trying to convince Trevor to get off trail. He refused. I said things I regret, which only led him to digging his heels in further. "Dad, if I get off trail now, I'll lose the PCT forever. When I'm at the top of these mountains, when I get to look out over the landscape, it's as if I can see the soul of the planet. I'm *not* coming home." I threatened to withhold funding and supplies. All I did was make him angry.

After those days of arguing, finally realizing there was nothing I could do, I relented. We would finish this conversation when he got home, and, moving forward, I would do my best to keep him safe. We knew there would be long food carries as he would try to avoid town stops as much as possible.

For the next ten days, Trevor was living his dream. While he and his hiking family would periodically check for COVID updates on their phones, they were isolated from what was going in the rest of the world. They were isolated from COVID. It was just them and the trail.

Trevor got to drink a beer at Montezuma Valley Market, pose for pictures at Eagle Rock, spend the night at Mike's Place, and devour a breakfast burrito at Paradise Valley Cafe. Aside from COVID, things could not have been more perfect.

I spoke with Trevor on the evening of March 26. He and his hiking family had just finished a long, punishing climb into the San Jacinto Mountains and decided to camp at the trail junction with the Fobes Saddle Trail at NOBO mile marker 166.5. He stated that it had started snowing once they hit six thousand feet. He was tired after doing eight straight days of "twenties" and was looking forward to taking a zero [a day of no hiking] in Idyllwild. His mother and I told him that we loved him, to be careful, and that we would talk to him the next day. Sadly, tomorrow never came.

Trevor woke up the next morning with his tent covered in two or three inches of fresh snow. He only had fourteen miles between him and a hot shower and soft bed. He and his trail family hiked two miles before reaching Spitler Peak Trail, the last bailout point between Apache Peak and Idyllwild. Historically, there had been a warning sign at the trail junction alerting hikers of this, but it had burned down during the forest fires of 2016 and never been replaced. Oblivious to the trail conditions ahead, they continued on into the freshly fallen snow.

Reaching the northeast-facing slope of Apache Peak, they found the trail invisible, covered by snow and ice from a storm that had moved through the area two weeks prior. Cut into the side of the mountain, the trail could not be seen, only a few disguised footprints covered by the fresh snow.

Apache Peak is described by many as the most dangerous section of the entire PCT, even during good conditions. The northeast-facing slope holds snow long into the hiking season and goes through many cycles of melting and refreezing until the warmth of the Southern California desert melts it away for good. The forty-five-degree slope above and below the trail is unrelenting. One false move and catastrophic injury or death awaits. Within the first two hundred miles of their thru hike, many hikers haven't even developed their trail legs and are unprepared for the danger. Hikers simply don't know what they don't know. In 2020, the Riverside Mountain Rescue Unit conducted weekly rescues (sometimes more than one per day) on Apache Peak.

The Apache Peak section of the PCT had been closed for several years due to forest fire damage but reopened in 2019. As a result of the closure, this was a section of trail we had overlooked in our research. Our concerns focused on Fuller Ridge, some twenty-five miles ahead. Trevor's ice axe and microspikes were awaiting him at the Idyllwild post office, so close, yet so far away.

Trevor and his companions headed across Apache Peak. Normally, early morning is the ideal time to traverse such terrain—with spikes and ice axes. But on this morning, Trevor had no microspikes and no ice ax, and the freshly fallen snow covering the trail had yet to bind to the ice beneath it. Jannek, from Germany, led the way. Trevor, second in line, and fifty feet behind, felt confident as Jannek made it safely through. But, in an instant, Trevor slipped, then regained his footing for a moment before falling to the ground. Cody, an Australian hiker and third in line, saw Trevor pause for a moment before he started sliding (belly down and feet first) down the mountain. With nothing stopping his fall and a sheet of ice beneath him, Trevor picked up speed and began pinballing off boulders before cartwheeling out of control. Jannek and Cody watched in horror before Trevor disappeared out of sight nearly three hundred feet beneath them.

Jannek and Cody first tried yelling to Trevor but heard no reply. They tried calling his cell phone and were directed to his voicemail. After a few paralyzed minutes, they activated their emergency beacons. In shock, Jannek and Cody waited for search and rescue (SAR) to arrive.

Nearly ninety minutes passed before SAR arrived on scene by helicopter. Weather conditions did not allow for a paramedic to be dropped. SAR identified Trevor's location and called to him via a loudspeaker, but Trevor was unresponsive. They pinged his location and moved to the safest drop location they could find, five miles away. After bushwhacking for nearly ninety minutes the medic made his way to Trevor before confirming he had perished from the fall.

I had been working from home that day when a friend called to notify me of the accident, which had been reported by the local newspaper in Palm Springs. At that moment, no one knew the perished hiker was Trevor.

I tried calling my son. No answer, but I was not concerned. I thought Trevor was some fifteen to twenty miles north of the accident site, and I knew that he had his driver's license on him. I thought that if the fallen hiker was Trevor, I would have been notified. As minutes turned into hours and the light of day turned into darkness, I knew Trevor would have made it into Idyllwild by then. We had agreed the night before that he would call us upon his safe arrival at the hotel there. I also knew my son: even if he forgot to call, his phone would be on.

By 8:00 p.m. in Texas, my concern had grown exponentially. I called the Riverside County sheriff who put me in touch with the coroner. They asked for a photo of Trevor in an effort to rule him out as the unknown hiker they had in their custody. An hour later, those three otherwise benign, innocuous words etched their way into my brain in the most painful, devastating, unimaginable way possible when the coroner called and said, "We have Trevor."

Trevor was an experienced hiker. He was physically fit. He prepared himself mentally for the challenges ahead through yoga and meditation. Even the best hikers would have had difficulty traversing Apache Peak that day.

Some people have publicly shamed him on social media for poor decision-making and bad preparation. Others ridiculed him or suggested he deserved it, that he had received justice for his decision to stay on the trail during the pandemic.

But Trevor was none of these things. He was like most thru hikers: uber-prepared, ultra-focused, and pursuing his dream. It was not until several weeks after Trevor's death that I found his journal, awaiting his return on his desk in his bedroom. His last entry speaks to why he was on the trail and why he had refused to come off. His decision to hike the PCT was not "to find himself" or to simply go on some epic adventure. It was spiritual for him. He had dreamed about this for years, prepared mentally and physically, and made commitments to himself. He was not going to let himself down. How do I know this? Here is the final passage from his journal:

A Note to Self

Whenever you're reading this, if you're reading this, and regardless of whatever happened—WOW! All these years of planning have culminated into the most incredible challenge I would have ever imagined. Tonight, specifically has cemented the reality and responsibilities of my impending fate. I hope I've achieved my goal. But if it is for a deserved injury, or quitting on a bad day, then it is time to reassess the commitments you make to yourself. Regret lasts forever. If this isn't the case however, I hope the experience was greater than anything I've ever imagined.

From the other side of metamorphosis,
You

Stay safe everyone. Make good decisions on the trail and always remember to #embracethealternate.

The hashtag, #embracethealternate, is associated with Doug Laher's efforts to educate others on how to approach risks, gauge safety, and make sure PCT hikers know of the dangers of Apache Peak and that section of trail.

FULL CIRCLE: SAN BERNARDINO FOREST TO THE DESERT FLOOR

PATTI "GLOW IN THE DARK" McCARTHY

From August 30 through September 2, 2013, Patti "Glow in the Dark" McCarthy and Lynn "3 Guy" Shapiro walked 44.3 miles along the PCT in the mountains of the Transverse Ranges, south and east of Big Bear. Some of the PCT stories we have found most inspiring have involved hikers overcoming health obstacles to return to the trail. Whether they describe walking with two new knees, terrible blisters, or any number of other maladies, these stories inspire and serve as a measure of what is possible even in the most seemingly impossible moments. Patti McCarthy who at the time was undergoing treatment for cancer, shares a story that is no less amazing and is certainly a prod to all of us who stay at home because of minor aches and pains. Patti, undeterred by a series of physical challenges was determined not to let anything get in her way, not even her dislike of the desert.

In 2019, Patti and her husband, Lynn, served as southern terminus hosts. Who better to send off NOBOs? "It's exciting to see the hikers leave," Patti and Lynn observe. "Each time someone takes off, we think he or she takes a little piece of us as we wish we too could be on the trail."

NEAR BIG BEAR

Labor Day weekend last year (2012) was our twentieth wedding anniversary. We celebrated by hiking from the private zoo and Onyx Summit area of Big Bear north to Deep Creek Bridge near Lake Arrowhead. We then had done 122 miles of the PCT. I was on top of life.

This Labor Day weekend we hiked from the Onyx Summit area south to Cabazon. During the past year we hiked an additional 186 miles for a total of 308 miles. Only 2,342 more miles to go, give or take a few.

Those 186 miles were hiked in between thirty-four doctor appointments, 102 medical procedures (including six kick-my-ass chemo treatments, thirty-five radiation treatments, and fourteen Herceptin infusions), and ear surgery. These miles were hiked in between dealing with anxiety, thrombophlebitis, low immunity, neutropenia, rock-bottom B12 levels, macrocytic anemia, cellulitis, shingles, and other stuff that would be TMI. As my aunt says, as she went through cancer, "We'd be justified being on the couch all day."

What keeps me going? I don't know. There were times on the trail, especially in the desert, when I was dizzy and exhausted. I'd think, *Why the hell am I here? Why do I insist on doing this? Irish stubbornness? The nature I love? Because I can.* Because I refuse, or try to refuse, to let this stupid disease defeat me.

Yes, life feels good!

Usually on the trail I can relax. This time, my mind just wouldn't. I developed a mild case of shingles before we left. I did *not* want to see another doctor, but I didn't know what this weird rash was, didn't want it getting worse on the trail, and it was starting to hurt. The doctor gave me a steroid, prednisone, to help it heal faster. I was still taking it during the course of our hike.

I forgot the effects of steroids. This pill was like the Decadron I had to take before the kick-my-ass chemo that kept me awake and moving until I knocked myself out with wine and Xanax. It was a vicious cycle.

So we were hiking along, and I said to Lynn, "What are you thinking about?" He said, "Nothing, just the hike." I was like, "Are you kidding?" I was thinking about solutions to work problems that didn't really exist, Relay for Life (I have a team in Encinitas), Halloween, my daughter's marathon, my sons, retirement, errands to run, and kitchen tables—all at the same time! Three days after being off that steroid, I found my brain still on a hamster wheel and was rearranging couch cushions at eleven at night because, for some reason, it needed to be done right then and there.

The hike itself was beautiful. I love being in the woods. It rained the first two days in the San Bernardino Mountains, but even that was fantastic. It brought out all these wonderful smells of pine and sage. We hiked 13.6 miles. Not bad considering we didn't get on the trail until noon, after spending half an hour trying to find the trail. That was only the beginning of how often we would get lost. The trail isn't clearly marked, and we got lost a lot. Our first night of camping was at the secluded Mission Springs Trail camp. There were only two other campers there, and that was a holiday weekend.

The second day, we were still in the forest. During the rain, we got lost again and found ourselves in a gully. It was raining harder. When I heard thunder, I realized, *Oh, crap, there could be a flash flood, and here we are in a prime area for trouble!* We scurried out, made shelter and waited it out for an hour. We hiked 10.9 miles that day. We followed Mission Creek for about seven miles. It was great hearing the sounds of the running creek in the distance. That night we found a spot that was our own private beach. We gladly took off our boots and walked around in the sand after cooling our feet in the cool creek water.

The third day we were in the desert sooner than we had expected. It confirmed my feelings about the desert—I don't like it. We know better than to hike midday. Had we known, we would have set our alarms for dark o'clock to take advantage of the cooler morning hours, but we had been too tired. So we plowed through. I have no idea how hot it was. Frickin' hot. I believe records were set.

That night we had a nice surprise. We found Whitewater Preserve. It used to be a trout farm. Now it's a beautiful conservation area, in the middle of nowhere, nestled in the San Gorgonio Wilderness. The camping was free. The rangers were really friendly. Again there were only two other campers there. It had a wading pool, a trout pond. There were flush toilets, a real plus. Our last water source was the Whitewater River. The river did look superficially white, but the water we collected was brown. Luckily, this place had safe water from a faucet.

On the last day of hiking we did get an early start. We had only eight more miles to go to get to Cabazon. It was so hot. It took us longer to get there than planned. Shade was rare. We stopped at any shade we found. At one rest stop we heard this weird animal sound. We realized it was a lone cow. We figured she was bitching about the heat too and looking for her buddies. The cows were the only animals we saw, although we did see what we think was a bear print in the mud. Water was infrequent but enough to get us through. Electrolytes would have helped: we had run out of Gatorade mix the day before.

We ended the hike back at Ziggy and the Bear's. Ziggy and the Bear are trail angels who live in Cabazon. They've been helping the hiking community for years. They are absolutely wonderful people. The last time we were in Cabazon for a hike, the California Highway Patrol tagged my car. Even though I put a sign on my car stating I was hiking the PCT, they were giving me seventy-two hours to move it. With us not wanting to do that again, Ziggy and the Bear let us park at their place. They also opened up their home to provide us with much-needed rest and Gatorades after the hike.

With three more chemo-like (Herceptin) infusions to go, we look forward to celebrating at the end of my treatment. It will have been 399 days from diagnosis of breast cancer to final treatment and worth a big celebration. We've considered many options: an exotic vacation, a big party, a private nice dinner. Nah. What more appropriate and better way to end such a traumatic year than to take another hike. We are going to do another four- or five-day stretch somewhere from Tehachapi to Deep Creek. I can't think of anything more healing than this.

A WEDDING ON THE TRAIL

CLAIRE HENLEY MILLER

Romance can be found along the trail. The intensity of the trail experience—the opportunities to talk, the bonding around shared challenge, the sheer amount of time together—creates an intimacy that sometimes results in romance but more often in enduring, lifelong friendships. Most intimate relationships are short-lived. Some last longer. In the first month of her hike, Claire Henley discovered that she had met the love of her life, Caleb Miller. Claire and Caleb's spontaneous connection remind us that timing can be everything. Their relationship progressed from introduction to courtship to marriage at lightning speed.

Hikers say that a day on the trail is like a month in real life. The connection you experience between people on the trail is so instant, so raw, so true, that after hiking with a person for only a few days, it feels as if you've known them for years. This was certainly the case for Big Spoon and me. For in a mere two weeks, from mile 235 (where Big Spoon caught up to me) to the KOA at mile 444, we spent our time on the trail together, showing each other our unmasked selves as we hiked through trying cold weather and tough uphill terrain. On this life-altering stretch we asked each other the big questions about the meaning of life, our desires and hopes, and how they fit in with our beliefs about the Great Beyond. By mile 369, in the town of Wrightwood, Big Spoon and I knew intellectually, spiritually, and emotionally that we were meant to be together: we both knew and felt that God had led us to each other, and though we had only known each other for a few weeks, we didn't want to wait to seal the deal God had devised for us as husband and wife.

Thus, what you are about to read is the story of how Big Spoon and I got married on the trail. And it is a story to tell indeed, because once the ball got rolling to finalize our lifelong commitment to each other as husband

and wife, the events that occurred as a result were nothing short of Divine Intervention.

It was the morning after Big Spoon and I stayed the night in Wrightwood, in the charming log cabin of trail angels Clayton and Jan. We were sitting in the living room drinking coffee and signing the hiker guest book when Big Spoon leaned over and whispered in my ear, "Let's elope."

I had already thought the same thing myself so didn't pause to consider the proposal and answered confidently, "Yes, let's."

The next several days on the trail we planned out the wedding logistics. On Thursday, May 21, the trail led us to the KOA in Acton. By this time, we knew that we needed to obtain a marriage license, but we weren't sure how or when we would go about the actual ceremony. A mile before reaching the KOA, we stopped on the trail to determine if any county clerk offices were nearby. Big Spoon pulled out his phone and immediately found the Los Angeles County clerk in the town of Lancaster—a thirty-mile hitch from the KOA—where we could both obtain our marriage license and have the wedding ceremony. The divine kicker being that Friday was the only day the office performed any weddings.

It was a good thing we looked up things when we did, because at the KOA the cell reception was weak and there was no internet connection. Thus, our next task was to figure out a ride to Lancaster for the next day, Friday. Big Spoon and I convened in the KOA lobby where the phone number of a trail angel named Mary was posted on the wall. "Let's go outside and give her a call," Big Spoon said.

We walked to the gravel parking lot to make the call, and who but Mary pulled in right as Big Spoon dialed her number. Mary was a wife, mother, artist, and joyous ball of energy who was there to pick up a fellow hiker. She was trail angeling that season by driving hikers where they needed to go because she was fascinated by the thru-hiking culture, saying, "It's just so cool to hear about you hikers' motivation behind such a giant journey."

So when Big Spoon and I told her we were getting married the next day and needed a ride to Lancaster in the morning, Mary jumped for joy, hugged Big Spoon and me tightly, and said without hesitation, "I'll be here tomorrow morning at seven o'clock sharp."

Big Spoon and I called our parents next. We made the nerve-wracking calls one parent at a time. We dialed my mom first. The first thing she said was, "I'm shocked." I explained to her that Big Spoon and I would have a formal wedding ceremony back home in Chattanooga after we finished the trail, but that because we already knew in our hearts and minds we were meant to be married, we didn't want to wait the four months before starting our lives together. By the end of the conversation she said, "Well, Sweetie, I guess I'm not surprised. Because remember I told you before you left this would happen, that you would find your husband on the PCT."

Next we called my dad whose reaction was loving and level-headed. Dad said he understood that Big Spoon and I had finally found each other and that it made sense we wanted to be with each other in every way, especially while on the PCT—our journey of a lifetime. He said he believed God had his hand in this and that he trusted my judgment. During this call, Big Spoon asked my dad if he could take my hand in marriage. "Thank you so much for asking me, Caleb. That shows your quality and style," my dad responded.

The conversation with Big Spoon's parents and grandmother was shorter than with my parents, but it was nevertheless full of joy, support, and beautiful love. Big Spoon told his family it had slapped him in the face that I was the one, and he didn't want to prolong an engagement. His mother, Ave, welcomed me to their family, "I've always told Caleb the greatest joy I know is being able to share life with the one you love." His father, Barry, said in a solid tone, "God bless." And Big Spoon's grandmother, Mary Elizabeth, wanted to make it very clear to us that we were not eloping, because if we were eloping we would be sneaking around behind everyone's backs and not telling anyone about it. Oh, no, we weren't eloping, the grandmother declared. Big Spoon and I were getting married.

That night, amid a field of thru hikers who were bundled in their tents, I sat with Big Spoon on the grass beneath the silver stars. Earlier in the day I had written him a letter in which I told him I knew we were getting married a lot quicker than most couples, but that I believed this was a marriage that would last like gold, and one in which I would be true to him and love him until death did us part. He read the letter while we sat side by side, and when he finished he took my hand and officially asked, "Claire, will you marry me?" I answered yes.

We woke the next morning at sunrise. I readied myself in the KOA bathhouse with the help of Pandora who was coming with us to Lancaster as our witness and maid of honor. Throughout my life, I never imagined I would look and dress the way I did on my wedding day. I wore my white desert-hiking shirt that was stained with dirt and sweat. My nose was sunburned and peeling, and my lower lip was split open and chapped. I had no makeup to wear, and my tangly hair was tied up in a bandana.

Pandora and I met Big Spoon in the parking lot. He wore his robin's egg blue hiking shirt that brought out the soft blue in his eyes. "How are you feeling," he asked me. "So sure about this," I said. "And you?" "The same, Claire."

Mary pulled in right on time, got out, and presented me with a bouquet of bright pink roses. She had a rose for Pandora too. They smelled heavenly sweet and completed my unique bridal ensemble. It was a bright sunny day, the first in a while. Once the office opened, Big Spoon began filling out our marriage license. I watched over his shoulder as he wrote my new name, Claire Henley Miller, and I didn't feel nervous one bit.

It cost $131 for the combination of the marriage license and wedding ceremony. A beautiful woman named Nichole with blue streaks in her hair and six-inch high heels told us to wait by the door. We moved our packs to the heavy door, and, as we waited, Big Spoon, Pandora, and I huddled up and prayed to God to bless this marriage.

The next minute the door opened, and we were pleasantly surprised to be let into the small, simple chapel by Nichole who now wore a long black judge's robe. I called my mom, put her on speaker, and set the phone on the podium where Nichole conducted the ceremony. Big Spoon and I took each other's hands. The day was May 22, 2015, exactly one month after we both began the PCT. The ceremony began with Pandora reading a meaningful Bible verse. Then Nichole recited the traditional marriage vows, and afterward Big Spoon and I proclaimed, "I do." "Do you have rings to exchange?" Nichole then asked.

Because everything between us had happened so fast, we hadn't had time to get rings. However, we did have tokens of our love and commitment to each other to use for now. Mine for Big Spoon was a rainbow-colored rock I had found near Silverwood Lake. It was the size and shape of a small spear head and had crystallized quartz at the end. "A solid rock to symbolize the solid marriage we're entering into," I said.

To my great surprise, Big Spoon then pulled out the Herkimer diamond his mother had given him. The diamond was fashioned so a chain could be strung through it to make it into a necklace. Big Spoon had turned the Herkimer diamond into a necklace with thin black twine. Nichole announced to Big Spoon, "You may kiss your bride."

By now, we were all starving, but daylight was burning and we had ten miles to hike that day to Agua Dulce. Thus, in concurrence with the nontraditional day, Mary drove us to a fast food restaurant for bacon double cheeseburgers and curly fries. From there, we ran our resupply errands: first to the bank to get cash, then to the grocery for food, and lastly to the post office where I shipped home my now unnecessary tent.

We were back on the trail by 2:00 p.m., after saying a grand goodbye to Mary, the lovely trail angel. I carried my roses on top of my pack through the famous Vasquez Rocks that rose above us like ocean waves. We made Agua Dulce by dinnertime. Our plan was to eat a celebratory dinner at the Mexican restaurant Maria Bonita, then hike a couple of miles out of town to camp.

We walked into the busy restaurant with our backpacks on and were seated at a booth in the far corner. Pandora ordered a round of margaritas and said for Big Spoon and me to get whatever we wanted, this meal was on her. We ate, drank, and were merry. Near the end of our meal the waiter came up with another round of margaritas.

"From that couple over there," the waiter said and pointed to the middle-aged couple at the other end of the restaurant who were looking our way and waving. Doug and Candi had seen us walk in with our packs and wanted to do something nice for us. Big Spoon told them that we had just gotten married and so the offering of the margaritas was doubly special.

Doug and Candi stopped by our table on their way out of the restaurant to congratulate us. They asked where we were staying for the night, and we told them our plans to camp a few miles down the trail. They looked at us like we were crazy because it was now dark outside. "We have a motorhome outside our house with a back bedroom and pull-out couch in the front if you three would like to stay there. We would be more than happy to have you." The answer to their proposal was a resounding yes. "The only catch," the couple said as we loaded into their pickup truck, "is that we have three peacocks that caw very loudly at night."

I wouldn't change a thing about my wedding day or night. The motorhome slept us beautifully, and the next morning Doug and Candi made a mouthwatering breakfast, using the fresh eggs their chickens laid. We drank gourmet coffee at the dining room table and fielded questions about life on the trail.

After breakfast, we hugged Candi goodbye, and Doug drove us back to the trail. It was a sunny Saturday, and I was a married woman now— married to a man of terrific talent, intellect, and love. All was brilliantly well with my soul.

"You're my wife," Big Spoon said to me before we started walking.

"And you're my husband," I said back to him.

Then we took to the beautiful trail—together having a long, hard, and glorious way to go.

From *Mile 445: Hitched in Her Hiking Boots*, by Claire Henley Miller (CreateSpace Independent Publishing, 2016). Reprinted by permission of the author.

The HoneySpooners, their eventual shared trail name, are still together. They make their lives together in Tennessee, where they have begun walking the long journey of parenthood.

FAREWELL TO ANGELS

ERIC SMITH

Eric Smith writes a much-deserved tribute to some extraordinary trail angels who have retired from "angeling" and whose generosity has benefited countless PCT hikers. These people and their big hearts (and their refuges) have become a part of trail lore in Southern California. Who, if anyone, will replace them is an unanswered question. As the number of hikers using the PCT continues to increase, the challenge of opening one's door (and heart) to one and all can be overwhelming.

Terms like "the kindness of strangers" and "unconditional support" come to mind when we think of these angels and the countless others along the trail who give rides, stock water caches, and provide food or a bed. Countless hikers, including both of us, have experienced their hospitality and perhaps wondered what the world would be like if more people embraced their philosophy of generosity. Trail angels are truly part of the magic of the trail.

When I learned that several of the most well-known trail angels of the Southern California PCT were stepping back or retiring altogether, it struck me that this signified the end of an era. Their absence will likely have a profound effect on most future thru hikers.

I attempted a thru hike in 2018 and was fortunate to encounter these amazing people who have selflessly opened their lives and homes to thousands of people who try to walk the trail. My experience was greatly enhanced by their generosity.

To anyone who is not familiar with what a trail angel does, imagine incredible generosity and thoughtfulness offered by someone you've never met and who wants nothing from you in return. In everyday life, unsolicited kindness is not commonplace or expected, so to encounter so much of it on my PCT hike was a real eye-opener.

I have to admit that I had always been somewhat skeptical when considering the concept of altruism and doing something for fellow humans that did not in some way benefit the giver. But even before I took one step on the PCT I learned just how wrong I was.

FRODO AND SCOUT

Let me begin with Frodo and Scout [Sandy and Barney Mann—see "Trail Names" and associated sidebar earlier in the book], a couple living near San Diego who have helped countless northbound hikers begin their odyssey by arranging transportation from whatever depot (bus, plane, or train) the hiker arrived at to their home. There they gave hikers a place to stay and an inaugural dinner before driving them the next day a not insignificant distance to the trailhead on the Mexican border.

When you consider the logistics of just getting to the trailhead, the help given by Frodo and Scout was invaluable. The amount of coordination and energy they put into assisting complete strangers was impressive, and they had managed to recruit and sustain an impressive number of volunteers to aid in all facets of the effort. Looking back on my own experience, I can truly say that beginning my hike was almost too easy, as all I had to do was show up, and they handled the rest.

To show my appreciation I offered Scout a donation to help with their operation. He politely declined and suggested I make a donation to the PCTA. I also recall Frodo making an impromptu speech during dinner about the increase in what she called "hiker entitlement," the apparent feeling of many thru hikers that they deserve a free place to stay, rides to town, and meals. Most trail angels do what they do without expecting anything in return, but, at the very least, hikers should not take their offerings for granted. Thanks to Frodo, I gained a better appreciation of what constitutes good thru-hiker etiquette.

CARMEN

My next significant encounter with a trail angel who no longer practices such deliberate acts of kindness was in Julian, California, at Carmen's Restaurant. I was fortunate to come through when I did, in the spring of 2018, because, while Carmen had sold her business, she was still allowing hikers to stay at her place.

What I remember first about my experience was that Carmen had hung a sign on the railing in front of her business proclaiming "Hiker Trash Welcome." And after the restaurant closed for the day, she allowed upwards of thirty people to camp out in and around the café, displaying absolute trust in complete strangers who had access to the property after she went home.

HIKER HEAVEN

In much the same way as Frodo and Scout took the trail angel ethos and industrialized it, the Saufleys hosted an oasis in the desert of Agua Dulce called Hiker Heaven. On their property they created a combination post office, campground, shower and laundry, and haven from the relatively inhospitable environment surrounding them.

They accepted resupply boxes mailed or delivered to hikers and helped hikers send "bounce" boxes [boxes containing extra supplies or equipment needed later in the trip and sent to a mail stop up the trail] from their converted garage. The Saufleys' outdoor showers allowed filthy hikers to wash off miles of trail dirt, and they offered loaner garments so hikers could launder their stinky clothes, thus briefly improving the appearance and smell of legions of hikers.

They also had a cadre of volunteers offering rides to and from Agua Dulce's stores and restaurants. Although I did not stay with them, I made a pit stop to shower and do laundry and was extremely grateful for the opportunity.

CASA DE LUNA

In many ways Terry and Joe Anderson epitomize the trail angel. Like the others mentioned above, these good folks took it upon themselves to welcome every single thru hiker to their place, season after season. Hikers were given the chance to rest and recover while enjoying a variety of couches and loungers in the Andersons' front yard. A manzanita forest was their backyard.

Evenings featured a taco salad dinner where Hawaiian shirts were required (and provided), and afterward hikers were given the opportunity to dance for Terry to earn a coveted PCT bandanna. She also had only one absolute requirement from each visitor—a hug. In addition, a bedsheet hung in front of the Andersons' garage served as a canvas for thru hikers to record their visit—a visual trail register.

THANK YOU

As I encountered these incredible people, I always took a moment to express my gratitude for what they gave. Before I set off on the journey of a lifetime I had no idea that people could be so gracious, caring, and generous. Besides the obvious benefit of refuge, food, and clean clothes, these amazing folks gave me another gift I had forgotten existed—the kindness of strangers.

To all who helped make my experience so memorable and meaningful, please accept my heartfelt gratitude and appreciation for your time, energy, and dedication. I know I speak for countless PCT alumni in saying this. You will be missed.

"STUPID SHOULD HURT" AND OTHER OBSERVATIONS

SCOTT GNILE

Scott Gnile offers observations about such things as the silence that often accompanies walking and the smells along the trail that you can't capture in a photo. He also captures the conviviality that occurs at refuges like Hiker Heaven, where hikers laugh, relax, share stories and information, and relish being clean and indulged. Gnile's insights and observations about things familiar to hikers allow armchair readers to experience the PCT vicariously.

Gnile also points out the uniqueness of Vasquez Rocks, a 932-acre state park created to preserve these distinctive sandstone formations. More than two miles of the PCT wind through this geologic garden that may seem strangely familiar to many hikers. Vasquez Rocks has been used as the backdrop for over one hundred television episodes, many music videos, countless commercials, and more than forty movies, including *Austin Powers: International Man of Mystery* (1997), *Blazing Saddles* (1974), *Hail, Caesar!* (2016), *Little Miss Sunshine* (2006), and *Planet of the Apes* (2001). Well before the movie fame of Vasquez Rocks, Tiburcio Vásquez, one of California's most notorious bandits, eluded capture by law enforcement in 1873 and 1874 by hiding in this area that now bears his name.

I hear rustling through my earplugs. It's loud. It's Sweep packing his stuff. I remove my earplugs. Everybody near me is moving. The sound of rustling nylon as things get jammed into stuff sacks and packs. It's dark. I rustle through my sack to find my iPhone. It's 3:30 a.m.! They're all getting up early to beat the heat on the next stretch to Hiker Heaven. Okay then, since I'm awake. Time to get up. I stuff my stuff too. I'm not hiking yet, though. It's overcast and cool. It'll be cool all morning. Why hike in the dark if I don't have too?

Time for breakfast. The more I eat now, the less I have to carry in my pack. I eat the last of my granola, my last instant breakfast, my last Starbucks VIA Caffé Mocha, the last of my raisins, and the last of my dehydrated tropical fruit. And for dessert I cook chicken ramen with freeze-dried beef chunks.

I start hiking when it's light enough to see without a headlamp. I leave by myself. Walking through the dim light along the creek and out of the camp. The damp overcast makes it impossible to determine my direction. I reach a fork in the trail without being able to tell which one to take. I use the compass app on my phone. North, north is the way I want to go, north to Canada. The weird thing is: without the compass I was convinced I was facing south. I trust the compass and walk against my feelings, north. North and up. Up into the clouds. The clouds with huge monolithic rocks looming like giants in the gloom. The trail leads me under their feet and around and over the hills. Down, then left, right, up. Zigging and zagging through the mist until I have no idea which direction I am heading except the trail leads somewhere, Canada I hope.

My knee feels essentially normal, until, oops, nope. It's not normal yet. Oww—the tinge of pain is more ephemeral, but it's real. Once it triggers, every step hurts. I immediately slow down. Rats! I am hopeful a zero tomorrow will heal this up. It's definitely better but not enough to hike at the speed I want to hike.

One of the things that is hard to explain by writing is the smell of hiking. The smell of damp grass, sage. The blossoming wildflowers, the dank rotting wood under the trees. The dry dusty smell of the trail through this arid region. Technology provides a way to record things to see and hear, it would be cool if they invented a scent recorder. So I try to describe the smells, but understand that my olfactory pictures are black-and-white stick figures in the rich range of scents that encompass a PCT thru hike. Not all are pleasant, but by far most of them are.

It's utterly silent. No, I mean *utterly*. No plane in the sky, no cars, no talking, no wind, nothing. The fog completely seals me into a silent world of my own. The sound of the gravel crunching under my feet is quickly absorbed and muted. I see a giant in the gray twilight before me: the trail passes beneath huge high-tension electrical lines. They hum and crackle in the misty humidity, the sound of work being done at a distance. Power produced one place is doing stuff someplace else. Here I am under the wires listening to the hum, sixty cycles per second. The cool mist blows softly onto my face. I think about the thru hikers who chose to hike out of the KOA camp last night. They are camping in this. I wonder how many neglected to set up a tent and cowboy-camped under the stars until they were obscured by the gray mist off the ocean. Wet stuff, cold and wet, sleeping bags, everything soaked. I pass some of them, no tent.

I think about all of the different hikes all happening at the exact same time. Every hike unique in its own way. Each reflective of the choices of each individual thru hiker. "Hike your own hike" is a common phrase in the thru-hiking world. It's an important concept. Encapsulated in it is the idea that bad things happen when you try to hike someone else's hike. If you hike too fast you could injure yourself. Listen to bad advice, and you can run out of water at the wrong time. You feel the consequences of each bad decision. As a wise person I know once said, "Stupid should hurt." With thru hikers it does—and rather quickly. It's a price you pay day after day as you face the consequences as a reminder, stupid really does hurt. Perhaps that's one of the things that I so love about thru hiking. It's real, with real ups and downs, pains and ecstasies. This is living now!

My trail takes me through Vasquez Rocks Natural Area Park. Fascinating rock formations with rocks embedded in other rocks. The embedded rocks were already rocks when they were embedded. A sign of inconceivable time spans. Of the ancient times when those rocks were free agents. All I know is that this place is special.

I walk right up to the coffee shop in Agua Dulce and sit down and order breakfast. It's somewhat surreal. One minute we are hard-core thru hikers pounding trail in the wilderness. The next minute we are dirty vagabonds discussing the quantity of sugar in our coffee. "Will that be one lump or two?"

The coffee shop is filled with thru hikers. I order pancakes, bacon, and eggs. I know I already had breakfast at the gazebo. Let's think of this as Sunday brunch. Whatever, it's good food. I immediately decide I'll be back tomorrow. We watch as a van pulls up and as a bunch of thru hikers without packs hop out. Some come to eat. Others walk into the grocery store across the street. We learn about the shuttle to Hiker Heaven. I finish my breakfast, pay my tab, and hop into the shuttle. On the glory road to hiker heaven!

Hiker Heaven is open again this year, and from all appearances it has attracted a bumper crop of thru hikers. Tents sprout from the dry dusty ground like giant fungi. Packs hang from trellises like sides of beef. I learn that the packs have been hung to keep the five dogs that roam the place from raiding them for food. There's a mobile home with a kitchen and satellite TV just for hikers. And an internet igloo and a shipping igloo. The igloos are not made of snow, they're made of PVC pipe and tarp. There are places to repair your equipment, order new equipment. Snacks and sodas can be had for a nominal sum. Thru hikers are bringing cases of beer from the local store. It may be a loud night. We are given the orientation tour. Go there and get your towel and loaner clothes, go to the shower door and add your name to the bottom of the list. Set up your tent and change into the loaner clothes. Put your clothes and stuff you want washed in a laundry bag and put it at the end of the line of bags in the garage. Then relax, you're in heaven. The Saufleys are some of the most generous people on the planet. Providing all of this free of charge to any thru hiker that shows up. It's an amazing, wonderful place. The one rule: you can only stay two nights.

I rest, relax, visit with friends old and new. I see people I haven't seen for weeks. Others who I just met. Here we are in this magical place. I take my shower, get a shuttle ride to the pizza place and stuff myself with pizza. I walk next door and buy a pint of Dreyer's Butterfinger ice cream. I eat it waiting for the shuttle back to Hiker Heaven.

I sit on the porch and watch the animated conversations of people who share a common experience of incredible hardships, pain, and deprivation of a little over 450 miles of the PCT trail. There is no certain demographic or ethnicity that defines a thru hiker. My Czech friends who I haven't seen since Mount Laguna are here. Hatchet is here. My favorite Israelis too. Moses, a new friend, is here after escaping a kidnapping. It's way past hiker midnight [on the trail, most hikers drift to sleep not long after sunset], and I doubt Sweep will be saying anything about it. He'd just be ignored anyway. For me, my waking hours are done. I start my zero day here in Hiker Heaven tomorrow.

WINTER HIKING IN THE TEHACHAPIS

KAREN "WHISPER" FRIEDRICHS

This is a story about winter hiking in the Tehachapis. It is not beyond one's imagination to think the Tehachapis might lend themselves to a winter hike with the right preparation. Certainly the days would be short, and the potential for bitterly cold and windy weather is significant, but the area tends to be dry, and storms do not tend to linger. Even if the storms don't linger, the memories stay with you for a long time. Karen Friedrichs made this frigid two-night journey as part of a more extensive effort to splice together short segments of the PCT north to Tehachapi through the fall and early winter of 2012.

No matter the season, the Tehachapis are not to be taken for granted. This is a landscape buffeted almost cruelly by winds throughout the year, winds generated by the inevitable unequal heating and cooling of the Mojave and the coastal regions to the west. Consider reading "Climbing a Ridge in Wind," by Linda "Blue Butterfly" Bakkar in *The Pacific Crest Trailside Reader: California* as a companion to Friedrichs's story. Like Blue Butterfly, Karen and her hiking partner, Catherine, also find unexpected challenges.

*Friday, December 28, 2012, Cottonwood Creek Bridge
to Gamble Spring Canyon*
The forecast for Tehachapi has been very much on our minds. It was stormy over Christmas and for the next two days. We decided to wait until today to begin this section that would take us up to 6,300 feet as we cross the Tehachapi Mountains.

We began our slight but steady uphill. The PCT follows several dirt roads through the ever-present wind turbines. We made rapid progress in the cool midday. The forecast for these three days is for highs in the upper thirties and lows around 20 degrees Fahrenheit. Okay, so a few weeks ago I bought yet another down bag, bringing my total up to five, apparently there being no such thing as having too many. Knowing that I'm a cold sleeper I knew I'd need a zero bag to be comfortable.

We climbed through several canyons and along ridges that gave us great views back to the Antelope Valley. Above Tylerhorse Canyon we encountered the beginning of snow on the trail. It was just a few inches, but when we descended to the small campsite in the canyon it had a foot of snow in places. As we continued we would get the usual snow on the north-facing slopes and clear trail on those facing south. When we arrived on the ridge above Gamble Spring Canyon it was about 4:30 p.m. and would soon be dark and much colder. Once in the canyon there was an obvious sheltered tent site out of the snow, and I quickly set up the tent while Catherine used her excellent fire-starting skills to get a cozy fire going despite the wet wood. We cooked and ate a few inches away from the fire and were quite comfortable. Our wet boots and socks dried nicely as we enjoyed the wonderful warmth. We both slept soundly in the silent canyon.

Saturday, December 29, 2012, Gamble Springs Canyon
to Oak Creek Bridge
Cold, very cold, colder, much colder, even colder. I'll try not to whine while describing today's events. When we woke up I was puzzled by the white sleeve on my black jacket. I turned on my light and realized that the inside of the tent was covered in frost or frozen condensation. I haven't experienced this before. My squall tent has netting on all four sides and has only collected a minimum amount of condensation. It was twenty degrees on my thermometer at first light.

I was wrong about these last hundred miles of the PCT. I had believed that once I reached Acton, I would be out of the San Gabriel Mountains and into the desert. I thought, "Great, some nice winter desert hiking." I thought this would be like Anza Borrego where I could walk along the trail, no jacket needed. Not in this desert. There's an abundance of cacti, agave, yuccas, Joshua trees, even Mormon tea covered with snow. Would that be iced tea? It certainly looked like desert, but it felt like tundra.

We had some hot cocoa and packed up quickly. Climbing out of our little canyon was just what we needed to get our heart rates up. Once on the ridge we entered the snow-covered mountain tops that we would trudge through for most of the day. We estimated that at least 80 percent of our route was covered in snow. For several hours I led as the snow depth varied greatly. I became increasingly annoyed at the extra work and energy required as a result of sinking down each step with a loaded backpack. After a particularly deep section, I asked Catherine to lead. My mood improved almost instantly from the relief of plopping my boots down exactly in her footprints.

Occasionally the sun would come out and warm us a bit. Near the highest point of our day there was a small cabin just off the trail in the woods. Soon after that there was a water cache, complete with hiker log, snow-covered beach chair, water bottles, and trash bag. There was even a makeshift roof of branches to keep the hot sun at bay during the spring. We decided that it probably was 70 degrees colder here now than when most of the thru hikers passed this way.

When we made a stop for lunch, it began to snow. We needed to keep moving to stay warm so I ate my sandwich as we continued. A little while later we were treated to the sight of eleven black horses and one colt just across a small ravine. They were following an obvious leader northbound on the PCT. It was a very dramatic moment, watching the jet-black horses run in a queue through the white snow. They wanted to get away from us but continued to move north, adjacent to the trail, so we got to see them several more times. The next unusual sight was the "tiger tank," an old watering trough with a bit of ice in it and a six-foot shower attached. A shower was the last thing I wanted, not that it was anywhere near operational.

We moved as quickly as possible, yet it took seven hours to do just under thirteen miles. It felt more like twenty to me. There was no water at Oak Creek, and initially we were glad we had made the effort to stash a gallon nearby. When Catherine went to retrieve it, she came upon a water cache of several more gallons near the road. Just over the bridge there was a little campsite maintained by the Tehachapi Mountain Riders, a horseback riding group. It had a picnic table, a hitching post, and a sign that stipulated "NO FIRES." I was so cold just before we arrived and had been fantasizing about another warm fire. It was not to be. The site was situated just below several wind turbines and less than a hundred yards from Tehachapi Willow Springs Road. We were both in our bags at 4:00 p.m., exhausted but happy to be beyond the snow-covered tread.

Sunday, December 30, 2012, Oak Creek Bridge to Tehachapi

We awoke to frost once again on the inside of the tent, though not as much as yesterday morning. The picnic table appeared to have a white tablecloth. We packed up quickly and departed.

The sky was overcast, and the wind was already significant at 7:00 a.m. Of these three days, this was the one that had a forecast of possible precipitation. We moved along at a rapid pace through the barren foothills. The colder I am, the faster I walk. It was 25 degrees when we exited the tent, and I'm not sure of the wind speed. There's a reason why we've passed hundreds of wind turbines on these three days.

The trail was very well-engineered along this eight-mile stretch. Our swift pace was interrupted occasionally by patches of snow, but otherwise the trail went by rapidly with only one short diversion. I zoomed right by a sharp switchback and continued straight ahead on a trail-like cow path, of which there are dozens in the area. Had the PCT not been covered in snow here it would have been obvious which one was the trail. We ended up on an adjacent hillside that had a power line from the wind machines anchored about a foot off the ground. It just didn't seem right. Catherine noticed a very nice wooden bridge in a gully behind us and correctly determined that we had wandered off the trail.

We finished at 10:00 a.m. I'm not certain when I'll return. I'm going to need to warm up first.

UNEXPECTED

RACHEL NEWKIRK

Rachel Newkirk and her husband, Ian, live outside of Tehachapi. They are part of a well-organized trail angel community that provides comfort and support to hikers passing through the area. The Newkirks exemplify what it means to have an open door policy. Not unlike the Manns, Carmen, Ziggy and the Bear, the Saufleys, and the Andersons, the Newkirks epitomize the wonder and delight of trail magic. Experiencing their hospitality firsthand leaves one in awe of the Newkirks and moved by their warmth and generosity.

Upon arriving at their home, one is struck by its liveliness. The guests at Rachel and Ian's place get melded into its fabric, and the two typically host at least a couple of large and small groups of PCT hikers daily during the thru-hiking season. There is a lot of sharing going on here, from whatever is in the pantry to bathrooms and laundry facilities as well as easy conversation. When I was there, Rachel put more than one meal together for a group of us hikers and for her family. The Newkirks' home was now our home. We took over their living room and eventually sprawled there for the night. In the morning they shuttled a group to the next trailhead north of town. The Newkirks effortlessly manage the comings and goings of their kids and the hikers who visit their home. They do all of this calmly and apparently naturally. What a welcome break from the wind farms along this stretch of trail.

Rachel's reflection on what she gets from the flood of PCT hikers that find their way to her home during the several months of the thru-hiking season is gratifying. It also suggests that giving is a two-way street (or trail). What is given is often returned in remarkable ways.

—HS

We had our first hikers of the season stay for the last two nights. An Israeli had emailed me at 5:00 p.m. on Sunday evening, hoping that we could take him and two others in for the night. I emailed back and said, "Sure. Here is my number." After a quick call I told them I would pick them up in ten minutes. As they came in, I showed them around: laundry, clean towels, and food. "Make yourself at home. Dinner is done, but you are welcome to make something for yourself."

Our busy family of six began opening our home to hikers about nine years ago. What started as dinner invitations to hikers quickly turned into hosting. Filling our couches, porch, floor, and occasionally the treehouse with hikers. Our home is not near the trail or in town, so I like to think that trail magic has a way of playing into how and which hikers make it to our home. We cannot host every night and definitely not every hiker, but we would average about sixty hikers a season. A small fraction of the hikers on trail, yet this small fraction always seems to carry a huge, positive impact in our home and family.

I kept hearing through mouthfuls of food, "I did not expect this!" These young men (like most hikers that come through our home) do not expect to be so at home for a night. Their expectations are as simple as a place to put their tent. This leaves so much room for the unexpected, and that is where I always seem to find magic. Magic fills me with happiness. I can so relate and am so often finding myself before the universe, going, "I did not expect this!" I love that feeling so much. It seems to be one of the first things to dwindle, with our emphasis on stability, security, and consistency, in our lives. I guess it really boils down to our desire for control. With all the expectations that build up from doing daily life with others, opportunities to respond with excitement, spontaneity, awe, and gratitude are stolen. We slowly begin to expect so much from each other and find ourselves saying less and less "I did not expect this!"

I am continually learning the art of expectations and their absolute essential value, that they add to a healthy life. We have our realistic expectations. We expect food at the grocery store, we expect drivers to stay in their lanes, we expect our children to do well in school, we expect the banks to hold our money, we expect to be held by a loved one when we are sad, and we expect to laugh with friends. We also hold onto so many unrealistic expectations: we expect to win the lottery when we play, we expect our children and ourselves to know how to navigate life's challenges, we expect for there to be more money in our accounts—always. These unrealistic expectations often result in disappointment. Instead of a sprinkle of magic, these results tend to feel like a slap in the face—a letdown from the universe—intended to bring you firmly back into the realm of reality. Often the disappointment of unmet expectations covers me in a blanket of inadequacy.

We need expectations in life, both realistic and unrealistic ones. I have learned and continue to learn that expectations need to be communicated clearly, that they take a lot of energy, and that they are essential for a healthy life and a healthy self. Yet it is these moments of "I did not expect this" that fill me with gratitude.

Gratitude is the oxygen for my soul. Such amazing, good things come from gratitude. Presence, laughter, altruism, humbleness, awareness, joy, peace, acceptance, freedom, love, and sparkle to life. So how do I let go of expectations while still holding onto expectations? How do I get over the unrealistic expectations and just jump to all the "I did not expect this" moments? I think that I will just continue to hang out with hikers. Their level of surprise and gratitude are contagious. They enter my space and fill it with minimal expectations and then proceed to explode my world with gratitude and spontaneous outbursts of "I did not expect this!"

Something in my heart joins the hikers every time. I did not expect this either, and thank you.

SOUTHERN SIERRA RANGE OF LIGHT

COVERING CALIFORNIA
SECTION G–SECTION I

Walker Pass • Mount Whitney • John Muir Trail •
Tuolumne Meadows • Sonora Pass

RATTLESNAKE AND BEAR

SUE KETTLES

Sue Kettles says, "I discovered the PCT in 1985, when the last of our four kids were born. An article in the *Oregonian* newspaper told about someone who hiked this trail from Mexico to Canada in one summer. I just sat there with my mouth open and cried. I thought that by the time I would be free to do the whole thing, I surely would be decrepit and not able to move anymore."

Even though she and her husband, Alex, knew nothing of backpacking, she talked him into an inaugural trip from Mount Hood to Cascade Locks. "We pretty much did everything wrong," she continued. "We packed all we could imagine we would need: massive parkas, a stove we hadn't started to see if it still worked, huge sleeping bags, and many changes of clothes. We bought most of our gear at garage sales. It was old and heavy."

By the time they reached their first camp, Kettles had wrenched her knee and blackened a few toenails. She had blisters and a "numb thing" going on with her shoulders. They had brought steaks to cook and, of course, the stove didn't work. They threw the steaks in the bushes and ate gorp.

"We woke to cold, wet weather. I could hardly move, my feet hurt so badly, and my knee couldn't take any more hills. We decided to creep back up to Timberline Lodge. I was dejected and heartbroken. I thought my dream was over before it even got started." But Kettles was determined. She returned to the trail, learning more and more with each outing. Her gear got lighter and lighter. By 2012, Sue had walked every mile of the PCT and many more than once. "It's in my blood now."

The brief vignette from the trail illustrates the truth that by seeing just what is in front of us, we miss the bigger picture. A delightful allegory for what so often happens in life.

By the time Papa Bear and I made it to Joshua Tree Spring, we were incredibly hot, suffering from unquenchable thirst, and super-tired. So we found a bit of wonderful shade and took a short, sweet nap.

It was August, and we had started at Walker Pass and planned to leave the trail at Kearsarge Pass. Drew "Papa Bear" Hendel and I had met a few years earlier in Southern California while section-hiking from Cajon Pass to Agua Dulce. Like me, he was also trying to complete the PCT in sections. He lives in Seattle, and I see him every year at Kick Off.

We knew this route through the High Sierra would be pretty dry this late in the summer. So we got dropped off after dark and hiked by magical moonlight. After maybe four miles or so, we set up a dry camp. The next day, we got an early start in an attempt to beat the heat and make Joshua Tree Spring, the first reliable water in that section. After reaching the pleasant surroundings of the spring, I settled in for a nap.

When I woke up, I meandered a few yards down to the spring and sat down on the rock to get spring water, which flows from a pipe into a horse trough.

As I looked to my right, I saw a rattlesnake slithering away from the rock I was sitting on. I guess I had interrupted its nap or trampled its hunting grounds. It was foolish of me not to have seen it earlier. In my sleepy daze I wasn't very snake-smart.

I jumped up and started yelling to Papa Bear: "Rattlesnake! You gotta come look!"

My shrieking must have awakened the bear that had been sleeping in the tree above us. As we watched the snake move slowly away, the bear lumbered from its perch. Papa Bear grabbed a handful of rocks. But this junior bear had little interest in us. He moseyed slowly down to the spring and kept walking away. Papa Bear and I just looked at each other with big smiles, each asking the other without words: did that just happen?

We decided to camp away from the bear tree, so we ate lunch and, after it cooled a bit, headed up the trail.

I feel so blessed and fortunate for my experiences and to have seen these things.

RETURN TO OSA MEADOW

GREG "STRIDER" HUMMEL

Greg Hummel passed away on the last day of 2014, just two and a half months after his return to Osa Meadow, of complications from ALS. Hummel was cofounder of and always a recognizable presence at the Annual Day Zero Pacific Crest Trail Kick Off (ADZPCTKO), a seventeen-year tradition that ended with the 2016 Kick Off. The event was timed such that thru hikers could walk the desert before the scorching heat, navigate the Sierra with a manageable snowpack, and reach Canada before winter weather arrived. Seasoned veterans gathered with new hikers, vendors, and trail angels for socializing with old and new friends, classes on everything from food and safety to leave-no-trace techniques, and the annual class photo.

As the numbers of hikers grew over the years, participation in the Kick Off overwhelmed the infrastructure of Lake Morena County Park and contributed a large crowd of hikers who were unleashed on the fragile desert ecosystem to the north. For that reason, the board and organizers of ADZPCTKO decided not to hold the event beginning in 2017.

Hummel's longtime friend and 1977 thru-hiking companion Paul "Nohawk" Hacker honored Strider at his memorial with an ode that included these lines:

> It wasn't all that long ago
> That you and I together strode. . . .
> Through forest glen
> Cross mountain stream
> To places only we have known
> We spoke of only lofty things
> Of higher places we would climb
> But now I see an endless sky
> Where your silhouette used to occupy

In the early history of the PCT, the entrance into the Sierra Nevada was at Weldon, a small town on Highway 178 west of Walker Pass. Weldon consisted of a post office, a small country store, and a KOA campground. That temporary route ran a ridge to the north of town, climbing four thousand feet in just two miles. From the top of that ridge, the path included trail and Forest Service roads, stringing several beautiful meadows together to the west of the current permanent route through Kennedy Meadows.

In 1977, a lot of the thru hikers bunched up at Weldon in early May to resupply for one of the longest stretches without easy resupply. Many of us aimed for the town of Independence, approximately 108 miles north. The trail in the southern Sierra wound up to Bonita Meadow and Beach Ridge, just skirting Osa Meadow to the west, before going through Casa Vieja Meadows, Templeton, Big Whitney Meadows, and up and over Siberian Pass.

A minor Forest Service road "shortcut" took me off the temporary route and right through Osa Meadow. A fire had destroyed the forest on the ridge on the western side of the meadow a year and a half before, and the crew of a Forest Service contractor was replanting Jeffrey pine seedlings all across the ridge.

Joyce, the supervisor, greeted me and asked what I was doing. After her disbelief of my answer and several questions, she asked me if I'd like to join the crew, making five dollars per hour (in 1977 not a bad rate!). I told her that I was on a timetable, had barely enough food to get to Independence, and couldn't afford to stop. She then upped the ante.

"I'll fill your pack with all of the food you can carry when you leave if you'll work for me for a few days," she said.

I agreed and was soon schooled on the leather belt with a side pocket in which we carried the saplings, and how to properly prep the ground with the pick ax.

From my journal, May 5, 1977:
There [are] a couple trailers and a car sitting there and some people working up on the burnt area. . . . So here I am after working 7 hours planting trees and being fed very well. I figure I can use the money and as long as Joyce is feeding me it is no food out of my pack. . . . The guys are nice, the work is hard, the food is good and I will work tomorrow too if it doesn't rain or snow tonight. I never saw the people behind me today. Clouds blew over all day and threaten constantly. My arms and hands are sore but it's a nice break for my blisters.

More from my journal, May 6, 1977:

> *Woke up to a half-inch of snow on the ground so we waited until 10:30*
> *am to work so that the snow would melt off. Worked hard in the cold*
> *until 5:00 pm and then called it quits. About an hour later the snow*
> *[continued] dropping and by dark there was an inch on the ground.*
> *[The crew] all went into Kernville for the weekend, leaving me with the*
> *trailer to sleep in tonight and plenty of food. Someone found a baby*
> *rabbit today . . . so he's my company tonight. I made $50 and planted*
> *two thousand trees in two days.*

Fast-forward to October 18, 2014: It had been on my mind for a long time: to go back and see if I can find the stand of trees I had a hand in planting so many years ago. Thus, I found myself going up Highway 395 this morning with my wife, Laurie, and my two youngest children, Travis and Molly, to meet Paul and Trisha Hacker at Pearsonville. We would explore the network of Forest Service roads north and west of Kennedy Meadows to find Osa Meadow.

The past year had me looking back a lot more than usual after being diagnosed with ALS in June. This brought my family closer to me and has placed a heavy toll on my wife, a nurse. The disease has diminished the muscle I built on the trail so long ago, one step at a time. Although the disease deteriorates my body and muscle control, my mind and memories remain clear.

We picked up sandwiches in Pearsonville and drove to the Kennedy Meadows campground to enjoy lunch on a beautiful fall day. From Blackrock Station you have a choice of two roads going north toward Osa, and, with two professional geologists directing, we chose the left-hand or westerly of the two. We drove for three hours, on dusty, poor dirt roads, getting lost in the maze of roads and finally found our way back to Blackrock Station around 4:30 p.m. with the sun getting low. Stupid geologists!

We decided to persist and continue up the eastern road. This road was paved, with good signs, and in just thirty minutes we stood in Osa Meadow in the bright sun just above the ridge. Travis and Molly helped me to walk the short distance to the edge of the meadow.

In Travis's words:

> *I could sense the enthusiasm in my dad's steps, but the uneven ground made it very difficult to help him keep his balance. I decided to lift him up with each step to make it easier for him to walk. With branches trying to make him stumble, with each step we had to walk slowly. I was very scared at each moment [that my father would fall]. My muscles started to shake as we finally got to the brim of the meadow. I was exhausted and we had only gone 20 yards at the most. We stopped and admired what my father had contributed as the sun was setting. As we turned back after taking a few more steps I was not sure I was going to be able to get him back to the car. . . . I was fearful that I would lose my balance and bring my father down with me; my face was starting to show the pain and a tear went to my eye. If he were to have fallen it would have been okay because I was prepared to go down with him.*

There, across a meadow of golden grass, gleaming in the bright sun, reaching toward the deep blue sky was a forested ridge, reminiscent of the denuded ridge I recall from 1977. The forested ridge, with trees all of similar size, thick with deep green, now looks natural, not planted by humans. The sweet vanilla smell of pine and musky grass filled the air.

Sure, I had agreed to plant those trees for monetary and nutritional considerations, but the pride swelling in my chest at contributing in a small way to the beauty of the Sierra will carry me for the rest of my life.

PLEASE DON'T DROWN, HE SAID

GAIL D. STOREY

The risks most on the minds of hikers when walking the PCT tend to be the precipitous edges, the exposed ridgelines in storms, and the bear or rattlesnake encounter. In reality, fording streams could well be the most dangerous, even life-threatening challenge, hikers face. As Dennis Lewon notes in *Backpacker* magazine, "Runoff-swollen rivers pose one of the backcountry's biggest threats." Often such crossings are deceptively hazardous. Even a shallow but swiftly flowing current can knock you off your feet. The epic snowpack of 2017 created treacherous conditions that resulted in the loss of two lives from drowning, Rika Morita while crossing the South Fork of the Kings River and Wang Chaocui in Kerrick Canyon.

While not a demonstration of best (or worst) practices for stream crossing, Gail Storey's account feels exceptionally real. Tyndall Creek is one of many formidable crossings hikers face in the High Sierra, and fortunately she lived to write about their experience.

Four hundred miles long and sixty miles wide, the High Sierra is the most remote wilderness of the Pacific Crest Trail. My husband, Porter, and I had been preparing physically and emotionally for the Sierra during the first 750 miles of our 2,663-mile hike from Mexico to Canada. In our mid-fifties, we were having our two-thirds life crisis—he as a hospice doctor and I as a hospice doctor's wife. He craved renewal in the cycles of nature, and I'd come along to make sure nature didn't do him in.

But nature seemed out to get me in crisis after crisis—injuries, sliding down scree, struggling out of ravines. I never much cared for nature, or rather, thought it okay as long as it stayed outside. Porter was an experienced outdoorsman, whereas I had hardly ever hiked or camped before the PCT.

The deeper we hiked into the High Sierra, the more its silence deepened around us, until we'd hear the distant roar of a waterfall. I'd watch snowmelt pour down the mountain and hope for a chance to redeem myself.

The trail led us through one rushing stream after another. *It's just cold water*, I told myself, don't freak out. I boulder-hopped across streams where rocks broke the surface. From the bank, I planned my route by the width of my stride and the weight of my pack. Once I committed to it, it was best to keep going, rather than wobble on a sharp or mossy stone. Sometimes when I got there, the space between rocks was too wide. I had to search for another or backtrack, waver while my trekking poles sought purchase in the rocky creek bed. If the rushing current grabbed the basket of my pole, or its tip got stuck in the rocks at the bottom, I plunged in and got wet to my waist, along with my gear.

We came to a creek so deep no boulders reached the surface. All that was available was a fallen log.

"It's all about momentum," Porter said.

I watched in awe as he bounded onto one end, bounced a little to test its strength, then strode purposefully across. He was most magnificent the last few yards, when he ran and jumped to the bank.

I could straddle the log and scoot, but the bark would tear up my pants and inner thighs even if I managed to hang onto my pack as I pushed it ahead of me. So pack on my back, I stepped up with shaky legs.

"What's the worst that can happen, right?" I called to Porter. "I could fall off, be carried away by the current, and drown."

"Please don't drown," he said.

You got this, I told myself. I took a deep breath and inched across, one foot in line with the other. I kept my eyes on the log's knots and bark and watched for slippery smooth spots. I tried not to look down into the water, afraid I'd lose my balance in its flowing motion.

"You're doing great," Porter encouraged me from the other side. I felt him psychically will me across. The most frightening moment was the leap from the end of the log to the bank. By then I was exhausted from courage.

He braced one foot on the bank. "You're almost there." He reached out his hand and I grabbed it. There was a grace to it, this wilderness minuet, one we'd do over and over again. The love with which he thrust out his arm, the trust with which I took it, would become the defining gesture of our hike of the Pacific Crest Trail.

Many of the streams lacked either boulders or logs, so we had to ford them. We stopped first to take off our boots, peel off our socks to keep them dry, then put our boots back on to keep our balance and not cut our feet on the sharp, slippery rock bottoms.

After each crossing, we paused on the other bank to pour the icy water from our boots, dry our feet, and put our socks back on. Our socks still got soaked, so after each ford we alternated to the slightly drier pair airing under straps on our packs.

I had no idea we'd be fording so many streams, up to twenty a day. Twenty!

"The guidebook says Tyndall Creek is 'formidable,'" I fretted that night at our campsite.

"You're doing fine at crossing creeks," he said.

"More formidable than what we've been through?" I asked.

"We'll ford it somehow."

We had no alternative, this high in the High Sierra.

The next morning we pried open our socks, frozen and stiff as boards, and forced our cold feet into them. Our boots were frozen too. Even the laces were stiff, hard to tighten and tie with our freezing fingers.

After cold fords through Wallace and Wright Creeks, we arrived at swollen Tyndall Creek. It looked even more dangerous than reputed. I held my breath as Porter crossed first to test the power and depth of the current.

"Undo your pack's hip belt," he called from the other side. "If you lose your balance in the current, shrug off your pack so its weight doesn't drag you downstream."

"And lose my pack?" I hollered back.

"Better than losing your life."

Frozen on the bank, I stared into the deep rushing water.

Finally I stepped in and lurched drunkenly even with my trekking poles. Facing upstream for balance, I slowly sidestepped across. But my foot got caught between two rocks on the uneven bottom, and the rapids knocked me down.

First there was white, the cold foam of swirling bubbles. I sputtered and gurgled, fought hard to get up, but I couldn't. I thrashed harder, and the water gave way beneath. My legs flailed above me. I sank, butt-heavy.

I landed softly on the bottom, half-reclining on my pack. I watched my sunhat rise above me to the surface. It was bright up there, but deep down here everything was blue. I was drowning in blueness. I bounced in the upwelling, downwelling. I slipped into a blueshift of time running backwards.

But someone was parting the air. He was a shadow, head to water, leaning from the sky. I looked up through webwork under water, saw the fine lace of trees, sunlight latticed through their branches. The world was halved by sunlight.

Porter plunged in and dragged me out, body, pack, and all. I sliced the air with my icy bones. We collapsed on the rocks. Water poured from us in rivulets. A waterfall of snowmelt myself, my teeth chattered like clacking pebbles.

I sat there reeling with stillness. Inside, I felt like the river, a wider, deeper version of myself. My skin tingled from the bracing cold, my eyes opened at the brightness of everything around me. Nature, much more powerful than I, was letting me live.

From *I Promise Not to Suffer: A Fool for Love Hikes the Pacific Crest Trail*, by Gail D. Storey (Mountaineers Books, 2013). Reprinted with permission of the publisher.

FROM WHERE I STAND

JOHN MUIR AND THE COMPLICATED ISSUE OF WHITE WILDERNESS

From my earliest readings of John Muir's stories and subsequently his biographies, I have been mesmerized by his courageous adventures, his vision of and advocacy for nature, and the way he learned through astute observation. His imprint on the modern environmental movement through his twelve books and three hundred articles is enduring, as are his efforts to successfully protect Yosemite and his role in the creation of the most influential environmental organization of our time, the Sierra Club. I will always laud him for those achievements.

But there is no question that despite his original and independent thinking, he was also a man who reflected many of the prejudices common in his time. As a result, Muir helped to shape a national park system and an environmental movement that still struggles to feel relevant and welcoming to people of color.

When Muir, then twenty-nine, embarked on his epic thousand-mile journey in 1867 from Kentucky to Florida, crossing an impoverished landscape ravaged by the Civil War, some of his descriptions of Cherokees and African Americans promoted cruel stereotypes. In *My First Summer in the Sierra*, as Muir drives sheep into Tuolumne Meadows in 1869, he characterizes the Indigenous peoples he encounters as "dirty" in a "clean wilderness" and as "shuffling, shambling . . . creatures" contrasting with the flowers, birds, and snowy banks he had been admiring.

In this way, Muir articulates a hurtful dichotomy. The beautiful wilderness landscape had no place for these "shuffling," "dirty" people. In fact, wilderness became an area absent of people, an uninhabited Eden where humans are only temporary visitors whose primary purpose is recreation. Mark David Spence documents the systematic removal of Indigenous people from Yellowstone, Glacier, and Yosemite National Parks as a part of their creation. These were precedents that continued as the park system grew. While Muir was but one of many voices instrumental in creating this exclusionary understanding of wilderness, he was certainly one of the most important.

Similarly, in this early history of the conservation movement, there was no recognition of the role that Indigenous people had played in preserving these beautiful wild lands for countless generations. It seems only recently, as we revisit our approach to fire management, for example, that there has been recognition of the wisdom of the controlled burning practices used by Native Americans for centuries.

Muir's attitudes about Indigenous peoples did evolve over time. He articulated respect for the minimal impact that Indigenous people had on the land, unlike "white man's marks made in a few feverish years." And he came to appreciate the knowledge Indigenous peoples had about such things as "how to get the starch out of fern and saxifrage stalks, lily bulbs, pine bark, etc.," saying, "Our [white people's] education has been sadly neglected." As American literature professor and mountaineer Richard F. Fleck concluded, Muir's impression of North American Indian cultures "changed markedly after he had actually lived with natives [on his five trips to Alaska] in the wilderness." He came to feel considerable sympathy for California Indians who, Muir wrote, were "being robbed of their lands and pushed ruthlessly back into narrower and narrower limits by alien races who were cutting off their means of livelihood."

Yet Muir was, at best, a tepid advocate for Indigenous peoples. It may well have been because around the beginning of the twentieth century, some of the premier conservationists (several of whom served as early Sierra Club board members) also became leaders in the eugenics movement—Madison Grant, Gifford Pinchot, Joseph LeConte, Henry Fairfield Osborn, and David Starr Jordan among them. It is not clear the extent to which Muir was sympathetic with these individuals beyond their interest in preservation, but it is clear that Muir was most outspoken in his advocacy for nature and not human injustices.

Because of his early hurtful writings and his later detachment from human welfare, in July 2020, the Sierra Club issued a statement that acknowledged, "Muir was not immune to the racism peddled by many in the early conservation movement. He made derogatory comments about Black people and Indigenous peoples that drew on deeply harmful racist stereotypes, though his views evolved later in his life. As the most iconic figure in Sierra Club history, Muir's words and actions carry an especially heavy weight."

On a personal level, this has diminished the sheen on Muir's image. But, more than anything, it has served to remind me of just how much work I have to do.

—*Rees Hughes*

WALKING THRU: A COUPLE'S ADVENTURE ON THE PCT

MIKE TYLER

Years ago when walking the Washington PCT, during the days before reaching the Egg Butte (also known as Knife's Edge) section of the Goat Rocks, I read Schaffer and Selters's cautionary words from their Wilderness Press guide over and over: "You can expect this narrow footpath to be snowbound and hazardous through most of July. Crampons may be required, particularly in early summer." Those words quickly became etched in the fear and worry centers of my brain. We had no crampons or ice axe, we were relative novices, and it was July 4. I was almost sick with anticipation. Yes, we did make the harrowing crossing. I could identify with the building fear in Mike Tyler's account of navigating the snow chute on the south approach to Forester Pass that began when they first saw photos of that precipitous traverse, and I could relate to the sense of relief once on the other side. For all but the most fearless (and perhaps overconfident), there will always be obstacles ahead that are cause for concern—the gnarly stream crossing, the exposed trail, the icy ridge.

Forester Pass (on many old maps it is called Foresters Pass) was named by the supervisor of the Sequoia National Forest to honor the foresters who discovered the pass. The trail over the pass was constructed in 1930. There is a plaque near the summit honoring Donald Downs, who was injured while building the trail and subsequently died during surgery.

—RH

"I hope it doesn't get too cold up here," Margo said, as we finished laying out our sleeping bags inside our tent.

"It sure looks barren," I replied, scanning the plateau. "It'll be chilly, but as long as the wind doesn't pick up tonight, I think we'll be alright."

At about twelve thousand feet above sea level, no trees can survive, just some short, scrubby grasses punctuated by tiny red, white, and purple wildflowers. Large patches of late spring snow still covered much of the plateau, and a stream ran in a gully below our campsite. Sheer granite walls rose up on three sides of us, with the valley dropping off steeply to the south, the direction we'd come. Up ahead in the distance an imposing granite wall loomed above us. At the top of this wall was Forester Pass.

This is the pass that everyone had been talking about for the last several hundred miles. It's the first high pass that the PCT crosses. It's also the highest point on the entire PCT, 13,153 feet above sea level. At this elevation, the snow sticks around until late in the hiking season. There's a chute on the south side—the side we would go up—that was everyone's top concern. We'd seen pictures, and it looked frightening. It was a steep chute that was choked with a wide tongue of snow. The tongue was long enough that there was no way to go above or below it. We'd have to cross it.

Without an ice axe, if we lost our footing while crossing it there would be no stopping a fall. Since we'd decided not to carry ice axes, relying instead on microspikes in order to keep our packs a little lighter, our strategy on this pass was simple. Don't fall.

"You can see the pass right there," I said, pointing at a barely visible notch in the soaring granite in front of us. "And just below it, there's the snow chute we've got to cross. It doesn't look so bad from down here."

"That looks like a long way up to me," Margo replied.

Just then, Mars and Coyote came walking across the trail toward our camp.

"Hey, guys." Margo waved at them as they approached. "See Forester up there?" She pointed to the notch in the ridgeline.

"Is that it?" Mars asked, eyeing the wall. "That's way up there."

"I'm pretty sure that's it," I said. "I hope that snow chute's not too sketchy."

"Same here," Mars replied.

"Where are you guys heading for tonight?" I asked.

"It looks like there's one more stream about half a mile ahead, so we'll camp there. We're going to head out super early tomorrow to hit the snow when it's still frozen. What about you?"

"We're planning on starting around 5 a.m.," I replied. "We really want to be off the other side before the snow gets soft." Everyone had the same basic strategy for going over these passes—go over early in the morning and be on the other side and off the snow before the midday warming sets in.

"We'll probably see you up there somewhere," Mars said, as they hoisted their packs. "Enjoy your night up here."

"Thanks," I replied. "You guys too. Stay warm."

"Well, this is definitely it," I said, looking across the snowfield in front of me.

"It's not that far across. Just don't look down," Mars said. We'd met up with Mars and Coyote again just as we started the straight-up-the-wall part of the hike, and we stuck together for the climb to the snow chute. Maybe we could get one of them to be our guinea pig, to go across the sketchy snowfield first.

"Yeah, that's a steep drop," I replied. The snow chute was maybe fifty yards wide. It wouldn't take too many steps to cross it. But the chute was steep. The snow tongue continued down for about two hundred feet below the point where the trail crossed it, and ended in a jumble of sharp rocks. Without ice axes, we would not be able to stop ourselves if we fell on the slick, steep snow. We'd slide down to the end of the snow and then hit those sharp rocks. No one had to say it, but it was obvious that a fall here would be very bad. Like "you could die" kind of bad.

"Let's just go across one at a time," Margo suggested. "Slow and easy."

"Yes, slow and easy," I agreed. "I'll go first." So much for guinea pigs.

I took my first step on the chute. The snow was frozen solid. "My micro-spikes are gripping it. They're gripping it really well." My footing felt very secure. I tried not to think about the icy chute plummeting down just below my left foot.

I stuck my hiking pole into the frozen snow and picked up my right foot. I planted it down a foot in front of me, making sure the spikes gripped the snow. Then I picked up my left foot and moved it forward, again making sure it was planted as securely as possible. Each foot placement was important. If one foot wasn't secure, when I took a step and picked up the other foot, well . . . things would turn out badly.

I repeated the procedure across the chute, one step at a time. Step, plant foot, plant pole, step. Over and over. My concentration was intense.

Nothing mattered other than my feet and the ice below them. I was 100 percent in the moment.

Crossing the chute only took a couple of minutes, but while it was happening it felt like forever. When I reached the other side, I turned to see Margo, Mars, and Coyote on the other side, watching me intently.

"It's not as bad as it looks," I yelled back across the chute. "Just focus on where you put your feet. And don't fall."

Margo started across next and took the same slow, careful approach to crossing. I could tell that the rest of the world faded from her consciousness, just like it had for me. She was focused on her feet and the ice; at that moment, there was nothing else for her. Finally, she also made it across safely.

Mars and then Coyote followed in the same manner. Once we were all across the chute, it was a quick climb up a mostly snow-free trail to Forester Pass. We were up on the top by 7:00 a.m., at the high point of the PCT.

We were all elated. All of us had been dreading this pass. Since it was the first of the high passes, it was one everyone had been focused on. We had studied pictures of the snow chute online and talked endlessly about how to cross it. Now that was all behind us. We had made it to the top of our first major pass.

"What an amazing view!" Margo exclaimed as she crested the ridge. From here, the views were spectacular. Looking back to the south we could see everything we'd walked over the previous day, as well as Mount Whitney in the distance. The trail wound down across the plateau and into the tree-filled valley beyond it. Looking north, we could see a whole new world that we would hike through over the next few days. Snow-covered peaks ringed the basin in front of us. From here we could see several big, crystalline lakes reflecting the early morning sun. It looked like a mountain wonderland.

"It looks like we've got more snow to go through," Coyote said as she came up the pass and looked north. Snow still covered much of the north face of the pass, so we'd have an hour or maybe two of hiking through snow on the way down.

"Yeah, we shouldn't mess around up here too long," Margo suggested. "We want to be off that snow before we start post-holing."

"Okay, a quick snack and then we go," I replied. "Congratulations on making it to the PCT high point!"

We all exchanged high fives, snapped a bunch of pictures, and headed off into that beautiful mountain wonderland that awaited us to the north.

From *Walking Thru: A Couple's Adventure on the Pacific Crest Trail* by Michael Tyler (self-published, 2019). Reprinted by permission of the author.

A BATTERED, BRUISED, AND HUMBLING KIND OF DAY

ANDY DISCHEKENYAN AND LAURIE KRAMER

Andy Dischekenyan and Laurie Kramer met on the top of Mount Whitney on the final day of their respective John Muir Trail thru hikes in 2012. Living four hundred miles apart, their relationship started with many phone conversations and weekend getaways, all rooted in their shared love of nature and adventure. Three years later, they took their relationship to the next level and moved in together—not to an apartment or a house but to a seven-foot-by-five-foot shelter. They have now field-tested their relationship across many years and many trails and offer advice about hiking as a couple.

"Sure," they write about their PCT thru hike in 2016, "there were moments, hours and miles of irritation and frustration but the difficulties felt few and far between compared to the perks of sharing this experience together." They attribute their success to good planning, open communication, a willingness to adapt—and having separate food. "Thru-hiking makes one hungrier than imaginable, which creates feelings of scarcity and possessiveness. Knowing we each had enough food fostered feelings of abundance which led to sharing with one another and other hikers."

The two articulate many positives of hiking together. They noted, "It was nice to always have someone to share the highs and lows with. It felt like the highs were higher and the lows more bearable having someone to commiserate with. We made decisions together, and it was nice to have someone to bounce ideas off of." Laurie observes, "Hiking as a couple afforded us the opportunity for conversation and silence. Eighty percent of our days we hiked within twenty feet of one another but would go miles without sharing a word. It was comforting knowing Andy was right behind me and allowed my mind to wander in ease." And, of course, couples can share loads.

This is how they tell their story of a very long day during their 2016 thru hike as they made their way over snow-covered Glen Pass and a series of challenging river crossings north of Rae Lakes.

Today was an ass-kicker.

We woke up at the usual 5:45 a.m., but gave ourselves permission to sleep in until 6:30.

The last two nights had resulted in minimal sleep, and our guidebooks warned about climbing Glen Pass too early and encountering lots of ice. We also figured the descent down Glen Pass would be icy since it was north-facing, so extra time would only make the snow softer and more enjoyable.

Were we wrong!

We left camp at 8:00 a.m. and hiked to the bottom of what looked like a loose rock wall. From there our path alternated between loose dirt, rocks, and snow. At times the switchbacks were visible, but most were hidden under a deep blanket of snow.

It was not fun. And Laurie had no energy today.

We both felt like it was hotter than it had been in the desert. We were sweating and smelling ripe. It was only half a mile to the top, but it felt like an eternity.

We took many breaks and slowly made it to the top at 9:00 a.m. We enjoyed the views, took a few pictures, celebrated our accomplishment, and headed down the other side. There were good tracks to follow, but the snow was soft. We started post-holing immediately, sometimes thigh-deep.

It was exhausting. With every step we didn't know whether we would sink or whether the snow would hold our weight. After an agonizing four hundred feet of this, Laurie saw a glissade track. Tired of post-holing, she gave it a go but slid very slowly due to the soft, wet snow.

At the end of this glissade she stood and walked about thirty feet to another glissade track. This one was much faster. She was headed for a pile of sharp, exposed rocks. Laurie self-arrested using her ice axe, which did not hold well but slowed her enough to stop her short of the rocks.

Andy, who had continued on in the tracks above, saw Laurie sliding on her side and then go out of sight. He called to her, and only after she had stopped was she able to respond.

It was scary for both of us and made for an even slower descent now that Laurie preferred walking over glissading.

We post-holed our way down. Going less than one mile per hour we eventually made it down to Rae Lakes around noon.

Toward the bottom and on a much gentler slope, we both glissaded. Andy went first and Laurie followed. It was important to her to have a corrective experience since glissading is the best part of hiking in the snow.

Laurie is such a strong person. You'd have to be strong to attempt something again that led nearly to injury a few hours earlier.

We hiked down toward Woods Creek Bridge. Once we dropped below ten thousand feet, the trail was mostly snow-free. Our new challenge was crossing the streams that had turned into rushing rivers.

Andy walked across one with boots and gaiters after getting soaked feet just trying to find where it would be easiest to ford. Laurie wore Crocs, and the strong current seized one about halfway across. She was able to snatch it when it came to rest on a downed log and before it disappeared downstream.

A few miles up the trail Andy attempted to walk barefoot across the gushing White Fork, but the current was too strong and the stones too sharp, and he turned around and retreated.

Swelling with meltwater, the streams are largest and strongest at the end of each day. We discussed camping and waiting until morning to cross, but there were no flat spots other than the trail and it was not wide enough for our tent. We decided to try again above the trail where the current didn't look as strong. This time Andy wore his shoes for protection. Laurie again wore Crocs, and, as before, one came off.

Andy's chin got scratched by a tree we used to help stabilize us toward the end of the crossing, but we made it over safely, cold and wet but relieved. We hugged and caught our breath. We had been prepared for the snowy passes but not for these small streams turned into rivers. At least not this many of them.

Bear Creek and Evolution Creek, still days away, are notoriously difficult on heavy snow years. In the blogs and photos we had seen of hikers ahead of us, these crossings seemed manageable, but things change in a hurry out here.

We were hoping to hike another mile and a half, but there were two more stream crossings to go. We opted to camp early and see what the streams were like in the early morning. We hope they will be less intense.

We have learned from today's posthole hell that we need to start early—no matter what the guidebooks say.

We have crampons, and if we encounter ice we can manage. It will be easier and faster than post-holing. Plus, there are at least eight streams tomorrow, so the earlier we cross them the better.

We have decided that we would be better off with trail runners rather than our waterproof boots. The boots are great on snow, but once they get wet they don't dry quickly. We hope to find a way to get our trail runners sent or brought to Mammoth. It is nice that we can adapt and learn as we go.

We got to camp around 7:40 p.m., and it is now 9:45 p.m.

Today was demoralizing.

Glen Pass was sketchy going up, long and arduous going down, and the scary creek crossing at 7:00 p.m. was the icing on the wet cake. Neither one of us talked about getting off trail, but today as a whole was not fun.

Hopefully tomorrow will be a better day. Time for sleep since our alarms are set for 4:45 a.m. Ouch. Tonight we are grateful for each other and Band-Aids.

Andy and Laurie may soon be experts on hiking as a family. On April 1, 2019, they added a son, Miles, to their team, and Miles went along on ten day-hikes on the PCT in his first year.

CLEANSING DIRT

CRYSTAL GAIL "THE GIVER" WELCOME

Although the lack of people of color walking the PCT has long been an issue, only recently has the inequity come into the consciousness of the broader PCT community. The conversation has been elevated by resources like Crystal Gail Welcome's "Taking Up Space in the Middle of Nowhere" in PCTA's Summer 2021 *Communicator*, Rahawa Haile's "Going It Alone" published by *Outside* magazine in 2017, and the online discussion sponsored in 2020 by ALDHA-West (American Long Distance Hiking Association) with Elsye "Chardonnay" Walker, Will "Akuna" Robinson, and Amanda "Zuul" Jameson.

I believe that one of the first steps in making the trail a more welcoming place is to understand white privilege as it relates to walking the PCT (or virtually any other trail across the country). White privilege is never having to give a second thought about how you will be received in some of the small trail communities you visit for resupply. White privilege is using hitchhiking as a transportation strategy when going into town or back to the trail. White privilege is not being monitored by staff in retail stores you visit along the trail.

In a piece published by *The Trek* in 2020, Welcome said that she had to "forewarn locals" about her presence when walking the 310-mile Superior Hiking Trail in Minnesota. "As a Black person in the outdoors," she continued, "you don't get to go out and explore 'unannounced' or 'uninvited' without making an effort for people to know 'who you are' and 'why you are there.'" We have a long way to go to make the PCT as comfortable and safe for all people as it has been for us as white people.

—RH

As a "Black" female, I am a rarity among backpackers. By "Black," I mean the societal construct whereby I experience discrimination and socio-economic and a slew of other disadvantages because of how race is conceptualized in the United States. However, my skin is the color of the soil, the earth tone "raw sienna" is a more precise modifier.

I was an awkward child, often an outcast. I was made fun of and misunderstood. I found solace in running. Running was an outlet. It offered an escape and filled the void of loneliness that I felt. Running was freeing, and I loved it. Unfortunately, that love diminished as I joined team sports in high school. It continued to fade as I journeyed through early adulthood. I gradually gained weight, and at my heaviest my body had quadrupled in size. Then, in my late twenties, I developed a nonfatal rare brain disease. This was followed by a period of sadness, which turned into a deep depression. I would often lie in bed reminiscing about the more active time in my life.

After many surgeries I received a neurological implant. The implant proved beneficial, and I began running again. I ran farther and longer than I ever had before. The evening after my first half-marathon, a friend took me to a nature preserve. In that moment, with no knowledge of back-packing, hiking, or any backcountry knowledge, I made the decision to hike a trail I had only heard about. Seven months later I was at the southern terminus of the PCT.

I began my hike on April 5, 2016. Along the journey, I met hikers from all over the world, though most were from the United States. Most were experienced, with years of backcountry knowledge, with the means to take time off work, and almost all were white. I did not meet a single Black hiker on my journey. I have often heard white outdoorsmen say that there is no racism on the trail. As I grapple with this, I question why I didn't see a single other Black person.

In the trail towns, I would have interactions with townsfolk who were pleasant enough. But I never felt the hiker welcome that other hikers seemingly received. They would socialize freely and had no need to declare themselves hikers, while I usually had to explain my reason for being in town. Once at Big Bear Lake, a guy asked me where I was hiking from. When I replied "the Mexican border," he told me, "Wow, you speak English good" (with no sense of irony), adding, "I'm glad you made it across the border safely."

In some ways, being on the trail was a bit of culture shock. One day, I was called "hiker trash" by a woman in her early twenties. Her smiling demeanor appeared friendly, yet the words seemed derogatory. As a Black woman, I am often a victim of the misuse of words. This term "hiker trash," I later found out, is frequently used to signify a bona fide hiker, but I suspect being called any term followed by "trash" off-trail would be perceived as demeaning. On the trail, I encountered hikers who would down-talk my hiking gear. They would say "that's crap" or "that's too heavy" or "that's not going to last." Those interactions reminded me of my childhood growing up poor and attending an all-white school where my dad was the custodian. Sometimes the negativity was too loud. I would listen for the chickadees. They sang of joy, without expectations. They whistled about stillness and taught me about the community that surrounded me, Nature herself. I only had to connect.

I also met some really amazing folks on the trail. For example, there were three hikers from Vermont who I spent four days hiking alongside. We spent an entire day lost together, heading south during a trail closure. We hitchhiked together and had meals together. One evening, out of nowhere, it snowed. I was grateful for them. At the time, I was clueless about how to stay warm—they built a campfire that evening. And when we finally said our good-byes, they gave me Vermont maple syrup as a parting gift. We have remained friends since.

Being a solo hiker meant that even though I met people and sometimes spent time with them, I was often alone with Nature. And this was the truly amazing aspect of my trek. When I was lost, I never fretted, because I trusted that she wouldn't lead me astray. When I felt I was running low on water, I would listen for the birds—whenever I heard them, I knew water was nearby. I would watch the clouds for evidence of shifts in weather. Instinctively, I knew the earth and was connected to the earth. The dirt was cleansing. Solo hiking felt natural, as if I had been backpacking my entire life. I understood I was safe among all things natural. The only things that could harm me were the humans, especially the ones who didn't look like me.

One afternoon while I was headed to a Mohave campsite, I was confronted by a rattlesnake. I knew little about how to approach a rattlesnake. I was in the middle of a ridge that I couldn't hike up or down. I didn't want to backtrack, so my only option was to forge ahead. I thought about how I would feel if I were sleeping in my home and someone came in and woke me up. It might end in tragedy, especially with me as a Black woman. I knew I couldn't awaken this snake, so I opted to wait it out. Time passed, and the snake didn't wake up. I was familiar with waiting, from my experiences of growing up without: waiting for paychecks, for new shoes or new clothes. Out of respect, I decided to turn around, figuring it was a sign that I wasn't meant to pass. As I was walking back toward the trailhead, two men came along with two llamas. They reminded me of the wise men in biblical times. They offered to help, and, as I held on to the llamas, they used my hiking poles to push the snake off the trail so we all could pass. I listened as the snake hissed in fear and anger. That night in my tent I felt the anguish of the snake. I cried—major, body-shaking sobbing that racked my body, each wail coming in a wave, and with every sob I let out a whimper. Even though the snake was not killed, we had disrupted the balance in Nature, and she cried with me. I think it may have rained twice during my nearly eight-week trek, and this was one of those times. As I cried, the rain beat against my tent. But the next morning I was greeted by the sun. I took this as a sign of forgiveness. I understood that we are all co-creators of the earth. Any harm that we do to others comes back onto us.

Toward the end of my trip I was hiking in the sweltering midday sunshine of Southern California. Apricity covered me like a cotton-lined fleece. I found myself drawn to an oddity on the trail, a Manzanita tree with a twisted trunk. My sienna complexion was reflected in the roots of the tree, a link to the earth that harmonized within me and offered peace. Its presence, its mahogany-cinnamon color in an otherwise bland landscape, served as a focal point. I was mesmerized by its aesthetically appealing weather-beaten leaves. I could tell they'd suffered, just like my ancestors. I honestly believe that a Manzanita tree can teach us more about the human condition than any textbook.

These trees exhibited strength. They survive within their means, growing not too high and not too low. They have exactly what they need to sustain themselves. They reminded me of my dad, a hardworking single father of four. He worked multiple jobs to ensure that I would have a life where I didn't need to struggle. A life where I could hike in the California desert with no major worries or threats.

Sitting underneath the Manzanita tree, I watched as a group of white hikers passed. They provided brief salutations but no relatedness. The tree offered solidarity, and our bond strengthened. We were together in a landscape with complimentary hues—I felt I belonged there.

Like many Black people I know, Manzanitas are resilient. They are equipped with rather unusual survival mechanisms. Because we derive from nature and we are one with nature, it is important that we protect Manzanitas. But it is not only the trees and the landscape that need our protection. We must also address the injustices that systems of oppression have inflicted on Black, Indigenous, and People of Color (BIPOC). This has made it impossible for so many BIPOC to know true acceptance and the unconditional love of the Manzanita. Like nature, I believe in an inclusive and diverse outdoors where even a twisted Manzanita tree can thrive. Where a raw sienna–skinned "Black" woman can find shade, comfort, safety, and kinship in the cleansing dirt of Southern California, sitting underneath a Manzanita tree.

A FUTURE FILLED WITH GRATITUDE

STEVE GHAN, ANNA MARSTON, AND BRAD MARSTON

Through the stories included in this anthology, we have made an effort to explore the ways the PCT experience is evolving because of influences like the growth in popularity, the impact of technology, the changing demographics, and the effect of climate change. Where does it all lead? If we look beyond what is near and stretch our imagination, we may be able to better contemplate our future and the future of those that come after us. Pushing out ten years seems challenging enough to predict, but the Marstons and Steve Ghan have imagined ahead six decades. This provocative PCT story suggests a more hopeful and far less dystopian future than many possible scenarios, yet it is still sobering. We also encourage you to read and reflect on Mark Larabee's "It Seems That Every Year Is the Year of the Fire," Alice Tulloch's "Crossing Paths," and her accompanying sidebar, "From Where I Stand: Leave No Trace—From Ultralight to Post Carbon Hiking," later in this volume.

Sitting on the electric bus that will take me home from Canada, I flip through my journal, reading the entries from my PCT thru hike. Some hikers think that bringing a book along is a waste of space and weight, but I believe that writing is a good way to process my experience and connect with nature and my surroundings. Also, my trusty journal weighs a very respectable 4.8 ounces, so when anyone says, "OMG, you brought a book with you?" I just tell them: "Hike your own hike."

March 1, 2080, Campo
On my way; the bullet train to San Diego was incredibly fast. And the e-bus service to Campo was exciting: I met many other hikers on it. Hiking now was the right choice. A month later and the heat would be unbearable.

Three miles down the trail and I was already soaked in sweat. The breeze was like a breath from an angel, giving me a break from the heat. And it only smelled faintly of smoke!

The air had been surprisingly clear during my hike. The last time I'd hiked in the West, the air had been thick with wildfire smoke. Maybe the risk of megafires will start to drop soon. Fingers crossed.

March 8, 2080, Warner Springs

86 degrees today. My grandparents told me that when they hiked the trail in 2018, most people started at the border with Mexico in late April. Scissors Crossing would be much too hot if I started that late. I'm so glad my grandparents' generation created a sensible climate policy that has limited global warming. They knew the desert would be barren by now if they had not made serious changes, such as reducing carbon emissions by 90 percent.

Hiking gave me opportunities to think. While I made my way down the trail, I thought about how my grandparents had walked along this very path. The same path that, while different, would still be recognizable to them today.

March 13, 2080, Idyllwild

I walked through a dead standing forest today. Thought about the fire that had forced my grandparents off the trail near here. Despite that setback, they still finished the whole PCT in four months. The trail changed them, and they began advocating for meaningful climate policy. They had a lot of vision for their generation. It's even more impressive when you realize that was a time when people still used gasoline engines. It's crazy that they dumped carbon dioxide into the air that way. What were they thinking? The manzanita is doing incredibly well. I hope to see some snow on San Jacinto Peak tomorrow—it's been so long since I've seen any!

Climate policy was successful in preventing long dry stretches and the desertification of highlands and forests, but it wasn't the magic solution. Too many fires still rage along the PCT. Many more trees stand dead than sixty years ago. Plants now flower months earlier. But it would have been much worse if activists had not had the courage and perseverance to push for change.

March 18, 2080, Big Bear

I've hiked through more dead forests this past week, past San Jacinto and San Gorgonio. Even though dead trees aren't good, they still have a certain beauty. Baby Ponderosa pines are growing to replace them. It's poetic, the young and the old, together. Also, I got my wish—there was snow! Only a little, but still. I chucked a few snowballs for the fun of it. Our climate seems to finally be stabilizing.

The climate is stabilizing, but it still has far to go. In my grandparents' time, you could walk this path in the summer. Now that's impossible. With the heat, increased risk of fires, and diminished water supply, hiking through the desert during the summer is crazy.

March 23, 2080, Wrightwood

It's a cute little town that used to be known for skiing. No snow in Wrightwood now, but it still has some evergreen trees.

I wonder what it would be like to ski. My grandparents said it was a popular sport in their day. I wish I could have had the chance to do it.

April 3, 2080, Tehachapi

This was a tough section. At least the PCT is finally rerouted through the whole Tehachapi Range, avoiding the floor of the Mojave Desert that was SO DAMN HOT six decades ago. Volunteers worked long, hard hours to make that happen, and to maintain the existing trail even as the weather turned more extreme. Still, there was almost no water in this section. Shade was nonexistent for long stretches. So many wind turbines and solar farms. I seriously considered leaving the trail but ended up sticking it out. I was glad I did. Although exhausted, I felt so accomplished afterwards.

Grandpa told me that passing climate legislation was difficult. A disinformation campaign about the human role in climate change confused many Americans. And the warming was so gradual people didn't notice it for a long time. People couldn't imagine a future world that could be better than the polluted one they lived in. They refused to accept responsibility for the impacts of the pollutants that they were putting into the air. It wasn't until a new generation clearly saw the effects and the terrible future that they faced that the demand for action became unstoppable. Many years passed before Congress acted, but the results were worth it. Carbon dioxide concentrations have stopped rising, hopefully soon enough to save most of the ice in Greenland.

April 10, 2080, Kennedy Meadow
More dead forests and manzanita along the way, and lots of rabbit brush and sagebrush. Beautiful! But now I want to get to the High Sierra. I want it so bad.

April 14, 2080, Bishop
Wow! We walked over lots of snow and forded rushing rivers. We climbed Mount Whitney and crossed Forester Pass. I saw my first marmot and heard my first pika! Pikas are so rare now. And the flowers are beautiful. I'm so grateful to my grandparents' generation. The snow, trees, flowers, and creatures add so much to the delight of being here. Thank you! And I finally got my trail name: Thankful. I guess I say that a lot.

Improving forest management was a great move. Rangers start controlled fires during cool seasons in wilderness areas. This keeps the fuel load down, so the megafires don't happen as frequently now. You can plan hikes around the prescribed burn season, and, while it doesn't guarantee a fire-free hike, it gives you better odds. And the soil isn't as dry as it would be if the snowpack had been depleted by an even warmer climate. I understand the "no campfire" policy on public land. At least we can still use our biofuel stoves. The likelihood that you won't come across any fires on a future thru hike is growing.

April 21, 2080, Tuolumne Meadows
So many people! After being with just a few friends for so long, my people senses are being overloaded. The introvert in me wants to hide in the forest. Instead I'm writing in my journal. I'm taking a zero day and will resupply from the store tomorrow. Resupplying from a store makes more sense than mailing food from afar.

I've always wondered why people thought mailing food to hikers was a good idea. Um, hello, you just added lots of carbon to the air? The atmosphere must have breathed a sigh of relief when hikers finally realized that resupplying at a nearby store treated the planet more gently. Plus, it helps the local economy.

When my grandparents saw how much the Lyell Glacier had receded by 2015, they knew that they had to act to save the ice remaining on the other mountains along the PCT. The ice on Mount Lyell is gone now, and the glaciers on Glacier Peak have receded one thousand feet, but now that the climate has stabilized, most of the glaciers on Glacier Peak have been saved. Yay!

April 26, 2080, Sonora Pass
I love swimming in lakes along the way; the water is so refreshing. The e-bus system that took me to Kennedy Meadows North works like a charm. Although I'm pretty sure the other bus passengers thought I didn't smell so charming.

E-buses are my favorite invention ever. They're quiet and don't use fossil fuel. They hold lots of passengers for a mega-carpool. There are cushy reclining seats and the driver-bot is funny. *And* they have free internet! This trailhead access was made possible thanks to the foresight of the PCTA which made it easier for hikers to find their way by public transit. Who could ask for anything more?

April 31, 2080, South Lake Tahoe
Arriving here was like stepping into a dream. Or more accurately, stepping into the water. The lake is amazingly blue and so clear I can see the bottom. The sun is shining and the sky is gorgeous, open and blue. I could live here my whole life.

I finish reading the entries and close my journal. I am so grateful to the activists all those years ago who made it possible for me to end up in this moment. If they hadn't acknowledged the threat of climate change, the PCT would have been destroyed. I can see why Grandpa and countless others fought to save it. Through droughts and fires and rising temperatures, the wild survived. It will survive, longer than any of us. But even survivors need help sometimes. The wild has no voice. It cannot speak for itself. Only those willing to speak up can give the trail the voice it needs. I will be one of those voices. I owe it to those who saved the wild, and to the wild itself.

THE PERFECT GIFT

GLENN WILLIAM JOLLEY

The cooler shaded by a clump of mesquite, filled with cold drinks and perhaps fresh fruit. A driver who offers a ride to town for resupply and brings you back to the trailhead. The RV parked near the trail handing out burritos to famished hikers. The gracious hosts like Rachel and Ian Newkirk who open their homes. These examples and many others are all trail magic, that enchanting feature of PCT culture that is mentioned elsewhere in this anthology (such as Rachel Newkirk's "Unexpected" and Heather "Mama Bear" Burror's "Weathering the Storm"). Best when unexpected and given freely, the magic vanishes when taken for granted but thrives when paid forward. When so many of the stories we have curated involve conquering a challenge on the trail, it is refreshing to include a simple story of kindness. Yes, this is trail magic.

"We make a living by what we get. We make a life by what we give."
—Winston Churchill

The bright green, one-inch, single-blade Swiss Army knife dangles from the keychain where my truck key is inserted into the ignition, and, as I drive, it sways slowly side to side. Rather than a distraction, it is a reminder of Meghan and her sweet and simple act of generosity the day we both left the campsite at Reds Meadow along the John Muir Trail (JMT). I was headed forty miles north to Tuolumne Meadows. She was leaving for home in the San Diego area. The previous day she'd turned eighteen, and in two months I would be seventy-four. The chance that we would ever encounter one another again was slim to none. With a quick hug, we parted company.

Seven days earlier I had been sitting in the King Street Station in downtown Seattle waiting for the train that would begin my journey to Vermillion Valley Resort (VVR) on Edison Lake. Once across the lake, I would be at the trailhead to begin hiking northward four hundred miles on the PCT to Lassen Volcanic National Park.

I was eager to return to the peace and simplicity of the wilderness. Return to the simplicity of an entire day walking alone. Return to discovering places to set up camp along unnamed creeks and small lakes. Return to places where the nights are so dark that the entire sky is lit with billions of stars. Return to the taste of meltwater so cold that it hurts my teeth. Return to the smell of morning fresh air and fields covered with wildflowers. All these and more are why I treasure my wilderness experiences, as challenging and difficult as they have become.

People ask me when I will stop and pack away my camping equipment for the last time. After all, they say, I am getting older. And I tell them I will stop when my body tells me to stop. And then they might ask, "Aren't you just a little fearful of being alone in the middle of nowhere?" I tell them that when I am in the wilderness I am in the middle of the universe, and so, until then, I will be bold and grateful and mindful and return to the wilderness as long as possible. I am as old as I feel, and I am as young as I move, and each morning I awake to reinvent my own limitations.

So there I sat on a hardwood bench with my bulky, heavy-laden backpack between my knees, cleaning my fingernails with my trusty red Swiss Army knife, a gift from one of my children on my fiftieth birthday. I smiled thinking about how long I had kept that knife and how thoroughly obsessive I could be about not losing things important to me.

The trek from VVR to Reds Meadow was an arduous thirty-five mile warm-up on my way farther north. Adjusting to the blazing heat, the high altitudes, and limited water was a challenge. But the views and the beauty along the way were worth every hour of challenge. At least that's how I thought at the end of each day with my boots off and my feet soaking in an ice-cold stream while chewing on a candy bar. Around noon on the fourth day out of VVR, I reached Reds Meadow. I had been there three years earlier when I had hiked the entire JMT. Nothing seemed to have changed. Same small camp store, same quaint café, same old wooden tables and benches, and same welcomed sight to the long-distance hiker needing a day of rest and respite. Oh, and killer hamburgers and pies.

The store was where those hiking the PCT and JMT could send resupply boxes. I retrieved mine and bought a couple of cold sodas. About two hundred yards north of the café are the campgrounds for backpackers, and I headed there to set up camp and take a zero day. That's where I met Meghan and her friend Emily. When they saw that I was looking around for an empty campsite, they called me over and asked if I wanted to share their space so that we could split the camping fee. I agreed and set up my tent at the edge of the campsite under a large oak. I had packed clean clothes, a razor, and soap in my resupply box so gathered them up and headed for the showers. The shower was worth the five dollars for fifteen minutes! Meghan and Emily were taking a couple of zero days because Meghan had injured her knee and needed an extra day of rest. I could see her swollen knee, and her limp was obvious. I silently registered doubts about whether she was going to make it the next 160 miles over the unrelenting switchbacks and unforgiving passes to Mount Whitney. That section of the trail is a test even for the strongest and most experienced backpacker with all body parts in perfect shape.

Meghan and Emily were best friends from high school and over the past year had made plans to hike the JMT together. I don't think they had considered quitting, and Meghan believed that after a couple of days rest she'd be good to go. I was less optimistic because I had experienced what lay ahead. I would never attempt it with an injured knee. But I kept that counsel to myself.

As it turned out, it was Meghan's eighteenth birthday, and they were going to celebrate it with a package of rice and beans. That seemed inadequate for a celebration, so I invited them to join me at the café for hamburgers and pie. We headed there and gorged ourselves, eating real food for the first time in a week.

The next morning Meghan awoke with more intense pain and swelling. Her knee had blown up like a balloon. It was then, sitting at the wooden camp table eating our meager breakfast camp food, that I cautioned her about continuing. She was obviously strong and athletic and impervious to the same aches and pains I experienced nearly every day on long treks, but I told her of my own experience hiking from Reds Meadow to Whitney. It is grueling and should not be attempted unless a person is in full health. This was not information she wanted to hear. Emily gently told her friend that if she further damaged her knee, she might not be able to compete on their school equestrian team, where she was among the best riders. Meghan abruptly returned to her tent, where we could hear the sounds of a teenage girl coming to terms with a decision she didn't want to make. After a few minutes, she emerged from her tent with red, swollen, teary eyes and quietly stated that she would call her mother to come and take her home. But then, what about Emily, Meghan asked? Claire, another young woman at the table and herself on her way to complete the JMT, invited Emily to accompany her, though she would have to get permission from Emily's parents.

The planning and scheming began. How would they go about convincing Emily's parents to allow her to backpack the next two weeks with a total stranger? There was continuing support for Meghan in her decision to abandon her plans. Then there was Claire shifting her own plans. And me just hanging around, resting, and taking it all in before I headed to Tuolumne Meadows and beyond. It was quite the two-day drama at our campsite.

It all unfolded as planned. Meghan's mother arrived late that afternoon from San Diego. Emily's parents permitted her to continue her trek with Claire. And I was up early the next morning to continue my own hike north.

Sometime in the mix of all the drama of the past two days, I shared that I had lost my treasured pocketknife somewhere between home and Vermillion Valley Resort. I figured it most likely fell out of my pocket on the train from Seattle while I was attempting to position myself to sleep. With my backpack ready to be slung over my shoulder, as I was saying my goodbyes, Meghan approached and handed me her small, green, single-blade Swiss Army knife to thank me for my support.

Not all acts of kindness and generosity along the trail are large and dramatic. Nietzsche claimed that life consists of rare, small, unnoticeable, and isolated moments of kindness that in time become significant. In the economy of generosity, a small penknife given to an old man by a teenage girl can seem pretty insignificant, but to this day the knife dangles from my keychain as a reminder that all acts of kindness in a world that feels increasingly selfish and isolating are memorable and worthy of our consideration and gratitude.

Having resolved to leave the trail, Meghan told me with certain bravado that someday she would return to this place and finish what she had started, and if by some chance we met up again she would buy me a hamburger and piece of pie. I laughed and told her I'd hold her to it. Then I turned and walked north toward my destination.

From *Trail Angels: Tales of Generosity and Kindness on the Pacific Crest Trail* by Glenn William Jolley (self-published, 2019–2020). Reprinted by permission of the author.

THE PACIFIC CREST TRAIL: AN EPILOGUE

SHAWNTÉ SALABERT

Shawnté Salabert describes the feelings that many hikers experience after an extended time on the trail. That exuberance of being in the wilderness has imprinted her with an indelible desire to get back to her happy place.

Readers can feel Salabert's emotional response to life on the trail and also how that life follows us home upon our return. Sometimes the best remedy for that transition is to go back out there. Even sitting in the pouring rain, one may realize how meaningful these experiences really are.

Salabert's writing made me reflect on the origins of the verb "saunter." When pilgrims of the Middle Ages passed through villages en route to the Holy Land and were asked where they were going, they would reply, "A la sainte terre" (to the Holy Land). They became known as sainte-terre-ers or saunterers. For Salabert and many of us, these mountains are our Holy Land, and we tend to saunter (not hike) through them reverently.

—*RH*

Three weeks ago, I sat slumped against a picnic table outside of the Tuolumne Meadows Grill, knocking back beer and fries with ravenous, calorie-deprived abandon. It was the end of my summer in the wild, living as free as I ever have, which made it all the more jarring to find myself surrounded by clean, sweet-smelling people, my ears overwhelmed by constant traffic and multilingual tourist chatter. I felt unmoored and clung to my dirty, wandering brethren as we commandeered a small, smelly fraction of space, sharing tale after tale—ones we'd already told each other countless times and loved to retell—of rancid water sources, annoying gear failures, oppressive desert heat, disgusting bodily functions, and rabid Sierran storms. One last hurrah with my hiker trash family, a bittersweet tang to the proceedings.

Life is different now. More clothing options. Less dirt under the fingernails. More distractions. Less solitude. When I returned home, I slid the key into my back door lock, and every instinct in my body told me to yank it back out and run, run, run. Back to the desert, back to the mountains, back to the lakes, back to the scent of pine, to the scampering creatures, to the places where I felt elementally at peace.

This feeling lodged in my gut and burned there, day after day, until I eventually found myself careening down the highway at 3:00 a.m., with my backpack, a tall cup of coffee, and enough music to carry me five hours north. Upon arrival, I practically flung myself back on the dirt, my heart comforted by the "Pacific Crest Trail" etched into the wooden sign at Agnew Meadows. *Exhale, girl, it's gonna be alright.*

Still like twin pistons from two months of hard mountain labor, my legs cranked me upward, the smell of sage and view of distant peaks like comfort food fueling my body. The sun settled into its familiar embrace, my perspiration gathering in the usual places. Floating on that unmistakable hiker high, I barely noticed the white puffs overhead and all but ignored their eventual transition into the unmistakable gray blur that marks an afternoon storm in the Sierra. One drop, two drops. Ten, twenty, a hundred. Laughing, I launched into my well-practiced routine and slipped on my pack cover, then my jacket. *It'll blow over soon*, I thought.

It didn't. Instead, a hundred drops turned to a thousand, and the rain drove down hard, joined by sheets of sharp, cold hail that flicked any exposed skin like tiny electrical jolts. Thunder and lightning flashes coursed, and I ducked under some trees to attempt a nap in the melee. I slid my eyelids closed and danced around the fringes of sleep until a couple walked up with a dog named Tank or Truck or Samson or something similarly mighty. Despite its owners' insistent tugs, the pup sauntered over and plopped down at my feet in a pile of fluffy obstinance, a silent protest against the elements. "He doesn't care much for hail," offered one of his people. "Neither do I."

Eventually, Tank or Truck or Samson was forced along on his cold, wet journey, and so was I. The weather dragged on and pulled me down with it, until I stopped and took stock. Despite the discomfort, was there anywhere else I'd rather be? No, I decided. *No.*

As if magically ordained by the universe, the sky cleared as I approached my destination, glittering Thousand Island Lake, lodged firmly on my list of Official Happy Places. I skipped along the north shore and found the perfect perch high above. As I set up my tent, it felt like I was finally home. While I ruminated on this comfort, the sun suddenly broke free from its gray prison and illuminated the lake. Cheers, whoops, and hollers emanated from all directions, echoing against the granite, and I joined in the joyous chorus.

After the most restful sleep in weeks, I awoke before sunrise and savored the quiet. I knew that other backpackers lay scattered around me, slumbering in their tents, but it felt like I had the place to myself. I walked to the water's edge with my camera, careful not to trample the frost-flecked ground cover. The water was relatively still, soft tendrils of fog rolling across its surface as the sky shifted, and I sat as silent, sole witness to the sunrise. It wasn't epic or spectacular, but there was a subtle beauty, and that was enough for me.

When I finally pulled myself away and moved back down the path to make the trek home, I no longer felt so unmoored. I realized that I might have left the trail, but the trail will never leave me.

HARD WALKING

GWYNNETH SMITH

Gwynneth "Gizmo" Smith's story speaks of determination but also acknowl-
edges the beauty and wonder surrounding Smith and her hiking partner.
Smith also mentions "base weight," the elusive standard many hikers strive
for. Base weight is the total weight of one's pack without food or water.
Base weight has become a subtle competition in the hiking community
that often results in hikers carrying the barest minimum. There are those
who cut off the handle of their toothbrush or go without a stove or leave the
extra layer at home. Yet, despite the efforts to shave weight, many hikers
still include a few personal items—impractical, sometimes unmention-
able—that few will openly admit to. This is a topic Dorothy Brown-Kwaiser
speaks to in "The Things They Carried" later in this anthology.

California's Section I is indeed one of the most physically challenging
of the PCT. Fondly known by some as the Washboard, its continual ups
and downs are exhausting, especially when you have high expectations
for your speed or stamina.

We've only just returned to the trail when we run into two other PCT
hikers taking a break. There's a third pack next to them. "That's our
buddy's pack," they explain. "He forgot his wallet at camp."

"That's the smallest pack I've ever seen!" I exclaim. "Is his food in
there?"

"Yeah, that's everything. His base weight is six pounds."

"Six pounds?"

"Yeah. He's hungry and cold a lot." They pause. "He doesn't like it when
we tell people that, though."

J and I laugh. Having a tiny pack doesn't get you any trail cred if you're
miserable all the time. I have a sneaking suspicion that most super-
ultra-lighters are hungry and cold a lot but will never admit it. The two
hikers we're talking to do not fall into that category. One tells us that his
base weight is thirty-three pounds—four of which come from the didg-
eridoo strapped to his pack. Huh? If I were to give myself a four-pound

musical instrument allowance, I think I'd pick something with a wider range. But, six pounds, thirty-three pounds, or fifteen pounds (my base weight), here we all are, coming up on one thousand miles.

It's more granite and forest with every mile. I feel like we're on a slow taper out of Kings Canyon: still beautiful but easing up on the overwhelmingly spectacular. The huge ups and downs have turned into small ups and downs, the sheer cliffs only a rocky giant's playground. Hard walking.

A small lake—Miller's Lake—calls our name. Blue, almost warm, thronged with bright blue damselflies. For once, for a minute, the mosquitoes let us be. By afternoon, it's the same ol', same ol': behind on miles, hard walking. I can feel myself being increasingly neurotic about miles, and I hustle J all day, hustle myself: walk faster, walk faster, walk faster, walk faster! But I can't walk any faster. I'm exhausted. This section of trail is brutal. "Why is this section so hard?" I bemoan to J. She says, "Don't you remember the Davids telling us that this is probably the hardest section of the entire trail?" I sadly respond, "I think I missed that memo." I've gotten it now, though. Holy smokes!

At three in the afternoon we come out on the ridge over Matterhorn Valley. I've seen this valley before, I'm sure of it—perhaps in the book of fairytales I read as a child. This is where the Enchanted Kingdom lies. Too bad that's not where we're going. No time to waste. We should be walking faster.

We pass Smedberg Lake in the late afternoon. There are lots of hikers setting up camp. "There's room over here," calls out a fellow hiker. "We're going to do two more miles," we reply. Two of the worst, hardest, rockiest, steepest miles yet. Why do I always need to do two more miles?

The setting sun shines off the glacier polish and lights up Volunteer Peak, which is behind us now. Only eighteen miles today. We're going to run out of food if we don't start hiking faster. Maybe tomorrow.

THE PALM OF GOD

MARK COLLINS

There is something about the spectacular and totally exposed ridge walk south of Sonora Pass that lives on in a hiker's memory. Your only cover there is the windswept, beleaguered whitebark pines that cling to the stony slopes. Sometimes, if you are fortunate, you remember it simply for the incredible views. But more often than not it is memorable because of an afternoon thunderstorm there, with wild wind, rain, or hail. Mark "Flyboxer" Collins experienced it all during his 2010 thru hike as he placed his survival into God's hands and the humble whitebark pine trees.

"No Way" Ray Echols, in his essay "A Sierra Storm" in *The Pacific Crest Trailside Reader: California* captures the innocent beginnings of these storms: "How quietly it begins, with the smallest and simplest of things . . . like the gentle brush of a butterfly's wings or the first rays of sunrise. It's early morning, and I notice a small puff of a cloud, a nascent cumulus, riding low and all alone on the southern horizon." It does not take many thunderstorms for PCT hikers to become attuned to the subtle, unnoticeable seeds that may become this greatest demonstration of power in the mountains.

It was July 25, and I was scheduled to hike Sonora Pass. Not having heard of it or seen it before, I didn't know what to expect. The guidebook describes possible "lethal" snowfields on the final descent to Highway 108, but beyond that I was ignorant. Thunderstorms had passed through the area the day before, but that morning the air was fresh and the skies a stunning cloudless blue. As I approached the pass, it was clear that there was going to be at least a mile or two of hiking above tree line. I didn't know it was going to be a long five miles.

At 10:00 a.m., just as I reached the tree line after climbing out of Kennedy Canyon, I stopped for my morning snack. While eating, I was admiring the wonderful view and enjoying the fact that for the first time in three days, the mosquitoes had vanished. As I was finishing my snack, I noticed that clouds had started rolling in over the ridge. *Uh-oh*, I thought. *More storms?* Even though the clouds were just beginning to appear, I had a decision to make. Should I pitch a shelter and possibly wait all day until the storm materialized and waste an entire day of hiking? Or should I go for it and hope for the best? I decided on the latter, figuring it was so early in the day and that the storm would probably arrive in the late afternoon.

As I continued my climb, I kept careful watch on the clouds. Sure enough, more and more clouds began to accumulate, and they created dramatic, exploding bomb–like plumes over the surrounding peaks. For the moment, my situation seemed just fine. Bright blue skies were shining above me, and the views were spectacular. I began to grow increasingly uncomfortable, though, when I noticed the trail made no descent as far as the eye could see. The trail simply followed the side of the ridge above the tree line for miles.

The clouds quickly began an angry darkening, and I could see rain falling on distant peaks. I began running through storm scenarios in my mind, confident that the trail had to start descending soon. No such luck. It was around 11:30 a.m., and I was still hiking the ridge. Then I heard a sound that sent shivers down my spine. A crash of thunder on top of the ridge. It didn't seem to roll. It was like someone dropping a tray of plates, glasses, and silverware to the floor. *Shit*, I thought. *I've got to get off this ridge!* My sunny skies quickly began to collapse on me, as dark clouds closed in from all sides. CRASH! Another clap of thunder. I started to jog slightly as my mind continued to process my options. I was quickly running out of time. Once again, I witnessed a wall of water falling across the valley and heading in my direction. I began running down the trail, but there was simply nowhere to go. The storm was going to overtake me within minutes, and I was stuck up on the ridge.

Just then, I noticed there were stunted clumps of whitebark pine to my left that formed a perfect cave. At these altitudes, these pine struggled to grow as bushes just a few feet off the ground and very close together. I saw a huge streak of lightning to my west, followed by a deafening crash of thunder. *Get off the mountain!* my mind screamed. If I could have jumped, I probably would have. I had thirty seconds to make a run for it or hunker down in the bush. Another giant streak of lightning, this time even closer. Get in the bush, my mind ordered. I dropped my pack, grabbed my rain gear and ground pad, and crawled into the bush. It was the most amazing place I've been on the trail. It was like crawling into the palm of God. The bush formed a perfect shelter. I assumed the lightning drill position and said a prayer. *This might be the end*, I couldn't help feeling. All of a sudden, the winds began to howl. It sounded like a jet plane flying two feet over my head. Rain came down in torrents, and hail pummeled the mountainside. Lightning and thunder crashed all around me. While I sat snug in the palm of God, my only regret was that I could not see the storm rage around me.

Then, as if someone flipped a switch, the rain and hail stopped. The violence was over. It had lasted for fifteen minutes. I sat in the whitebark a little while longer, waiting for the clouds to move farther east. As I emerged from my green refuge and saw blue skies to the west, I couldn't help but let out a victory howl. I'd made it. I had survived! I finished the rest of the pass feeling high as a kite. My hike had been resurrected from the depths of mosquito hell. That evening, I was blessed with a rainbow while standing atop Sonora Peak. *Maybe I'll make it to Canada after all*, I thought.

NORTHERN SIERRA

MOUNTAINS AND RIVERS WITHOUT END

**COVERING CALIFORNIA
SECTION J—SECTION M**

Sonora Pass • Echo Lake • Donner Pass •
Yuba River • Feather River Canyon • Belden

TO THE CLASS OF 2013 AND SNOW AND MORE SNOW

BARBARA WIEDEMANN

There has recently been an increasing identification with a particular "class year." For example, the PCT class of 2013 includes thru hikers and other long-distance hikers who walked the PCT during that calendar year. Classes may have a Facebook page, a class bandana, and a class video. In 2013, thanks to Barbara Wiedemann, they had a class poem.

TO THE CLASS OF 2013

To Puma who played a miniature guitar
to Lotus who greeted the sun
to Viking who lived in Iceland, though a German
to the retired aerospace engineer
to the ones who wore kilts
to the Japanese man who struggled with English
to the one who was seventy-six
to the speed hiker who averaged forty-one miles a day
starting at 6 and ending in the dark at eleven
eventually setting a record
to those who encountered a snowstorm on Sonora Pass
to those who forded a swollen river
and lost gear and ruined electronics
to those who hiked through blisters and bruised tendons
to those who hiked 1300 miles
and were only halfway and kept going
to those who spent five or six months on the trail
eventually reaching Canada
to Purple Haze, Siesta, Story Time, Songbird, and Giggles
to all the solo hikers

especially the women
to all the PCT thru hikers,
thank you for showing
what is possible.

SNOW AND MORE SNOW

It's another hard day
just north of Sonora Pass.
In the morning,
because the snow is frozen hard and slippery,
because the trail is on the side of a mountain,
I focus on each placement of a foot,
each placement of a trekking pole,
trying not to imagine
what would happen if I slipped.
In the afternoon,
because the snow softens,
I sink up to my thighs,
fighting for any progress.
Because the snow bridges weaken
I plunge into icy water,
struggling and crawling up the bank,
feet and socks wet for days.

In the evening
first reading a book by Alice Munro,
her last and final collection
of dark and depressing short stories,
then writing on those same pages,
defacing it, really,
I lecture myself.
"Enjoy this," I write.
"You're not doing this again,
enjoy the whole experience,
enjoy the desert heat and the numbing cold,
enjoy the rain and the hail, the snowpack,
the isolation, and the sometime loneliness.
Enjoy it all."

A PASS TO REMEMBER

KIT MITCHELL

In reviewing the stories we considered for inclusion in this anthology, we gravitated toward tales that entailed a dance with death. What is it about the stories where hikers do everything right that makes them less interesting? It is the tale of the hiker who runs out of food or water that holds our attention far more than—yawn—the person who planned well and ends with a little extra. It is the tale of a thru hiker who is still on the trail in late October and is overwhelmed by an autumn snowstorm in the North Cascades (duh) and staggers to safety after losing his way. In this case, Kit "Chinchilla" Mitchell and her husband, "Pyrite" send their ice axes home and keep their microspikes safely in their packs as they top Dicks Pass. If they had worn their microspikes and kept their ice axes, there would have been no story.

Kit talks about the complex dance we humans seem forever destined to do: balancing humility and hubris. It is part, it seems, of what it means to be human. She concludes with a plea to cherish every day with gratitude and joy.

> *"The world is older and bigger than we are. This is a hard truth for some folks to swallow."*
>
> *—Edward Abbey*

Pyrite and I were a little less than three months in, and about eleven hundred miles into our thru hike, when we reached Echo Lake near Lake Tahoe in early July 2011. We planned to meet Pyrite's parents for resupply and spend a zero relaxing in South Lake Tahoe. Facing a high snow year, we learned about the delicate balance between taking pride in our accomplishments and maintaining humility and a healthy respect for the forces and rhythms of the natural world. We carried tales of torrential river crossings and precipitous passes, and we were simply happy we had made it safely through the challenges north of Kennedy Meadows and in the High Sierra. Some days we felt superhuman and brimmed with delight. Other days the realities of slogging through, over, and under snow seemed insurmountable. To keep our spirits up, our thoughts turned to the possibility of once again walking on dirt. Talk on the trail said we would see more and more dirt as we approached and passed Sierra City. To lighten our load, and in anticipation of what was ahead, we ditched our ice axes at Sonora Pass, and carried on with trekking poles and microspikes.

Pyrite's parents graciously met us at Echo Lake, bringing supplies, and hiked out with us to spend a night at Lake Aloha in the Desolation Wilderness. Beneath the expansive granite peaks surrounding azure patches speckling the frozen lake, we spent the evening with them. They had a fresh perspective, which was a mirror for us to reflect on where we had been.

After coffee and breakfast the next morning, we said farewell and headed north.

Although still hiking through snow, our spirits were rejuvenated, and we felt empowered by our experiences to make smart decisions. We believed the most difficult part of the pilgrimage was behind us. Brazen with confidence, we continued on. The following is Pyrite's account on a pass I will remember.

We got to the top of Dicks Pass (a fairly modest pass at 9,380 feet). We barely glanced at the map before looking toward our descent. From the top of the pass it dropped quickly into a deep bowl, where the bottom of the bowl dropped away again into Dicks Lake, about 1,000 feet down from where we were. The edge at the top was a nearly vertical cornice, maybe 60 degrees. It was early in the morning, and the snow was icy.

Chinchilla and I looked around for the best route down. Nothing looked particularly good. The top of the pass was corniced, with rock above it. I started cutting steps, knowing that at least the incline of the snow would get less severe on the way down. I cut steps about five feet down, so my face was in line with Chinchilla's feet.

I looked up at her with apprehension.

"I don't know about this."

We agreed it wasn't very safe. It was hard getting my feet in, and each step was more unstable. I began moving back up.

It was then that I slipped and was suddenly sliding—plummeting—down the bowl. Fast. I reached out and stuck my fingers as deep into the snow as I could get them, clawing, trying to dig my toes in too.

I cursed, Chinchilla yelled "Stop!," and I *tried* to stop, frantically digging fingers, elbows, knees, heels, and anything possible into the snow.

I flipped and dug my heels in like a crab. I think it was my pack that finally added the last bit of friction necessary to stop my fall. I came to rest about three hundred vertical feet down from where I had begun my fall, maybe twenty feet from where the bowl started to drop even more steeply into the lake. My sunglasses and trekking poles were scattered across the slope. Deep gouges decorated the snow where I had stuck various body parts.

I stood up, looked at my hands, and thought that they were still cold so that's why I saw no bleeding. I waited, but no blood came. Hands intact, I was checking myself for further injury when Chinchilla called down, "How was it?"

"Not bad," I replied. I was uninjured but shaking from an intense adrenaline rush.

She responded, "Should I come down?" (We had earlier talked about the possibility of glissading.)

When I'd said "not bad," I meant literally not *bad*, considering that I had just come close to dying. Her coming down in a similar fashion was out of the question.

I thought for a second, grabbed the three-millimeter rope that I'd purchased to get across rivers from my pack, and headed back up the slope. En route, I retrieved my sunglasses and trekking poles. It wasn't as hard on the way up, without a pack. I had my trekking poles to self-arrest if necessary. I felt okay about getting back up to Chinchilla. The adrenaline rush erased my fear.

When I reached Chinchilla, we decided to tie the rope around her hip belt and then around my waist and use a carabiner as a belay device to lower her down. I kicked in deep foot pockets and guided the rope through the device. We only had one hundred feet of the rope, and the snow was damn steep, so I told her to dig her feet in and stand up. Slowly and carefully, I made the descent again. I had Chinchilla untie herself in case I went plummeting down three hundred feet again.

No sense in taking her down with me.

I thought of possible ways to rappel down, but it wasn't feasible. The tips of my trekking poles were in my fists (we had really lightweight trekking poles, so the traditional technique to self-arrest would not work). The second time was more successful, and I got to Chinchilla, kicked in again, and started the process all over.

Three hundred feet later, we reached my pack. I put it on, and we traversed east to the trees. I decided it would be a good idea to figure out where exactly we needed to meet up with the trail. I pulled out the map, took a good look, and realized that the trail went up from the pass, up a ridge, and didn't come down to our elevation until about a mile away. It struck me that I had done something not only horribly risky but also unnecessary. Tired at this point, and dejected after realizing our negligence, we worked our way around the lake to meet up with the trail successfully and without further incident.

This was by far the stupidest mistake we made on the trail. We were so accustomed to dangerous and sketchy situations in the Sierra and North Yosemite that we didn't stop to think that maybe the trail didn't go straight down from Dicks Pass. I kicked myself repeatedly the next couple of days while being thankful that nothing more serious had happened.

Thru hiking reminds me that we puny humans are not the center of the universe. Whenever we get comfortable and things are going well, we're likely to encounter the force that scares the crap out of us, purges the overconfidence, and reestablishes equilibrium. In these moments of understanding, when the rhythms are amplified, I am most grateful for being alive and that my best friend is alive and that I can share another day with him. Because it's not all about us, and we are insignificant. But, for a time, we are free, and we are here on Earth, and we are alive.

BOTANIZING THE PACIFIC CREST TRAIL

MATT BERGER

Matt Berger's passion for flowers and plants of the PCT is infectious. I got a taste of the breadth and depth of Berger's passion for the flora of the trail when I attended a multipart webinar he conducted that featured hundreds of spectacular images of plants (with some pictures of fauna and scenery thrown in), all of which he had taken while hiking the PCT. There were times I found myself thinking, "Did Matt walk the same trail as I did?" I recognize that I have had a serious case of what Berger labels "plant blindness." I am now learning to notice, really notice the amazing diversity of plant life that I pass. It is one thing to appreciate the fields of woolly mule's ears near the Peter Grubb Hut or the rhododendron festooning the forest north of Mount Hood or the stalwart foxtail pine around the Bighorn Plateau. It is another to notice the small delicate miracles that surround us along virtually every mile of the trail. May Berger convert us all to section- and thru-hiking amateur botanists.

—RH

The Pacific Crest Trail is a wonderland for a botanist or anyone with a love for flowers. The trail traverses so many diverse environments from chaparral, dry deserts, high deserts, coniferous forests, temperate rainforests, and subalpine to alpine tundra and ranges in elevation from 140 to 13,153 feet above sea level. On top of that, the trail winds over unique soil types, from limestone outcrops near Dunsmuir to vast serpentine exposures throughout the Klamath Mountains. This great diversity of habitats makes for the incredible number of plant species, literally thousands, a hiker may encounter along the trail. The length of a thru hike also means you'll be travelling through seasons, and plants that northbound hikers see may be different than what southbound hikers see.

For the ultralight plant maniacs, you can download the Jepson Manual as an e-book on your smartphone to look up and key out all the plants of California as you rest in your tent at night. I also found it very fun to use a clip-on macro lens for my iPhone to take close-up photos of all the species I saw. I suggest looking at the websites Calflora (for plants of California) and iNaturalist (for plants and animals found anywhere) before your PCT hike to familiarize yourself with plants you might see.

I first hiked the Pacific Crest Trail in 2014 and set out with the goal of photographing every plant species I encountered. During my time along the trail, I acquainted myself with plants of the western United States and identified what I could when I got to a town where I could look them up. Since I am from Ohio, many of the plants were unknown to me, but plant families and some genera were familiar, so learning was a fun way to spend my time while hiking. I took thousands of photos of plants I would not identify until years later. On top of this, I had the time of my life. Astonishing views were complemented by the diverse habitats I walked through. Botany and thru hiking had become an obsession.

It wasn't until my second hike, in 2019, that I was really tuned into the plants along the trail. I spent much of 2014–19 in California and worked as a rare-plant botanist for a time in Northern California. So in the winter before my 2019 trek I researched and hunted down all the rare-plant locations I could along the trail and marked the locations on my GPS app on my phone. When I'd get close to these points while hiking, my eyes were peeled for my targets. I had a lot of luck with this strategy and saw dozens of the gorgeous rare plants I'd hope to find. With modern smartphone technology, I can take photos of any plant and upload photos, GPS location, and other data to citizen science websites like iNaturalist or Calflora and publish the observations to be used by scientists who want to know where rare plants grow.

When I tell other hikers that I'm really into plants, one of the most common responses I get is something along the lines of, "The other day in the forest, I saw this big, bright red flower or fungus thing. I'm not sure what it was, but it was huge and red, and I loved it!" Then they show me a photo of the snow plant (*Sarcodes sanguinea*), one of the most unusual and stunning plants along the PCT. I really like seeing small obscure plants that may get overlooked by mile-crushing hikers, but this is one of the plants that makes just about every hiker stop and take notice. The plant is entirely scarlet, stem, flowers, and all. It has no chlorophyll and doesn't photosynthesize but instead is a parasite of fungi. The snow plant takes advantage of a symbiotic relationship between conifers and mycorrhizal fungi. The fungi help the trees take up mineral nutrients from the soil and in return receive sugars the tree produces during photosynthesis. Snow plant taps into the mycelium of the fungi and steals these sugars for its own growth, so it doesn't need to have any chlorophyll (which gives plants their typical green coloration) for photosynthesizing and sugar production of its own. Because it also has no need for sunlight, it often grows in shady forests where other plants wouldn't be able to gather enough light to survive. Let this be a lesson in the incredibly diverse ways plants have found to make a living.

One of the most exciting species I found was the Piute Mountains triteleia (*Triteleia piutensis*), which I photographed in 2014 when I had no clue what it was. I wouldn't realize what I'd found until 2018 when looking back through all my PCT photos and identified it as a super-rare species. This plant was first described to science in 2014, exactly one month before I saw it on my first PCT hike. I lacked photographic geo-referencing abilities in 2014, but in 2019 I recorded the plant in three locations along the trail, all of which were previously unknown occurrences. As the common name suggests, it only grows around the Piute Mountains of Kern County on dry rocky slopes, and often it can be found just feet from the trail. It looks like a small yellow lily on a stalk just a couple of inches high. To think that every thru hiker of the PCT has walked right past a showy little plant that was still undescribed until 2014 is so cool to me. There are plants left to find and learn about even in popular areas.

Another plant that made me shout when I found it for the first time was the pygmy poppy (*Canbya candida*). This tiny rare poppy often grows mixed in with many other sand and decomposed granite–loving annuals, making it difficult to spot. In fact, I spotted it accidentally when getting on my hands and knees to examine a slope that was covered in other small, blooming annual plants. It is often just an inch or two tall and has fleshy green leaves, with bright white poppy flowers rising above them. It is considered rare since it has a relatively small geographic range where it can be found and is just really difficult to see unless you are into what we call "belly botany"—in which you lie on the ground to get up close and personal with tiny plants.

Sometimes you find a plant that you weren't even aware existed. For me that was the case in 2019 when I saw the Mount Mazama collomia (*Collomia mazama*). This beautiful blue wildflower is only known to be found in the Crater Lake area and just to the south, and I found two new populations of this species growing right along the trail. It is a sticky little herb growing to about a foot or so high, topped with a cluster of blue flowers.

My hope is to get hikers excited and interested in the plants along the PCT and wherever they are. Many people have "plant blindness": all vegetation is just a green blur, a boring backdrop. I want to inspire people to take a closer look at each flower, to get on their hands and knees and look at the carpets of tiny wildflowers and see all the diversity that exists around them. Notice subtle differences in smell, texture, shape of leaves, and growth forms. For me, the more you know about plants, the more beauty is experienced along a hike. Seeing a plant I've never seen before makes my day feel productive and satisfying, and I hope to share that feeling with others!

PROTECTING THE PCT
ONE PARCEL AT A TIME

In 1993, the US Forest Service and the Pacific Crest Trail Association celebrated the completion of the PCT in Southern California's Soledad Canyon with the driving of a ceremonial golden spike. But the trail was complete only as a continuous path. The PCT's scenic viewsheds and public access weren't fully protected from nearby development—and they still aren't today. Approximately 10 percent of the trail remains on private property, typically with a narrow easement only allowing trail users to legally cross the land but not to wander unencumbered.

Land ownership throughout the West is frequently found in a checkerboard pattern, alternating between private and public ownership. That's the result of the nineteenth-century land grant program in which the federal government gave every other parcel to railroad companies to spur westward development and economic expansion.

Today the checkerboard presents significant conservation and land management challenges. As population pressures increase, private landowners big and small are selling their scattered parcels for residential development or resource extraction, drastically altering the biological, recreational, and public health resources of the West's last privately owned large landscapes. Roads cut to reach new homes destroy wildlife habitat, interrupt migration corridors, degrade the quality of rivers and streams, and cross recreational trails like the PCT.

One of the PCTA's most important mission mandates is to ensure that the trail and surrounding landscapes remain protected for generations to come. We accomplish this work through partnerships with government agencies, nonprofits, local communities, private donors, and willing sellers of private property.

Through the power of collaboration, the PCTA made a historic leap toward a fully protected PCT with the Trinity Divide acquisition project in 2019. The deal between the PCTA, Forest Service, Trust for Public Land, Wyss Foundation, and Michigan-California Timber Company protected seventeen miles of the PCT and the 10,300 acres surrounding it in the Klamath and Shasta-Trinity National Forests in Northern California.

The PCTA's land protection program would not be possible without the federal Land and Water Conservation Fund (LWCF). The LWCF funds local parks and playgrounds and protects national parks, wildlife refuges, wilderness areas, and historic and cultural sites. The program does this without using tax dollars, as money for the fund comes from lease payments made by companies drilling for offshore oil and natural gas.

Like the PCT, much of the congressionally designated national trails system depends on the LWCF to close the land ownership gaps and complete the trails. In 2020, Congress passed the Great American Outdoors Act, which included permanent full funding at $900 million annually for the LWCF, about double what the program had been receiving in recent years.

This consistent funding—while long overdue—is a major opportunity to protect valuable private land. It will be crucial if we are to complete and fully protect the PCT and the nation's other national scenic and historic trails before it's too late.

—*Megan Wargo, director of land protection,*
Pacific Crest Trail Association

GIRL IN THE WOODS

ASPEN MATIS

In Aspen Matis's 2015 *LA Times* interview promoting her memoir *Girl in the Woods*, she observed that the Pacific Crest Trail is "simply time with yourself." "For me," she said, "that time gave me the opportunity to think clearly through my thoughts—unfiltered and redirected by the thoughts of everyone else." For Matis, thru-hiking the PCT was her "salvation" after being raped on her second night at college. Traumatized and depressed, she returned to the trail where she had grown her confidence and asserted her independence. (She had hiked the John Muir Trail at the age of seventeen and nearly a thousand miles on the PCT a year later, just before starting her first year at Colorado College.)

Inspired by John Muir's classic *Travels in Alaska*, and wishing to "be as free and euphoric as he was . . . glissading, traversing boundless snow, alone," Matis had been pulled to the High Sierra. Fittingly, in this excerpt, we find Matis traversing boundless snow alone, well ahead of most thru hikers, nearly twelve hundred miles north of the southern border.

Unknown Place, the Northern High Sierra, June 18, Day 60
The mountains of the Northern Sierra rise and fracture like the shards of a dropped ceramic, impaling the uneven ground, erect. Sun-poured and slashed by shadows black and long. Deadly, lovely, angular faces thrilling to witness. Frightening; they morph you. You're merely a blackened speck. Long ridges cut the sky, drop down into fog-washed forest, hemlocks with arms like soft walls, sweep back up again to sharp summits, gray.

I stepped carefully, walking along a slick and rocky ridge, down toward timberline, down, down into woods that smelled of black soil and sage. In the forest, on my own, I felt like a dandelion seed, caught circling in gusting wind: lonely but also sometimes gleeful, riding on my own safe current.

My beauty and independence were new for me. They brought me pride and satisfaction; they changed my sense of possibility. I felt awake in my body. Living in the woods, building my little shelter each night, a silent shadow, drifting in and out of mountain towns, a ghost, I was entirely self-reliant. On the trail I had persisted despite fear, and walking the Pacific Crest had led me deeply into happiness. I felt amazing now. In this body that brought me twelve hundred miles, I felt I could do anything.

I emerged from the trees to a field of dense snow sheened with ice. I walked out onto it, feeling exposed, stepping carefully across the uneven sun-cupped surface of last year's snow, an ocean of shallow bowls, slippery and round. I tried to step only on the pockmarks' glossy rims. The holes' bottoms were soft snow, melting out. Step there, and you might fall through.

Two months earlier, I'd stood in the shadow of the rust-brown corrugated metal fence that rippled along the Mexican border as far as I could see. The desert dipped and swelled like the sea, and among the dusty waves I saw no one. I'd begun at the soundless place where California touches Mexico, with five Gatorade bottles full of water and eleven pounds of gear and lots of candy. My backpack was tiny, no bigger than a schoolgirl's knapsack. Everything I carried was everything I had.

From California's deserted border with Mexico, I had often walked more than a marathon a day. Yesterday I had hiked twenty-five miles. Today I'd hiked seventeen miles already. The miles flowed beneath my quick feet, a river of pale gravel, a river of branches against the sky, of stones on stones, of snakes, of butterflies and inch-worms and dead leaves that smell as sweet as black rich mud. For days I'd seen no one. But I wasn't scared of the solitude. People-less wilderness felt like the safest place.

The snowfield sloped downhill, and I began to run. My gait was wild now, careless, heels punching the glassy ice. My hard steps shot cracks through the ground like a hammer to windshields; my impact shattered the world again, again. I was enjoying the pop sound of cracking ground, the jolt of breaking through that extra inch.

Then I fell through, into the snow, up to my neck.

My body stopped. Adrenaline struck my heart; I wriggled. I freed my arms, tried to push out, free. But my legs were stuck. I couldn't shift my feet, not an inch; my heels were numbing. I thrashed; my ribs felt bruised. I couldn't even move my toes. Nothing. I pressed my hip left into the sea of snow; it burned me. I held my core against it until the hole melted wider, harder, dripping. I tried to contort myself out, breathe, pressed my bare snow-burned palms against the snow, pushed, pushed—determined. Still I was trapped. Fighting still.

And I broke out. In one slick thrust I popped my body free. I was euphoric—success!—I breathed, okay. But my right shoe was gone. It remained in snow, five feet deep down, stuck there. I didn't think. I didn't stop. I pulled off my fleece shirt, tied it around my exposed foot, and violently, maniacally dug.

I was wearing only thin black running spandex and a polypro shirt. I hadn't planned for this long delay on the snow. As the hole widened, my body heated; my right foot cooled, freezing and then burning. I knew how easily I could lose my foot. In an instant the mountains had morphed from my playground into my death trap. Even with all the survival skills I'd mastered in my thousand miles of walking, past basking rattlesnakes I'd stepped over like sticks, the glass-eyed bears, the shame and weight of my secret, after everything—this silly threatless snow spot could be where I—just nineteen years old, a dark dot of a body in boundless whiteness—would end.

I was desperate to live, digging. At last I produced my icy shoe. Shoved my numb foot into it. Limped north.

I placed my feet down on the holes' glassy ridges, tried to follow the shade where snow was more compact, not melted by the sun into soft bowls like death traps, but I couldn't always tell. I was alert constantly, meticulous.

I heard frantic squeaking—a tiny fluffed pika resting in a snow hole. June was still winter in the High Sierra. At long last, back in the forest, trees were dripping, everything melting, the sound of budding spring. I'd thought I'd gotten out of the cold without harm, lucky, but as my foot regained feeling, I realized I couldn't step comfortably. I saw that there was damage from the fall. My left shoe was torn open, its silver mesh now a flap clinging to a gaping hole.

I called my mother and asked her to mail new running shoes to Sierra City, the mountain-resort town with the next post office the trail would meander by. She said she'd already sent that post office dried strawberries and freeze-dried green beans and also a plastic baggie of children's Flintstone multivitamins I could chew so I wouldn't need to try to swallow a grown-up pill. She'd picked out the purple "grape" ones, leaving me with the oranges and the reds, as she knew I like those flavors better, and she didn't want me to have to carry any needless weight. She wanted to help me quickly; I wouldn't dissuade her. I felt grateful for her devotion. I simply thanked her.

A Chinese proverb says that a journey of a thousand miles begins with a single step. This journey had begun with the coercion of my body, with my own wild hope. I'd walked into the desert alone in search of beauty and my innocence lost—and strength. I had taken two and a half million steps in the direction of those things to get to here.

This is the story of how my recklessness became my salvation.

From *Girl in the Woods: A Memoir,* by Aspen Matis.
Courtesy of HarperCollins Publishers.

HOOFPRINTS AND FOOTPRINTS

ROSEMARY L. BROOME AND CHLOE S. LALONDE

In 1973 at age twenty, friends Rosemary Broome and Marily Reese left college, learned how to pack a horse, and rode the Pacific Crest Trail on horseback. They were among just a handful of people trying to complete the entire trail that year. With large segments of the PCT still incomplete, they traced unfinished portions of the trail onto topo maps to establish their route.

Fast-forward forty-two years to 2015, when Chloe Lalonde—Rosemary's daughter—and Chloe's college roommate Ceili Brennan set out on their own PCT journey, joining hundreds of other hikers. Unlike Rosemary, they benefited from a well-defined route and the many advances in backpacking gear and technology.

This story weaves together the very different PCT experiences of mother and daughter to give us a taste of their journeys.

INSPIRATION: CHLOE

Two of the more personal questions you can ask someone on the trail is why they are hiking and how they made time for it. My mom's influence on my decision to hike the PCT was fundamental. I like to think I would have decided to do the trail anyway, but it's impossible to tease it out. We did a family trip with a packhorse on the Rae Lakes Loop, which was enough to convince me that packing with horses was *not* the easy way to travel in the backcountry. I love horses, and I ride, but when our pack mare threw two shoes on top of Glen Pass and when often we were forced to camp in the buggiest, boggiest meadows for grazing, I decided stock made a good thing way too complicated.

We backpacked the John Muir Trail as a family in 2008, and I set my sights on the PCT someday. Ceili and I talked about walking the PCT while we were in college in Connecticut, and this plan finally materialized two years after we graduated.

TRIP SUMMARY: ROSEMARY

Marily and I dreamed up the idea for our trip in 1972 during a summer overnight horseback ride out of Squaw Valley. We rode with English-style saddles with sleeping bags trussed on somehow. We had many mishaps that weekend, but during a briefly idyllic period when everything held together, we fell into a trance imagining riding across the country. We awoke from that trance one foggy morning toward the end of May 1973 with our three horses and an immense pile of camping and horse gear dumped on the dusty ground of the US-Mexico border.

Forty-three years ago, the PCT was a compilation of existing trails, dirt roads, and sometimes just a line on a map. We set out intent on a wilderness camping adventure. We had two saddle horses (Dotty and Star) and one packhorse (Dude) to carry our primitive camping gear and pelleted horse feed in addition to typical backpacking fare of freeze-dried dinners and instant oatmeal. The horses would graze along the way, and we would resupply in local towns at about 10-day intervals. Communication was by landline telephone to Marily's parents, who were mailing our food boxes.

However, even the best-laid plans go awry, and ours proved no different. In retrospect, we did not sufficiently factor in the vagaries of the trail and the issues that arise when traveling with horses. We mostly camped out, but we also sought horse feed on many occasions. Our trail angels, who made their living from the land we passed through, came bearing alfalfa hay.

The extended entry from my 1973 journal gives a sense of some of those challenges.

> *Now we were left to the task of packing a horse we knew absolutely nothing about. Champ* had nervous eyes but didn't seem alarmed when we saddled him. Then, like idiots, we assumed there would be no problems and the panniers were slapped on. One bag flapped a bit and Champ was off and running. Marily took off after him while I initially just stood and stared until I finally hopped onto Star bareback to join the chase.*

* About halfway along their journey, their riding horse Dotty was unable to continue, and a replacement (Champ) was secured to perform pack duty. By then, Dude had proven to have problems as a packhorse, but they had grown attached to him, so he was promoted to saddle pony.

Around the lakefront cabins we all raced like the Three Stooges, one after the other. We eventually caught sight of Champ near the stables being held by a man. More soberly now, we packed him up again, inside the corral this time, and led him around among the trees, bumping the panniers so he would get a sense of his new size and shape.

We finally departed Serene Lakes with only half the grain we'd intended. Star had managed to pull one of the sacks into the pen the night before, and the horses had helped themselves to dessert.

We moved north of Donner Summit with Marily astride Dude, me on Star and leading our newly christened Thing II, as "Champ" just did not accurately reflect his personality. Dude was prancing and dancing, wasting more energy in vertical motion than in making headway down the trail. Our trail soon petered out, requiring an unavoidable cross-country stint. It looked straightforward enough, but from previous experience we knew what could happen. And, of course, it did.

We poured over the topo maps trying to match wrinkles on the map with features on the landscape before us. We started out up a scrabbly hillside with Thing II stumbling and dragging back on the lead rope. We hauled him up and then down the forested back side of that hill, discovering an old logging road but no White Rock Lake. Eventually, from a high spot, we saw a lake in the distance. We had apparently passed White Rock Lake and were now headed for distant Webber Lake. Thing II was oblivious to all directions and exclamations, bulldozing his own path. At last, we emerged into a meadow at the lake's outlet. We were in sheep country. We progressed rapidly to the other end of the lake in the fading light where we set up camp, sponged off the horses, and turned them out in the meadow with bells just as a fellow drove up to deliver the news that we couldn't stay. He was the caretaker and said the head sheepherder hates horses and would fire him if we stayed. We moaned and groaned that it was too dark to move on after such a hard day. The caretaker suggested that we have dinner and then he'd return to drive our stuff to another area a mile away.

The new campsite was a grassy spot but featured no water. He left his lantern as our flashlights, true to form, were again not working. Dude got staked and the other two hobbled and we went to bed. I awoke a bit later to find Marily leaving the tent as she thought the bells were getting too distant. Dude had broken his rope and had taken off while Thing II and Star hopped along behind. Fortunately, they tired quickly, enabling Marily to get the hobbled ones and leaving Dude to reluctantly return.

All three were then tied by their snouts. The following morning the caretaker returned for his lantern and gave us directions for a shortcut: "It'll save you at least ten miles." Shrugging our shoulders, after all it was his backyard, we skeptically headed out the recommended logging road. It wound around getting farther and farther away from the PCT. We concluded that he was quite wrong, but here we were and could follow dirt roads along the Feather River Valley. It was nineteen miles to Yuba Pass and four more to Bear Trap Meadows where we decided to stay.

The meadows were well cowed over, leaving a polluted, disgusting trickle of water down the center. It was a freezing cold night and we staked Dude but had a backup line ready in case the other two got to wandering. Once again, it was a night of trials and tribulations as the horses somehow escaped. By the time we had retrieved them we were shivering uncontrollably. Not surprisingly, we woke to see frost covering the meadow and ice chunks in our dirty cooking pots.

Logging-road angst set in as we continued north, so upon reaching Interstate 5 near Shasta, Marily and I, being almost a full month behind schedule, took the Interstate 5 on-ramp to Weed, bypassing the Trinity Alps [walking along the shoulder of I-5 a distance of about ten miles]. During this section, Shasta stunningly loomed for days, first ahead and then behind us.

TRIP SUMMARY: CHLOE

Despite a critical drought and zero Sierra snowpack, our journey started with a snowstorm on Mount Laguna on day three, and we spent the night on the floor of the Pine House Cafe & Tavern with forty other hikers. By the time we reached Idyllwild, we found ourselves in a group of hikers who stuck together all the way to Kennedy Meadows. We shared the kind of bond that first-time thru hikers do when facing long water carries in Southern California and discovering the exhilarating freedom of sharp, bright dawns from flat on our backs in the rocky sandy desert.

Unlike my mom, Ceili and I traipsed up Whitney and over Forester Pass under blue skies. Spectacular thunder and lightning storms punctuated our passage over sequential Sierra passes, but we found our own pace through these wilderness stretches.

Northern California also brought its challenges for us. We struggled with the monotony of the never-ending forests and how to occupy our minds, though our bodies were now fit and ready for higher-mileage days.

Smoke from wildfires completely obstructed our views of Mount Shasta, although as we passed through the Trinity Alps and our favorite hidden trail town, Etna, coastal breezes would sometimes lift the hazy curtain and present us with bright clear days.

Oregon was at once exhilarating and difficult in both 1973 and 2015. Despite fine trails and dramatic volcanoes, cold, wet weather led us to some miserable camping and miles. We both, by chance, sheltered from unrelenting rain at the same resort, Big Lake Youth Camp, in central Oregon.

For Ceili and me, alarmingly early snow and rainstorms over Labor Day weekend helped extinguish the fires up north, and we forged new friendships through the adverse hiking conditions. For my mother and Marily, they couldn't wait for Oregon to end.

THE END: ROSEMARY

Marily and I spent a few days in the Columbia River Gorge to regroup. The weather had closed in, and our time on the crest was done. The only option was to head up the eastern side of the Cascades through ranching and orchard country. Fueled by apples, we made our way through orchards, often in rain and snow.

Thankfully, we spent every night indoors, welcomed by hosts who then contacted friends and relatives farther north to arrange the next night. On November 9, we reached the Canadian border at the head of the Okanogan Valley. We met up with Marily's parents, who greeted us with a champagne picnic. Being too cold to linger, we soon loaded up to drive home through the pouring November rains.

Chloe and I both followed a dream from end to end across the years, and we have inspired each other: *Here Because of Her.* My PCT experience inspired Chloe to set out with Ceili, and her hike inspired me to relive my trail time in writing and photos.

I find that the Pacific Crest Trail still beckons. Chloe's birthday present to me this fall was a promise to do a PCT section in Washington near Stehekin with me next summer—on foot!

THE END: CHLOE

Washington had some of the toughest, most beautifully rewarding sections of trail. We again encountered snow and rain in the Mount Adams and Goat Rocks areas but finished in a last burst of summer after Snoqualmie Pass. We were blessed with ten perfect days through Glacier Peak Wilderness and into the North Cascades. Final days in Washington with our trail friends were bittersweet. It was a special moment when Ceili's parents and my mother hiked into Monument 78 to meet us with a celebratory picnic on the morning of October 5. We all hiked out to Manning Park together. The connection with my mother's experience gave me special insight into how the trail used to be. Yet, despite improvements in trail infrastructure, technology, and resources available to the multitude of hikers, our thru hike was no less unique and authentic.

I will close with an excerpt from my blog, written near mile 1500:

It is a magical, magical feeling to be alive in my skin, walking confidently forward along a clear, well-trodden path, knowing how many miles to my next water and how many days to my next town. Few things are simpler.

This is not real life. Many hikers would interrupt me right now and say: "There is nothing more real!" No, I maintain this is not real life. We are in a suspended state in which we are at once self-reliant and also dependent on the circumstances that have allowed each one of us to be here. But it is real right now, it is rare (for each person), and it is a joy. I'm so grateful.

TECHNOLOGY AND THE TRAIL

JACK HASKEL

A couple of years ago while walking south on the PCT on the reroute approaching Sierra Buttes, I asked a NOBO hiker about how the new stretch of trail navigated the terrain around the Buttes. His response surprised me, "Where are the Sierra Buttes?" When I, no doubt failing to hide my disbelief, said it was that mountain he'd just gone around, he admitted to relying exclusively on the blue dot and the narrow map of the trail on his phone. I confess to being somewhat of a Luddite and prone to knee-jerk reactions, but that encounter came to define my exasperation with the exploding role of technology on the trail. I appreciate Jack Haskel's much more nuanced appreciation for the impact of technology and the inevitability of its use. I am the dog that barks after the hikers have already passed.

The reality is that technology has enriched and will continue to enhance much of the PCT experience. My hope is that its application will be thoughtful and carefully considered and that the trail will be, as Haskel concludes, "free from most technology."

—*RH*

"Unlike television, nature does not steal time; it amplifies it."
—*Richard Louv*

I imagine that people have been fretting over technology since the advent of the first tools. And, as creatures of the wilderness, we've surely been debating tech and its place in the outdoors for, well, forever.

Now seems a good time to survey the situation of technology and the Pacific Crest Trail.

I'm an old millennial, born in 1983 into a home that was obsessed with "homebrew computers." I remember reading user groups about hiking as a small child, and I recall the day the first popular web browser came out (I was ten) and then spending far too many hours on the early World Wide Web reading about backpacking even before I was a teenager. On the internet I participated in the birth of ultralight backpacking. On the internet I found my first job after college: mapping the Pacific Crest Trail with a GPS in 2006.

My first memories barely touch the era before personal computing. I am the start of a new era.

In 2007, the first iPhone was released. That same year, Lon "Halfmile" Cooper collected the first significant user-generated data about the PCT. The information would become the indispensable Halfmile maps.

The internet and social media have connected all corners of the world. The average Jane can have followers and influence both widely and narrowly. The PCT has spawned thousands of websites and online touches that have reached millions of people.

Remarkably, we're just at the beginning of the digital era. Drones are just starting to take off, although the PCT's skies are still quiet. There are places, like much of the PCT, where accessing the internet requires clunky satellite adapters. The futurists' predictions of artificial intelligence, robotics, and genetic engineering still seem like abstract concepts of little consequence to the PCT experience.

In camps and online, we talk about how we experience the outdoors, debate the pros and cons of emergency beacons, and lament or speak in favor of listening to podcasts while hiking or watching movies in our tents.

"Backpacking, like other forms of camping, is a response to the pressures of modern urban life, including everyday technologies," geography professor Terence Young told me via email.

In his book *Heading Out*, Young dates the history of American camping to the summer of 1869. It turns out that the arguments we have today about technology and camping date to those early years. Since then, debate has raged about who is having the most authentic experience: People heading out with little technology? Or are they doing it wrong? Is backpacking better than car camping and car camping better than RVing? Is it purer to have less technology in your pack?

For the past decade, I've worked for the Pacific Crest Trail Association to support the trail's hikers, horseback riders, and community. The more I learn, the more I know that history repeats itself.

Young's book includes fascinating pieces of PCT history. He correlates the creation of wilderness and the PCT in the 1920s and 1930s with expanding technology.

"One technology was particularly important for the creation of the Pacific Crest Trail—the automobile and paved roads," Young writes. "An early PCT advocate, Clinton C. Clarke of Pasadena, began his quest for the trail in 1932 because he strongly disliked the new Angeles Crest Highway that was being pushed through his beloved San Gabriel Mountains. Clarke worked with the Forest and Park services to create the PCT through wilderness (unlike the Appalachian Trail, which ran between settlements). In this way, the PCT's backpackers would be able to avoid cars and wildlands would be protected from invading roadways."

Truly the PCT exists as a place to get away from technology. Dubbed "America's Wilderness Trail," it's a rare opportunity to spend months in primitive self-reflection.

The trail is a place for me to escape from a screen. But a screen also keeps me connected to the trail when I'm home.

"With over half of the PCT in designated wilderness, providing opportunities for solitude and exploration—core elements to wilderness character—is integral to the nature and purposes of the trail," says Beth Boyst, US Forest Service Pacific Crest Trail administrator.

The PCTA captures that in our official Statement of the Trail Experience, which guides the creation and management of the PCT.

Favoring landscapes that appear wild and free from development by humankind, the Pacific Crest Trail's nature and purposes are to provide for unparalleled journeys on foot or horseback along the high and spectacular spine of the Pacific mountain ranges. Primitive forms of travel hearken back to simpler and more rugged times. The trail's protected corridor offers a sense of solitude and closeness with nature, evoking extended retreat from civilization, even if venturing out only for a day.

The PCT experience should favor panoramic views of undisturbed landscapes in an uncrowded, non-mechanized, tranquil and predominantly natural environment. It should feature diverse, untrammeled ecosystems and historic high-country landmarks while avoiding, as much as possible, road crossings, private operations and other signs of modern development. Trail facilities such as campsites, water sources and other amenities for hiker and pack-and-saddle use should be simple.

That places the Pacific Crest Trail in direct response to technology.

Yet with every passing season, the tendrils of technology extend further into the trail experience. We leverage technology at the PCTA. We wouldn't know what lands to protect were it not for robust digital maps. We wouldn't be able to reach as many people if not for our databases and web presence. The scale of our work, and the PCT itself, would be greatly hampered if the digital age hadn't happened.

I am near the center of the drumbeat of technology encroaching into the trail.

We're in an era of total information—or at least we're nearly there. Huge volumes of words, photos, and videos are shared about the PCT each year. I can log in to Instagram and see photos from the summits of remote peaks taken just a few hours ago. Satellites show me the snowpack. Crowdsourced reports in apps and websites detail the status of once-unknowable things such as today's rate of flow at a desert spring. All this has changed the expectations of wilderness travelers. Similar to the rangers at the front desks of Yosemite and Kings Canyon, I get asked how a specific creek is flowing on a given day. PCT hikers of the past wouldn't even imagine that something like that could be known.

When I hiked the trail, we used a paper book and its little black-and-white maps. But it was me who carried that GPS. I am living the birth of this new digital future.

The PCT has become popular because of technology. The internet's effect on discovering obscure subjects, like walking across the country on the PCT, is immense. And once you discover a niche topic, you have the world's knowledge at your fingertips to research and obsess over.

To keep the PCT in fantastic shape in an era of increasing use, the PCTA and our community of volunteers, donors, partners, and advocates must adapt. We've seen hikers abandon paper maps in favor of smartphone apps that show more updated information and let people share comments and photos. But the crowd doesn't always have all the information they need. And they move in practical ways. If it's useful, it gets noted. Regardless of whether a campsite is too close to water or the trail, on private land, in endangered species habitat, it gets noted and used—even overused.

Dana Hendricks, PCTA's Columbia Cascade regional representative, piloted a review of smartphone apps and how they map campsites.

"We've been noticing that while there may be dozens of potential campsites along a stretch of trail, it's those sites listed in the apps that are full when hikers get there and that show most noticeable impacts when the season's over," she said. "To make things worse, many of these sites are much too close to the trail or the water."

Thankfully, so many care about protecting the trail.

"We attempt the admittedly difficult balance of providing hikers with the information they have come to expect in the internet age, while working collaboratively with trail maintainers and managers to get their message of stewardship to hikers," says Alice Bodnar, one of the owners of Atlas Guides, which makes the popular Guthook Guides apps for long-distance trails.

These days, phones are deeply engrained in PCT hikers' trips. Most people don't even consider the possibility of keeping their phone turned off. Phones are used all day—for photography, for music, for navigation, and for leaving comments in apps for the hikers coming behind you.

Technology has created a lot of work for people like me who are involved in land management. The Society for Wilderness Stewardship published a fascinating paper on emerging technology in the wilderness. It calls for further research into the issues, and it challenges land managers to keep up.

Research already shows that emergency beacons change some people's behavior in the backcountry. Many of us are more likely to travel solo or take unnecessary risks if we have an electronic tether to a rescue crew. But beacons save lives and take the search out of most search-and-rescue operations. Research could help educate users about how to approach beacons in a newly nuanced way. We also worry about how this connectedness seems to have resulted in backcountry travelers transferring risk onto others. Instead of being responsible for ourselves, we expect to press a button and be saved.

The Society for Wilderness Stewardship paper talks of the impact of technology on management systems: "When demand suddenly exceeds supply, there is often an incentive for either illegal use or, at a minimum, finding ways to 'scam' a system. In the past, managers had a chance to react to these pressures and make corrections because it took time for word to filter out about a desirable destination or how to 'beat' the system to get there. Now information spreads almost instantly via the internet."

Some technology is regulated. Bikes are banned on the PCT and in wilderness. Companies can't install cellphone towers willy-nilly in the Sierra Nevada. Drones can't be operated in wilderness. Road building has limits. The list goes on. The PCT is a protected place.

But some technology is not regulated. Largely, if it's handheld, it's not regulated. You can use your two-way radio, GPS, or phone without restriction. As managers, we try to not be overly judgmental of people's choices concerning handheld devices. Part of the PCT and wilderness experience surrounds the idea that an unconstrained experience is worthwhile.

PCT thru hiker Sterling "Leo" Montes, who has beautifully documented the trail experience through photography, thinks a lot about his generation's relationship with technology. I asked him about how smartphones are affecting our time on trail.

"Our phones are our portal into the world we left behind," he said. "It's important to embrace our disconnection from that, and the trail forces you to do that 99 percent of the time. I often found my phone fulfilling its more intended purpose. Instead of mindless consumption, I found myself intentionally sharing my experience with the rest of the world and staying in touch with those I missed.

"I kept trying to take photos of my friends, and they were always on their damn phones," he said. "The juxtaposition is cringeworthy. We still can't escape these crazy devices. I wanted us to all acknowledge how silly it is to keep these things in front of our faces among some of the most beautiful places on the planet where there's absolutely no *need* for a phone or a connection."

It's my greatest hope that the PCT will be around in one thousand years. As it is already today, it will be one of the last quiet places for a lengthy relationship with how nature once was: free from most technology. I can only imagine how the next story of technology and the PCT will be written.

SNOWSTORM: SIERRA CITY TO BUCKS LAKE

DAVID H. BAUGHER

David Baugher, who retired after a career as a fire chief, lives in Arnold, California, in the foothills of the Sierra. In 2014 he began hiking northward as a multiyear thru hiker (MYTH), with the goal of completing the trail by his sixty-first birthday in 2024. The following piece is a deeply personal reflection on the finite nature of life and the choices we must make along the way. Even though he feels a particular urgency because of his father's last years, Baugher resists the temptation to foolishly push ahead with his hike and aborts his journey. He will return again another day and finish that section. Turning back is one of the most difficult decisions a PCT hiker can make. Yet, as we have seen in reviewing countless stories from the trail, not doing so can have disastrous consequences.

With a heavy heart, I hung up my phone in cabin 1 at the River Resort in Sierra City. My wife, Luann, had called that quiet morning to let me know that her mom, Marilyn, had passed away. I had taken a nero [nearly zero-mileage day] in Sierra City and was planning to return to the PCT that spring morning. The resort owner, Jim, said "no problem" to my request to spend another night considering the circumstances. So, finding a comfortable chair on his expansive deck overlooking the Feather River, I began to ponder.

Alzheimer's is a terrible disease. Marilyn, diagnosed with the disease in 2003, had, like so many we know, descended into a faint picture of the person we had known before. In 1905, German psychiatrist Alois Alzheimer performed an autopsy on a woman who had suffered early cognitive failure. Alois discovered that one-third of the woman's brain had disintegrated, leaving plaque-tangled cell fragments. More than one hundred years later, Alzheimer's disease remains poorly understood and generally regarded as incurable.

In the morning light, sitting on Jim's deck with the river below, I thought back to my own experience with cognitive failure. Fifteen years earlier, my father, Hank, had been diagnosed with frontal lobe dementia. Like the sun setting below the Sierra, my father faded away before our eyes in less than eighteen months. Hank was only sixty-one when his light went out, and it was his death that prodded me to change my life and ultimately begin hiking the Pacific Crest Trail.

I was asked in 2013, "How long did your father live?" I was fifty-one that day, and the question hit me like a sack of stones. In ten years I would be the same age as when my dad passed. What was I going to do or achieve over the upcoming ten years? Work? Not an exciting thought. A quote from Steve Jobs drifted into my mind: "If today was the last day of my life, would I want to do what I'm about to do today?" My answer that morning was no, prompting a change of life for me.

I spent the remainder of that day talking with my wife and kids. Things calmed down after a while, so I borrowed a book from the resort's small library and then, in the quiet of the afternoon, read on the peaceful deck. By the following morning, things in the family had resolved themselves and settled down. Marilyn's passing had been expected, and there was nothing I could do here or back at home, so, with Luann's endorsement, I returned to the trail.

The PCT crosses Highway 49 above Sierra City at an elevation of forty-one hundred feet. Here the trail aggressively climbs toward the jagged Sierra Buttes, ascending four thousand feet to skirt the iconic landmark. Later I discovered that, in the winter of 1852, unusually deep winter snow had smothered Sierra City, then a village of tents, shacks, log houses, and a few frame buildings. Most residents abandoned the hamlet, struggling to reach the San Joaquin Valley. Five diehards stayed to work their gold mine and were there when the buttes suddenly discarded their top layer of snow. The avalanche wiped out the village and killed two of the five miners.

The PCT led upward, and the new Sierra City lay far below me. Several hours had passed when I encountered a couple of hikers walking toward me down the trail. Up ahead, they warned, was a solid wall of snow at seven thousand feet, and they were unprepared to cross it into higher snowbound elevations. I had extra clothes, crampons, and an ice axe, so I felt confident continuing.

These two guys were the first PCT hikers I had met since leaving Donner Pass four days before. Yes, there had been lots of snow but nothing that stopped my progress northward. My thoughts wandered as the trail passed under my feet. Indeed, I did hit snow, but the crampons did their job, and I continued. That day I covered fifteen miles before finding a dry campsite with an excellent supply of firewood. Soon my tent was up, soup was heating in my pot, and a campfire warmed the oncoming evening chill.

Morning broke cold and gray. As always, I procrastinated before leaving the tent and going out into the frigid mountain air. In the quiet, I packed up camp. The preceding night's fire was a faint warm remembrance, and the ivory banks of snow surrounding my dry patch of campsite looked foreboding. It was 9:00 a.m. when I shouldered my pack and noticing the soft snowflakes drifting down from a now gray smoldering sky. For all the serenity, majestic repose, and granite permanency, the Sierras can be as temperamental as an adolescent, and I was about to experience this firsthand.

Returning to the trail, I followed the PCT upward across rolling ridge after ridge where the trail played peek-a-boo with my navigation skills. Occasionally, the path was visible, usually along the sections with southern exposure, while on the northern exposures the trail was nowhere to be seen. The spring snowpack in these sections was ten to twenty feet deep, obliterating signs, blazes, and any indication that hikers had been through the area. My family, following my course remotely via a Spot satellite transponder, reported that my path seemed to zigzag haphazardly in these sections. They could only guess what I was encountering.

My mind echoed "Dave, you better watch out," as the snowflakes began falling in earnest. These were not gentle Frosty the Snowman snowflakes, this was a mean snowstorm with driving winds. Yet I continued, the cold pressing straight into my bones. After a couple of hours, thick swirling clouds of snow still whirled around me, and howling winds blew even harder. I started climbing a tall frozen ridge, with wind thundering across the trees, and now cold rain pelting my backpack, and tattered, ghostly clouds whipping overhead. Reaching the summit at noon, I thought, *You better consider taking a break and getting into some shelter.*

Breaking the ridgeline, I made for a stand of trees on a south-facing slope. Within the grove, I found bare patches of ground and managed to set up my tent while the wind screamed. After one glance around, I dove inside the tent with my pack, like a ground squirrel escaping a red-tailed hawk. It was high noon, Thursday, June 18. For the next three days and two nights, the storm raged outside my tent, roaring out of the west: rain, hail, sleet, and wind. Wow, did the wind blow. When the Sierra goes on a rampage, there is not much a hiker can do but take shelter and watch with awe. In this storm, lulls were brief, and then a high-pitched scream would start again in the treetops, and my tent would be slammed by the roaring winds.

Two mornings later, I woke at sunrise and crawled from the warmth of my sleeping bag. The storm had broken. As I pushed forward after breaking camp, a gray mist enveloped the ridgeline, completely restricting visibility. *Dave,* I thought, *you better watch where you are walking.* I looked over my map, which indicated that the trail followed this ridge for a half-mile before dropping to a lower elevation. Here the trail was visible under my feet, but ahead the trail disappeared into another large snowbank. I was unsure of my exact location, with no horizon to see, so I took a ninety-degree turn and walked about fifty feet to check out the terrain. At this point the ground disappeared into a gray abyss below. I was standing on a cliff. Carefully returning to the trail, I went the opposite direction, only to encounter a crumbling cornice of snow that also fell off into that gray abyss.

I hauled out my GPS, turned it on, and then followed the path exactly as indicated on the screen, precisely, step by step. There was not much room for error. I hiked down from the ridgeline, safely heading for lower elevations. My camp that night was nestled in the sunshine along an old logging road. Dinner and relaxation ensued in the fading light. That evening was quiet, and the night was *too* quiet.

When morning came, I emerged from my tent to discover another snow-covered landscape. Oh, man, not again. But I broke camp and continued downward, the trail dropping into Feather River Canyon. Later that day, I crossed the bridge over the Feather River and made camp along Bear Creek.

A dry morning greeted me after a night's sleep, and I hit the trail again. My goal was Bucks Lake. As I was climbing to the north fork of the Feather River Canyon ridge, a faint cell signal allowed me to call home. Still grieving from the loss of her mother and having seen no movement on the Spot transponder during the time I had waited out the storm, Luann was relieved to hear my voice. I asked her to contact lodging in the Bucks Lake area and find me a room for the night, then continued on.

My hosts at Haskins Valley Inn, Doug and Dixie, told me that I was the first PCT hiker they had seen that spring. Doug also let me know that the upcoming section between Bucks Lake and Chester was even more snowbound and dangerous than the trail I had just covered. After another call home, arrangements were made for Luann to pick me up in Quincy the next day.

The next morning, Doug, Dixie, and I drove down the mountain to Quincy. I was lost in thought. This had been an extraordinary spring backpacking trip. I reflected on the death of my mother-in-law, on Alzheimer's, and on my father's death, and how, in a roundabout way, those events connected me to Pacific Crest Trail. As I gazed out the window, trees passed by in a blur as we drove to town. Echoes of the wind screaming through treetops still resonated in my ears. The heaviness of heart I'd felt in Sierra City had lifted, replaced by my renewed determination to return and continue northward.

FRIENDS IN HIGH PLACES

MEGAN KIRKPATRICK

Nature is all about balance. How one species interacts with another often creates a symbiotic relationship that can have far-ranging impacts. Megan Kirkpatrick takes a detailed look at two critical members of the ecosystem that the PCT traverses. The whitebark pine and Clark's nutcracker are residents of this domain and decidedly influence everything from mountain hydrology to the abundance of squirrels in the woods and even bear-human conflicts.

Quietly a change has been taking place that may have a significant impact on all who take pleasure from the backcountry. Kirkpatrick raises our awareness of the importance of a "winged forester" and twisted and gnarled trees that are hundreds of years old. With all at the mercy of climate change, there are profound and provocative consequences. Whether or not we humans take action, nature is doing its best to respond.

I have always been in love with wilderness, so forest ecology was an inevitable field of study for me. I want to spend as much time as possible connected to wild spaces, to the wonder of the natural world, to the juxtaposition of its delicate relationships and their resilience. This is how I fell in love with whitebark pine and complex ecology.

Whitebark pine (*Pinus albicaulis*) is one of the nine North American species of five-needle pines, also known as white pines. Whitebark pine grows in some of the most fantastically beautiful landscapes in the United States. They shape the aesthetic of our high-elevation recreation destinations, and one must work to see them.

Anyone who has hiked the Pacific Crest Trail has come across this species. The PCT overlaps with a significant portion of whitebark habitat. From the High Sierra to Canada, the trail traverses the small portion of land where whitebark pines can be found: high, remote, rugged country.

Aside from biologists, backpackers and climbers are often the only people to come across this species. Its ecology, the numerous ways it influences life from the highest elevations to the lowest river valleys, is mind-boggling. Whitebark pine is a keystone species, meaning that it is such a vital component of the ecosystems that its loss would radically change the landscape. The diverse and complex dynamics of whitebark pine communities play a crucial role in protecting water resources and providing food and shelter for numerous species of plants and wildlife.

Whitebark pine has an important evolutionary friend, a bird called the Clark's nutcracker (*Nucifraga columbiana*). Whitebark pine is dependent on the nutcracker as the main mechanism for seed dispersal. Whitebark pine cones do not open on their own, but within them are fatty seeds packed with calories that the birds crave. The birds use their perfectly adapted strong beaks to get the seeds loose, and they store them in a pouch below their tongue. They carry these pine nuts to cache spots to be retrieved later in the year, a sort of subalpine pantry. They are capable of caching thousands of seeds each year, and uneaten seeds have the potential to germinate and grow. Because the seeds are large and do not have wings to be carried by the wind, this habit allows for seed dispersal the tree cannot accomplish on its own.

Whitebark pine is often found as the sole tree type inhabiting wind-swept slopes of high mountain ridges and crests, gripping the mountainside with the tenacity needed to survive in this harsh environment. It grows in the Rocky Mountain, Sierra Nevada, Cascade, and Pacific Coast Ranges. Constant exposure to wind often twists and contorts the trees, which can cause them to form a dense shrub-like mass known as krummholz. [It was a krummholz that protected Mark Collins in his story "The Palm of God" earlier in this anthology.] However, this tree can also reach heights of nearly one hundred feet. Stands in the US and Canadian Rockies are between six hundred and seven hundred years old, and individual trees can live one thousand years or more. Seeds that germinated in the Dark Ages became trees that are still alive today, with centuries of ecological data recorded in their growth rings.

Whitebark pine at these harsh sites increases biodiversity by providing shelter from the elements, which facilitates the existence of less hardy plant species. The tree itself provides nest sites for many animals, and the fatty seeds serve as an important food source for species other than the Clark's nutcracker, including grizzly and black bears, which rely on the fats, carbohydrates, and protein to sustain themselves through winter. Correlations between whitebark pine and reduced bear-human conflict have also been observed. A healthy crop of cones not only increases bear survival by providing critical nutrition, it also affects foraging behavior. A healthy supply of seed means that bears stay in higher elevations, where there is less risk of human contact.

Squirrels also depend on whitebark seed, and a reduction in seed availability may decrease their presence at high elevations where they are an important means of seed dispersal for other trees, facilitating regeneration. They also disperse lichen and fungi, which serve as an important food source for many species, influencing nutrient cycling. In addition, squirrels are themselves an important food source for many carnivores.

Humans are also influenced in a very real way by whitebark pine. Being the highest-elevation trees, they have a significant effect on hydrology. Whitebark shades and retains winter snowpack, which slows melting and regulates runoff. Their root systems hold soil together, which reduces erosion and increases water-holding capacity. This effectively maintains the headwaters of many alpine watersheds that provide crucial sources of moisture throughout the year for surrounding communities and ecosystems. This prevents flooding as well as summer droughts, an important factor in protecting water supply and agricultural operations and reducing the risks of wildfire. This process also contributes to the vigor of plant life at all elevations and helps the species that depend on them.

Unfortunately, whitebark pine is in trouble, having suffered significant mortality in recent decades from multiple sources. The introduction of a fungal pathogen to North America has profoundly changed the dynamics of whitebark pine communities, affecting them throughout their range. White pine blister rust (*Cronartium ribicola*) is a fungal disease native to Asia that was accidentally introduced to the United States near the beginning of the twentieth century. It is a major threat to the future of whitebark and all high-elevation white pines, which show low resistance and high mortality when exposed to the fungus. The disease has spread to thirty-eight states and found its way to high-elevation ecosystems, where it can create a devastating ecological cascade.

The rust causes characteristic "cankers" that girdle the branches, preventing water and nutrients from passing through the cankered area.

It can take years to completely kill a large tree. However, in that time the tree experiences reduced cone and seed production and lower vigor overall. Reduced cone production means less food for wildlife and less chance for tree regeneration. Unlike the mountain pine beetle, which only attacks mature trees, blister rust shows no preference and can kill a small tree in just a few years.

The mountain pine beetle (*Dendroctonus ponderosae*) is also affecting whitebark pine. This native insect has always been an important part of the ecology of our forests. They attack older and diseased trees, allowing for faster regeneration and a balanced ecosystem. In recent years, the balance has tipped. Historically, cold winters kept mountain pine beetle populations in manageable numbers and away from high elevations where temperatures are lower. Recent warming trends leading to mild winters and hot, dry summers have stressed our forests and not only allowed the mountain pine beetle to ravage lower elevations but also to climb to subalpine terrain where trees are already weakened by blister rust.

Finally, past fire suppression practices have threatened whitebark pines. Low-severity fires historically helped remove fire-intolerant trees such as subalpine fir and Engelmann spruce, creating openings that allowed whitebark, a fire-tolerant but shade-intolerant species, to thrive. Past firefighting practices are thought to have enabled these competitor trees to replace whitebark pine. When these fire-tolerant trees increase in an area that is historically adapted to low-severity fires, they act as ladder fuels, increasing the chances of a stand-replacing fire.

There is an ongoing effort to research ways to protect and restore whitebark pine, including programs to replant and thin competing trees, collect seeds, and increase levels of genetic resistance to blister rust. The Clark's nutcracker, however, may be the true key to saving our western high-elevation pine forests. The nutcracker can find other food sources at lower elevations, but the tree may not survive without this winged forester and its obsessive habit of seed caching.

John Muir wrote: "When we try to pick out anything by itself, we find it hitched to everything else in the universe."

I cannot think of a statement that better describes ecology in a nutshell, and I cannot think of a better example of this quote than the ecology of whitebark pine. It is amazing to think that so much can depend on the routine of one single bird.

So the next time you are backpacking and you come across a whitebark pine or hear the *kraaak!* call of the nutcracker, take a moment to appreciate the delicate bonds that surround you and the powerful ways they shape our world.

CASCADES AND THE KLAMATH KNOT
THE REALM OF FIRE

COVERING CALIFORNIA
SECTION N—SECTION R

Belden • Feather River Canyon • Lassen
Peak • Burney Falls • Castle Crags • Etna
Summit • Seiad Valley • California Border

THE MOVING
MIDPOINT OF THE PCT

The engraved stone at mile 1320.7 (according to Halfmile) that marks the PCT midpoint looks authoritative and permanent, but its placement is somewhat arbitrary. As reroutes occur along the length of the trail, the midpoint moves south or north. And should the 7.2 miles on the Canadian side of the border count in the total? There are also plenty of disagreements about the total length of the trail. Halfmile's GPS calculations place the midpoint at mile marker 1325.1. The *Pacific Crest Trail Data Book* places the location at 1326.9. I checked some of my old Wilderness Press guides. For example, between the third and fifth editions of the Oregon and Washington guide, published in 1979 and 1990, the trail from Seiad Valley to the northern border lengthened 22.2 miles. But in the eighth edition, published in 2020, that segment of trail was listed as 71 miles shorter, and the total length from border to border had shrunk to a measly 2,583.9 miles. The mileage in the relatively recent four-guidebook series published by Mountaineers Books totals 2,644.1.

So, wisely, years ago, the PCTA decided to settle on a number. "We can't re-print t-shirts and remake trail signs every season as the tread moves," the PCTA website observed. "The Pacific Crest Trail is around 2,650 miles and that's accurate to within 10 or so miles." That would put the midpoint at 1,325 miles.

Regardless, that marker not far south of the PCT's crossing of Highway 36 is always a welcome sight. And you will still have plenty of time to debate the totals for elevation gained and lost, even the height of Forester Pass or Mount Whitney, as you complete the second half of the trail.

—*Rees Hughes*

WALKING HAT CREEK RIM WITHOUT WATER

KEITH FOSKETT

Water caches are a subject of significant debate within the PCT community. Here's one side of the conversation. Those in favor note that persistent drought in California has diminished once-reliable natural water sources, and public campgrounds along the PCT often no longer have water (e.g., Guffy Campground, above Wrightwood, and Upper Shake Campground, north of Green Valley). The growth in numbers of hikers has further stressed the available resources, and, in recent years, more of these hikers have been inexperienced or have kept pack weight down by carrying minimal water. The other side expresses concern about hikers relying on unreliable caches, generally supplied by trail angels who often give considerable time and money to resupply a cache. As numbers of hikers grow, it is unrealistic to expect volunteers to service the immense demand (such as the Third Gate cache in the San Felipe Hills or the Kelso Valley Road cache). And do caches take away from the true PCT experience? There are no easy answers. Keith Foskett's experience makes a case for both sides.

The Hat Creek Rim rises some nine hundred feet above the valley below. Nearly a million years ago, the land that now forms the valley gradually dropped, creating the Rim's distinctive escarpment. This section of the Modoc Plateau is volcanic in origin, with permeable layers of lava that quickly allow water to percolate below the surface. As a result, as Foskett discovers, there is very little accessible water on this notoriously dry stretch of trail.

As recently as 1917, the Hat Creek Rim would have provided a perfect vantage point from which to observe the violent eruptions of Lassen Peak. The most powerful explosions of this most recent period of activity occurred May 19–22, 1915. A resultant wall of melted snow and mud swept down upper Hat Creek and would have been fascinating to view from the safety of the south end of the rim. Accounts of the night of May 19, 1915, are included in *The Pacific Crest Trailside Reader: California*.

Georgi "Firefly" Heitman, mentioned here by Foskett, was a long-time trail angel with her husband, Dennis, in the Old Station area not far from the south end of the Hat Creek Rim.

I woke at 5:00 a.m. to light rain tickling my face and disturbing the dried leaves. Weak sunlight filtered through the pines, and I peered up at dark clouds racing overhead. It was September 1, and my surroundings looked distinctly autumnal. Foliage had withered and faded, and California had chilled. My watch showed 48 degrees, and I shivered, wondering why the temperature had plummeted from the seventies the day before. Skipping breakfast, I set off quickly to warm up.

I reached Hat Creek and decided against calling the Heitmans because I knew, especially given the cold weather, that I'd struggle to move on if I stopped there. I went to the café and ordered the biggest breakfast they had. I chatted with two local hikers eager to hear about my hike, then headed off to make inroads into a brutal section of the PCT.

Hiking a long-distance trail is not about giving up a few months of your life. It's about having a few months to live. The harsh days, when everything goes wrong, when you doubt the whole idea of thru hiking, when rain flies in your face and you've run out of stove fuel—these are only ever just days. Lying in my tent after a brutal few miles, when I thought the world was against me, I knew the next day would be kinder. And the bad times came rarely; a thru hike is a heart-warming experience that made me glad to be alive.

I pondered the hard days as I approached Hat Creek Rim, a notoriously hot and dry twenty-six-mile stretch out of Hat Creek, so hot it's more typical of southern California. The Heitmans maintained a water cache at the start. After a short climb to the top, I drank some fluid. The clouds dispersed, and the temperature rose alarmingly. The next water cache lay eight hours away, plus breaks, with no water sources in between, so I filled my bottles and a further bag, which I usually used for camp. It sprang a leak, and a jet of water shot from the side.

"Shit," I mumbled.

I pulled out a waterproof compression bag and emptied the contents back into my pack. Filling it, I strapped it securely and strode off. Two hours later, it had also leaked, leaving most of the water on the trail. I had just one bottle, but rather than return to the cache, I pressed on: perhaps not the wisest of decisions. But any thru hiker will tell you that making miles is far more important than safety!

The heat was stifling, and Hat Creek was earning its reputation. Walking in that temperature, I should have been carrying at least 64 ounces, ideally 128. I had just 32 ounces. The rim dropped away to flatter lands. Scorched blonde grass waved weakly; the horizon blurred to a hazy apparition. Stunted trees appeared ill and withered. It felt more like the African bush.

Three hours and nine miles in, I stopped to eat. My throat felt rough as I coaxed the last few trickles from my bottle. I sucked on candy, hoping to elicit some moisture response, then picked up my pack and continued. I had no choice but to walk the entire rim. There was no water until the next cache, seventeen miles away.

A reflection caught my eye. Cattle had gathered round a shallow pond; they dispersed as I approached. It wasn't water, more a black sludge with green organisms floating on the surface. Flies buzzed round my head. I pulled out my filter and sat by the edge. It stank, cattle dung littered the area, and a cow eyed me curiously, trying to convince me otherwise. I relented, put my filter away, and walked off. Even at this stage, I still contemplated returning to the first cache; now ten miles behind, instead of sixteen miles, or five hours, to the next one. I had visions of diners in the café a week later, tutting and shaking their heads as they read the *Hat Creek Herald*: "English hiker found dead with no water."

Reginald at my Nerve Centre, trying to cope with my borderline dehydration, heatstroke, and sunburn, sent out orders faster than a thru hiker's mouth at an all-you-can-eat breakfast to his colleague responsible for my internal organs. Normally faultlessly efficient, she was struggling to stabilize. "I'm running way-above-normal temperatures down here, Reginald. Keith must know he needs water; I need two bottles just to maintain all systems. Anything above that is a bonus." "Do what you can," Reginald replied. "We're in a dry zone. I see parched, dusty soil. I don't think there's any water coming, so you'll have to shore up the defenses and wait."

Five hot hours later, I saw a white sign by the side of the trail: "Cache down here!"

Sheltered in the trees sat a solitary chair.

"Don't rely on the cache twenty-six miles in," Georgi Heitman had said a few days earlier. "It is maintained but not often; there's a good chance it'll be empty."

Ten large water bottles were tied to a tree. As I gingerly lifted each one, my hopes fell further and further.

"There's a good chance it'll be empty."

It was. I was coherent but in poor shape. I had a pounding headache, felt tired and lethargic. My throat was so dry I couldn't even muster a swallow. Then I noticed a cool box [ice chest] under a bush. I lifted it, and it felt heavy; my hopes rose. I pried the lid open and peered in. One lonely jug of water sat in the corner, and two sodas slid down and rested next to it. Speckled with thousands of condensation bubbles, they were still cold! I drank one quickly without coming up for air and subsequently spent several minutes burping. I swallowed more water and left one soda and some water in case someone was behind.

From the searing heat of the rim, I descended and camped near Lake Britton amid the gentle hum of nearby waterworks. The countryside in the morning was transformed and reminded me of home. Lush green grass, lakes idling between hills, familiar trees such as oak and elm. A low mist hovered over the water, and a heron fished. It was a world away.

From *The Last Englishman: Thru-Hiking the Pacific Crest Trail*, by Keith Foskett (self-published, 2018). Reprinted by permission of the author.

THE MOUSE CAPER

THE RAVENS

Tim and Ann thru-hiked the PCT in 1996 and returned in 2015 to hike the length of the trail with their two children, Will (thirteen) and Juniper "Joon" Jubilee (nine). On their 1996 hike, Tim and Ann became The Ravens because of the black clothing they wore on the trail. The 2015 hike certainly had an inauspicious beginning as Will fractured his wrist in an ill-timed skateboard accident about a month prior to their planned departure. Despite the delay, they reached Kennedy Meadows at the end of May, and by July 22 they had arrived at Castle Crags. Unfortunately, as they approached northern Oregon, Will (by that time "Bling") began to experience severe leg pain. Unknown to The Ravens, those sore muscles were a symptom of a stress fracture. For two and half weeks, Bling limped along until they neared the Goat Rocks, where his stress fracture became a major break. Will had no choice but to convalesce with his uncle in Winthrop, Washington, while the rest of the family walked on to the border. The Ravens returned to Washington the next summer in order for Will to complete the PCT, followed by the Continental Divide Trail in 2017 and the Appalachian Trail in 2019. Some families are into baseball and soccer. The Ravens are into long-distance hiking.

These two entries from the journal of The Ravens' 2015 hike give the reader a sense of what hiking with them might be like.

April 14, 2015
CA Section A
Desert View Picnic Area
Today's miles 16.7
A lot of people are trying to hike the PCT this year, and many of them have little to no experience. That means, in a lot of cases, they bring way too much stuff. We see many very large packs filled with everything. At some point these hikers usually start dumping gear. About mid-morning Will

found a full can of bear spray along the side of the trail that someone had discarded. He asked if he could spray it. I thought sure, why not. I pointed to an area away from us. He pulled the trigger, and an orange mist came out of the can. He shot it a second time. Will had his fun, [so] it was Joon's turn. I took the bottle to her, which is when the wind shifted direction. Suddenly we all felt burning in our noses. All four Ravens ran from the area as fast as possible. Everyone had burning eyes, nose, and throat. We did a lot of coughing and gagging while we moaned, groaned, and laughed. We used water to wash out our mouths.

I guess that was not such a good idea.

—*Papa Raven*

July 21, 2015
CA Section O
Squaw Creek
Today's miles 22.8

Because we camped in the middle of the trail last night, we wanted to get moving quickly in case another hiker came by. However, this did not happen. We just could not wake up because we were up half the night defending ourselves from predators. Around 2:00 a.m., a noise woke Ann up. Then she woke me. As we were lying there, we heard several large animals run down the hill behind the kids' tent. Since they seemed to be bouncing around, we figured they were deer or elk. Once we made sure they were gone, we settled down. In no time, we heard the scurrying and chewing of a much smaller animal. We kept looking around outside of the tent but could not see anything. With no luck we settled down to go back to sleep, but before we knew it we heard the noises again. This went on for a while. Finally we saw it. It was a mouse and it was *inside* our tent.

Of all animals we encounter hiking, mice are the worst. We have more problems with them than any other wildlife. They will chew through bags to get to food they smell, and they keep you up all night. How did we get it out? Well, we scared him to one side of the tent and moved bags and packs out of the way. With fewer places to hide, the mouse would run faster and faster around the tent. Several times it climbed up the mosquito netting. One of those times, I put the cooking pot over him and slid the pot lid between the netting and the pot. We had it trapped. Next we unzipped the tent door and threw him up the hill across the trail. We took a look around and found that the mouse had chewed a hole through the side of the tent, through our lunch bag, and into the bag of M&M's—sacrilegious! From past experience, we know this mouse and friends will be back. Under such circumstances there is only one thing to do. Ann crumbled up two Ritz crackers and placed them outside the tent. We have found that if we feed the mice, their tiny stomachs fill up and they leave us alone the remainder of the night. Once again this worked. As we lay there, we heard several mice scurrying around the outside of the tent and nibbling away on the crackers. It took a while to fall back asleep, but we eventually did. It is amazing that, despite all the commotion we made during the night, the kids slept through it all.

This day, like the last several, was the same: drop down, climb up, walk a ridgeline, and repeat. The hills are covered in trees, and at the lower elevations we encountered a great deal of poison oak. At times it was difficult to pass around it. When we could, we washed off our legs and arms. Today we encountered some of the worst we have seen on the trail. At one point of the day, Will entertained us by somersaulting down a hillside. Sitting in the middle of the narrow trail that was on the edge of a steep hillside, he stood up [suddenly]. In doing so, he used his poles to help push himself up, but the weight of his pack kept him rolling forwards as he somersaulted several times down the mountainside. He traveled about twenty feet. The only thing that was hurt was his pride. We all got a good laugh from the incident, including Will!

Toward the end of the day we encountered a bear. As normal, Ann was up front. She heard a loud crashing of a large animal breaking tree branches as it headed down the hill. The black bear stopped at the bottom of the valley below us. As it walked slowly up the other side of the valley, it made a soft clicking noise. Will spotted a baby bear near its mother. Baby and Mama kept calling to one another. Meanwhile, Mama would not take her eyes off us. We were a good distance away as we watched a bit more and then we heard another cub calling. We looked and looked, but could not tell where it was coming from. With one more cry from the unidentified cub, we realized it was roughly 50 feet behind us up the hill. At this point, we decided it was time to quickly exit the scene so mama and cub could reunite. Tonight we camped at beautiful Squaw Creek. The sky to the north was filled with huge billowing thunderheads that kept flashing bright due to the lightning storm taking place within them. It was a spectacular show!

WILD

CHERYL STRAYED

Although Cheryl Strayed walked eleven hundred miles of the PCT in 1995, it was not until 2012 that *Wild: From Lost to Found on the Pacific Crest Trail* was published. The success of that book and the subsequent movie in 2014 elevated the profile of the PCT around the world. (The book has been translated into thirty-seven languages.) A number of hikers, including Kathryn Barnes and Will "Akuna" Robinson, whose stories appear in this volume, were drawn to the trail after reading *Wild*. The excerpt we have selected may be the most famous scene in Strayed's story.

Section O of the PCT stretches from Burney Falls to Castle Crags, and for many years, along with portions of Section I in Washington State, it was reputed to be the least favorite section of the entire trail. The impact of industrial logging, as Strayed describes, had been brutal. However, when I finally walked that section in 2014, twenty years of healing had worked wonders. While not my favorite stretch, I appreciated magical camping spots along the singing waters of the McCloud River and the Indian-rhubarb-wrapped banks of Squaw Creek and the constant presence of Mount Shasta.

What follows here is adapted from "The Accumulation of Trees" in Strayed's book *Wild*, with ellipses showing where text has been omitted.

—RH

I forced my feet back into my boots and continued on, ignoring the foot pain as I ascended past an eerie pair of electrical towers that made otherworldly crackling sounds. A few times throughout the day, I saw Bald Mountain and Grizzly Peak to the northwest—dark green and brown mountains covered with smatterings of scraggly windblown trees and bushes—but mostly I walked in a bushy forest, crossing an increasing number of primitive roads cut with the deep treads of tractors. I passed old clear-cuts that were slowly coming back to life, great fields of stumps and roots and small green trees that stood no higher than me, where the trail became untenable in places, difficult to track among the litter of blown-down trees and branches. The trees were the same species as those I'd hiked past often on the trail, but the forest felt different, desultory and somehow darker, in spite of the intermittent expansive views.

Late in the afternoon, I stopped for a break in a spot on the trail with a view over the rolling green land. I was on a slope, the mountain rising above me and descending steeply below. With no other place to sit, I sat on the trail itself, as I often did. I pulled off my boots and socks and massaged my feet as I stared out across the tops of the trees, my perch on the trail essentially a ledge over the forest. I loved the sensation of feeling taller than the trees, of seeing their canopy from above, as a bird would. The sight of it eased my sense of worry over the state of my feet and the rough trail ahead.

It was in this reverie that I reached for the side pocket of my pack. When I pulled on the pocket's zipper, Monster [Cheryl's pack] toppled over onto my boots, clipping the left one in such a way that it leapt into the air as if I'd thrown it. I watched it bounce—it was lightning fast and in slow motion all at once—and then I watched it tumble over the edge of the mountain and down into the trees without a sound. I gasped in surprise and lurched for my other boot, clutching it to my chest, waiting for the moment to reverse itself, for someone to come laughing from the woods, shaking his head and saying it had all been a joke.

But no one laughed. No one would. The universe, I'd learned, was never, ever kidding. It would take whatever it wanted and it would never give it back. I really did only have one boot.

So I stood up and tossed the other one over the edge too. I looked down at my bare feet, staring at them for a long moment, then began repairing my sandals with duct tape as best I could, sealing the bottoms back together and reinforcing the straps where they threatened to detach. I wore my socks inside the sandals to protect my feet from the lines of tape and hiked away feeling sick about the new state of affairs but reassuring myself that at least I had a new pair of boots waiting for me in Castle Crags.

By evening the forest opened into a wide swath of what can only be called wilderness rubble, a landscape ripped up by its seams and logged clear, the PCT picking its way faintly along its edges. Several times I had to stop walking to search for the trail, obstructed as it was by fallen branches and clumps of turned-up soil. The trees that remained standing on the edge of the clear-cut seemed to mourn, their rough hides newly exposed, their jagged limbs reaching out at absurd angles. I'd never seen anything like it in the woods. It was as if someone had come along with a giant wrecking ball and let it swing. . . .

The sight of the churned, barren earth unsettled me. I felt sad and angry about it but in a way that included the complicated truth of my own complicity. I used tables and chairs and toilet paper too, after all. As I picked my way through the rubble, I knew I was done for the day. I mounted a steep berm to reach the flattened clear-cut above and pitched my tent among the stumps and upturned mounds of soil, feeling lonely the way I seldom did on the trail. . . .

I hiked away from my camp in the clear-cut at first light and saw no one all morning. By noon I didn't even see the PCT. I'd lost it amid the blow-downs and temporary roads that crisscrossed and eventually obliterated the trail. I wasn't terribly alarmed at first, believing that the road I was following would snake its way back to another place where it intersected the trail, but it didn't. I pulled out my map and compass and got my bearings. Or what I believed were my bearings—my orienteering skills were still rather unreliable. I followed another road, but it only led to another and another until I couldn't clearly recall which one I'd been on before.

I stopped to eat lunch in the midafternoon heat, my monumental hunger slightly deadened by the queasy realization that I didn't know where I was. I silently lambasted myself for having been so careless, for pushing on in my annoyance rather than pausing to consider a course, but there was nothing I could do now. . . .

I studied my map and walked on, down one rough logging road and then another, feeling a flutter of hope each time that I'd found my way back on track. But by early evening the road I was on ended in a bull-dozed heap of dirt, roots, and branches as high as a house. I scaled it for a better view and spotted another road across an old clear-cut swath. I made my way across it until one of my sandals fell off, both the duct tape and the strap that held it across the top of my foot having detached from the rest of the shoe.

"AHHHH!" I yelled, and looked around, feeling the strange hush of the trees in the distance. They were like a presence, like a people, protectors who would get me out of this mess, though they did nothing other than silently look on.

I sat in the dirt among the weeds and knee-high saplings and did more-than-extensive repair on my shoes. I constructed a pair of metal-gray booties by winding the duct tape around and around my socks and the skeletal remains of my sandals, as if I were making a cast for my broken feet. I was careful to wind them tight enough that the booties would stay on while I hiked, but loose enough that I could pry them off at the end of the day without ruining them. They had to last me all the way to Castle Crags.

And now I had no idea how far away that might be or how I would get there.

In my duct tape booties, I continued across the clear-cut to the road and looked around. I wasn't sure anymore in which direction I should go. The only views I had were those afforded me by the clear-cuts and roads. The woods were a dense thicket of fir trees and fallen branches, and the day had taught me that the logging roads were only lines in an inexplicable maze. They'd go west and then northeast and later veer south for a stretch. To make matters more complicated, the section of the PCT between Burney Falls and Castle Crags didn't go north so much as in a wide westerly hook. It seemed unlikely that I could even pretend to be following the trail's course anymore. My only goal now was to find my way out of wherever I was. I knew if I went north I'd eventually run into Highway 89. I walked the road until it was nearly dark and found a reasonably flat stretch beside it in the woods to pitch my tent.

I was lost, but I was not afraid, I told myself as I made my dinner. I had plenty of food and water. Everything I needed to survive for a week or more was in my backpack. If I kept walking I'd find civilization eventually. Yet, when I crawled into my tent, I shivered with palpable gratitude for the familiar shelter of the green nylon and mesh walls that had become my home. I squiggled my feet carefully out of my duct tape booties and set them in the corner. I scanned the maps in my guidebook, for the hundredth time that day, feeling frustrated and uncertain. . . .

In the morning, . . . I reinforced my duct tape booties with another layer of tape and walked all through the humid day. The night before, I'd made a plan: I would follow this road wherever it led me. I'd ignore all the others that crossed its path, no matter how intriguing or promising they looked. I'd finally become convinced that if I didn't, I'd only walk an endless maze. By late afternoon I sensed that the road was leading me somewhere. It got wider and less rutted and the forest opened up ahead. Finally, I rounded a bend and saw an unmanned tractor. Beyond the tractor, there was a paved two-lane road. I crossed it, turned left, and walked along its shoulder. I was on Highway 89, I could only assume. I pulled out my maps and traced a route I could hitchhike back to the

PCT and then set to work trying to get a ride, feeling self-conscious in my metal-gray boots made of tape. Cars passed in clumps of two and three with long breaks in between. I stood on the highway for half an hour holding out my thumb, feeling a mounting anxiety. At last, a man driving a pickup truck pulled to the side. I went to the passenger door and opened it up.

"You can throw your pack in the back," he said. He was a large bull of a man, in his late forties, I guessed.

"Is this Highway 89?" I asked.

He looked at me, befuddled. "You don't even know what road you're on?"

I shook my head.

"What in the Lord's name have you got on your feet?" he asked.

Nearly an hour later, he dropped me off at a place where the PCT crossed a gravel road in the forest, not unlike those I'd followed when lost the day before. The next day I hiked at what for me was record speed, spurred on by my desire to reach Castle Crags by day's end. My guidebook explained that, as usual, I wouldn't exactly be arriving at a town. The trail emerged at a state park that bordered a convenience store and post office, but that was enough for me. The post office would have my boots and my resupply box. The convenience store had a small restaurant where I could fulfill at least some of my food and beverage fantasies once I retrieved the twenty-dollar bill from my box. . . .

By the time I dragged into Castle Crags at three, I was almost barefoot, my booties disintegrating. I hobbled into the post office with strips of dirt-caked tape flapping along beside me and inquired about my mail.

"There should be two boxes for me," I added, feeling desperate. . . .

I waited for the clerk to return from the back room.

"Here you go," said the clerk, setting my resupply box heavily on the counter.

"But, there should be . . . Is there something from REI? It would be—"

"One thing at a time," she called as she returned to the back room.

By the time I walked out of the post office, I was almost whooping out loud with joy and relief . . . with the pristine cardboard box that contained my boots—*my boots*!

From *Wild: From Lost to Found on the Pacific Crest Trail*, by Cheryl Strayed (Alfred A. Knopf, 2012). Reprinted by permission of the author.

THE THINGS THEY CARRIED

DOROTHY "BACON BIT" BROWN-KWAISER

This story calls to mind the little extras that somehow sneak into our packs. In the ongoing effort to conquer the challenge of base weight, tension arises between what we need and what we want. Many hikers wrestle with this whether they are going out for a day, a week, or more. You may remember the discussion of base weight in Gwynneth Smith's "Hard Walking" earlier in this volume.

In this piece we are also reminded of those barely noticed items that buoy us emotionally. These don't weigh much but are the ounces of love, caring, and memory that can fill our hearts. For example, I have carried a picture of my family and an encouraging card from my wife. Brown-Kwaiser's concluding comment that we all have nonfunctional items that really don't count against the base weight of life resonates strongly.

Bacon Bit thru-hiked in 2012.

—HS

If I remember right, *The Things They Carried* is a book by Tim O'Brien that I read in one of Ms. Ruth Michaud's high school English classes. The title refers to what soldiers carried during the Vietnam War—some of it issued, some of it sentimental, all of it somehow necessary for survival. It was the descriptions of the personal effects the soldiers packed—the photos, letters, and keepsakes—that left a lasting impression on me. The PCT is not a war, but we have those sorts of belongings on the trail too. And on today's easy-breezy hike, I was thinking about mine.

But, first, I must explain that many of us PCT thru hikers know what each item in our pack weighs to the tenth of an ounce. We carry as little as we are comfortable with. My base pack weight (my pack without food, fuel, and water) is around seventeen pounds. I have sent home extra socks, my mug and replacement mug, my belt, the lid to my pot (I made one of foil), an extra sports bra, insoles, extra batteries, extra bandages, Tylenol, an emergency blanket, the *PCT Data Book*, my journal, and a T-shirt. All of this to shed ounces that turn to pounds. Yet I carry a handful of items of no physical use, and I would never consider sending them home.

I have two gorgeous and unnecessary stuff sacks that a friend came by in Guatemala. I love the colors, and I use them to store my electronics, which are not so beautiful. I think it gives them better energy. I also keep my MP3 player in a small, red Jazzercise drawstring bag that my Jazzercise women gave me. I don't need any of these sacks really, but they make me happy when I see them. My store-bought stuff sacks are great (and water-proof), but they have no meaning.

I have ribbons clipped to the outside of my bag with an alligator clip. The clip is from Jazzercise. The ribbons were on a gift from Ann Maureen Scully, one of the female rangers I work with and whom I deeply admire. The ribbons are what I hope this trip will be—light, bright, happy, color-ful, and springing with energy.

I have a stuffed mouse from my late kitty, Scout. That stuffed mouse has been killed too many times to count. Scouters was my little boy and my best bud. He was a bit over a year old when he was hit by a car. He had just turned from a cute runt with huge paws into a handsome, ath-letic, intelligent cat. I still miss him terribly and find myself replaying all moments up to finding him in the road. When the going gets rough, I reach into my pocket and squeeze that mouse. Scout and I had a shared passion for the outdoors.

And, last but not least, I have the written word: a couple of poems, cards, and quotes from friends. Two letters from my mate, who, it turns out, has a wise eighty-year-old hiding inside his twenty-nine-year-old body, and this side comes out in letters. The wise eighty-year-old woman inside me is also in love. All of these I turn to as needed or reflect on as I hike down the trail lost in thought. I have read most of them enough that I can just pull out lines and turn them over in my mind. There is plenty of time to think out here.

We all have things like this in our lives—little tokens and mementos that usually have no monetary value or physical purpose but that we would never get rid of. The values are intangible and cannot be measured. They do not count against the base pack weight of life. As on the trail, they are what make the burden bearable.

A GOOD PLACE FOR MANIACS

CHUCK MCKEEVER

Chuck McKeever shares some of the feelings that can envelop a hiker as they dutifully put one foot in front of another heading toward the next goal. This excerpt illustrates the introspection that comes along with the simple pleasure of taking a short break.

Here McKeever is in the Trinity Alps, heading toward Paynes Lake in the Russian Wilderness. Along the way he has suffered from painful plantar fasciitis and bouts of loneliness that have given him serious pause. Like others, he realizes that there is only so much one can control, leaving us at the mercy of our own physical and mental limitations. Only a short time before, McKeever has contemplated leaving the trail, sharing his doubts with his girlfriend, who is waiting for him in Seattle. Wisely, she encouraged him to wait a little longer before making that decision.

The prospect of quitting is not wrapped up in one big black-and-white choice to finish or not finish the whole thing. It's spread out among the many thousands of little things that add up mile after mile, day after day. Having to set up a still-wet-from-last-night tent, say. Or the eighteenth mosquito bite of the afternoon. Or running out of toilet paper a day from town. Or how it weighs on you to eat the same boring lunch day in and day out, experiencing food for the first time in your life as a chore to be endured rather than a pleasure to be anticipated. The days and days without talking to your loved ones. The fifth misstep, the third twisted ankle of the morning. They only need to add up wrong once against the sunsets and the joy of being alone and the joy of being with people and the knowledge that your legs are strong and that your lungs are full of clean mountain air, I think.

It feels ironic to know that any minute I could lose the forest for the trees. But, to my advantage, the thing about hiking alone is that after a while you come to realize that there isn't a whole lot else to do, so you keep walking, regardless of how you feel. In the earlier parts of this trail it felt great to bail on a day early here and there, with the promise of Scrabble with friends or jokes shared over dinner huddled close together, but now my days and nights are my own. So instead of socializing, I walk. Today that means 27.5 miles, because I get to my goal of 24 with plenty of afternoon left, and walking—for all its mundanity—is something to do.

The next day the trail is a little less friendly. There are chunks of rock everywhere, which is murder on the ankles, and for miles the trail seems to wind upward. When it isn't going up it's going south, which is equally frustrating, seeing as how the whole goal of this endeavor is to walk north. Still, I'm in good spirits all day. My heel is completely silent. It hasn't been totally pain-free in nine hundred miles, so to have a whole day where I don't have to think about it, save for wondering why it isn't hurting, feels miraculous. Again I'm reminded how foolish it would've been to give up just two days ago. I've cleared 50 more miles since then and feel inexplicably great. I eat lunch in the shade of some towering pines, in the quietest stretch of forest I've hit all day. A trail crew recently cut the blowdowns in the area, and the smell of the newly chainsawed trees is heavenly perfume. It takes a good deal of mental effort to get back on trail after an hour sitting there basking in it. To sit for a while in the grass with no shoes on, to squish that grass and burrow in the earth with your toes, to tilt your face to the warm sunshine and take in the backdrop of hills or mountains that frames your life that day—there are few better ways to pass a half-hour.

By virtue of being out here, fighting through tough days full of mosquitoes and heat and hornets and weariness, we are granted such perfect moments in time. We have to do our best to acknowledge them as they come and not let them pass unremarked. More climbing, more frustrating southward turns, and then the trail drops into a long burned-out stretch. Walking through the blackened and ghostly trees left in these sections of trail never fails to make me feel hot, regardless of the breeze, as though some phantom heat remains of the conflagration that devoured each one. The only hopeful-looking part of it all is the forest floor, where ferns and Indian paintbrush and fireweed all bloom with colorful aplomb. I make camp next to Paynes Lake, a small deep-blue body of water ringed in entirely by towering gray cathedral rocks.

As I make dinner it becomes clear that, for just the second time on this entire trip, I haven't packed quite enough food for this section. Tomorrow will be fine; Saturday and Sunday will be lean days indeed. I wonder how

I'll fare. It's a little bit thrilling, truth be told. Ziggy and City Time, absent since Castle Crags, show up while I cook dinner. I've been wondering when I'd see them, and it does my heart good when they roll into camp. My routine lately is a lonely one, and familiar faces are more than welcome. Just as welcome is the sunset of pure gold that lights up the ridgeline as we retire for the evening.

From *A Good Place for Maniacs: Dispatches from the Pacific Crest Trail* by Chuck McKeever (self-published, 2020). Reprinted by permission of the author.

McKeever did go on to finish the trail. After 146 days he returned to Seattle and his life there. He says, "Hiking the trail was an experience of coming to terms with all the things I didn't know I didn't know. This is still a daily discovery for me, but with regard to nature, I feel like I don't know less than I did before."

His final thought: "This trail has ruined me in all the best ways, hasn't it?" Many of us have been ruined in the same way.

FINDING HEALING IN NATURE

WILL "AKUNA" ROBINSON

Will "Akuna" Robinson came to the PCT to find his way out of a dark place. After serving in the US Army in Iraq, Robinson came home a changed man. Changed in ways that were hard to manage and harder to accept. His struggles eventually led him to the southern terminus and a sixteen-hundred-mile hike on the trail. Here he was able to come to terms with some of the demons that had followed him home from Iraq.

Even though Robinson describes himself as a relative novice to hiking setting out, his time in the army gave him a good base of skills. Along the trail Robinson also was able to find the love and support he had so sorely been missing since his transition out of the service and back into "the world." Robinson's tale of finding his way speaks to all of us with demons of our own to contend with. The PCT is not without its challenges, but it can also be a healing place. A place of reflection. A way to reconnect with one's inner and outer self. Robinson's story is not just about his healing journey but also the healing that can be found in nature.

My first attempt at thru hiking the Pacific Crest Trail was in 2016. Since then, I have completed the Triple Crown of Hiking [the PCT, the Appalachian Trail, and the Continental Divide Trail]. After all the miles and years, I can honestly say that the Pacific Crest Trail is my favorite trail. I have such a special connection with the PCT.

To understand this, I must take you back to a time before I knew what a thru hiker was or what "ultralight" meant. It was a time when I knew more about M16 rifles, troop formations, and marching, a time when I was surrounded by brothers and sisters dressed in desert camouflage thousands of miles from the PCT southern terminus.

In 2003, I proudly served in the US Army and was deployed to Iraq for Operation Iraqi Freedom. The time I spent there shaped the years to follow.

Things changed daily, and the stress levels were higher than anything that you could imagine. The days were long, the work was hard, and the daily fear affected us in ways we would realize only later. My fellow soldiers and I would constantly fantasize about everything going on back in what we referred to as "the world," anything that would give us a few moments to escape the environment that we found ourselves in.

My escape came in a box of books sent to us by a kind soul back home. In it I found a PCT guidebook. It became my sanctuary in Iraq. I constantly flipped through its pages and absorbed as much as I could. Sometimes I just sat staring at the illustrations, imagining myself there. I would tell myself almost daily that one day I would be standing at that terminus and attempting that hike. After a series of injuries, my time in the military ended, and the battle for my mental health began.

As it always has a way of doing, life went on, although it changed dramatically from what I remembered life being like as a civilian. Those years were dominated by doctors: orthopedic surgeons, psychiatrists, psychologists, physical therapy professionals, and a long list of different pain specialists. I spent the next thirteen years in a deep depression, fighting the symptoms of post-traumatic stress disorder more and more with each passing year.

Before I knew what was happening, the joy went out of my life. I no longer wanted to interact with people and didn't want to go places, and the things that brought me joy rapidly diminished to zero. I got to the point where I only left my home when I had no other option. I no longer felt like I was living—just existing.

One evening while lying in bed, one of my restless nights, the movie *Wild* came on TV. As I watched Reese Witherspoon struggling to carry a heavy pack, I immediately thought of the guidebook from so many years earlier. After some quick research I determined that the trail she was on was the one I read about and had hoped to hike. I don't know why, but instantly I knew that this is what I needed in my life. This was the thing that I'd do to bring myself back to a state of living. I had no clue what I was doing. I had never been hiking. Over the next few weeks I ordered gear that I really did not know how to use or wasn't quite sure I would need. In no time I was geared up and booking a ticket to San Diego to start this epic journey.

On April 2, 2016, I stood at the PCT southern terminus watching the taillights of my ride disappear. Staring north I wondered if I had made the right decision. It took less than one hundred miles for me to know that I was definitely in the right place. In a short time, I became part of a trail family. I saw myself quickly removing the shell that I had built up over so many years. I began to hesitantly embrace other hikers, socialize, and crave human interaction. This was the closest that I had felt to being part of a community since my time in the military.

Hiking every day gave me time to work on myself without the distractions of society. I had time to think about some of what I had been avoiding and the best ways to go about living. Sometimes just a primal scream into the wilderness was enough to let go of so much of what had been bothering me.

The people on the trail gave me so much love and support. My faith in humanity was renewed over the course of my hike. There's something special about people opening their homes or their cars to a stranger. These kind and generous people did more than help me in my travels. They showed me that even though PTSD had ravaged my life, I wasn't this outcast that people would not accept.

I did not complete the PCT in 2016. That doesn't matter. The sixteen hundred miles I hiked connected me forever to a new way of living. The very next year I found myself standing again at the southern terminus looking north. But this time I wasn't wondering if I was in the right place. I knew I was home.

After those years of PCT hiking, people who were experiencing many of the challenges that I had faced began contacting me. So I continued hiking and completed the Appalachian and Continental Divide Trails so I could share with other people the healing that I found in nature.

That's why it is crucial that we do all we can to preserve these public lands. Because of war, financial difficulties, mental health issues, or other problems, people are hurting everywhere in this country of ours. If I could find healing in nature, maybe they could too. My PCT experiences molded me into the person that I am now, and there are so many people out there who need this sort of transformation in their lives. I'm not saying that nature is going to be the answer for everybody or that it will solve every problem. But if nature can be the answer for a few, then we have an obligation to make sure that it's around for them to receive the same opportunity for healing that all of us have experienced.

Although Robinson got to the PCT on his own, Sean Gobin, veteran of both the Iraq and Afghanistan wars and a former marine captain, has started the Warrior Hike Program for veterans, based on his experience reentering society. He and a fellow veteran walked the Appalachian Trail after they returned from their tours, and they realized the value this thru-hike experience had in their reintegration. Now the Warrior Hike Program offers hiking opportunities on eight trails, including the PCT.

FIRE!

MICHAEL "PAUSE" MEYER

Just when it seemed unimaginable that the 2018 fire season could get worse in Northern California, the Delta Fire joined the Hirz Fire in early September south of Castle Crags and Dunsmuir, closing fifty-five miles of the PCT. The Delta Fire had grown rapidly, expanding to more than 40,000 acres less than four days after it started. These fires both moved quickly, gobbling up large swaths of trees and buildings. And then, as the fire season stretched into mid-autumn, the devastating 153,000-acre Camp Fire incinerated the community of Paradise in the second week of November. This fire season was one for the record books but was topped just two years later when 4 percent of California's total acreage burned (4.4 million acres) in a single year.

Michael Meyer was thru-hiking in the Trinity Alps and Russian Wilderness at the end of July 2018 less than a week after the massive Carr Fire ignited not far to the south. His story has become much too typical, as fire has become an increasing reality all along the PCT over the past decade or more. What was once considered an occasional event requiring a few detours is now commonplace in any particular year. The combination of drought, lightning, and humans has created scenarios like those Meyer recounts and have sadly become part of the PCT experience.

I can't get the image out of my head. It's messing me up. It threatens to ruin my hike. As if that matters, under the circumstances.

The Carr Fire has again doubled in size overnight, engulfing 89,000 thousand acres. Several hundred homes have burned, a dozen people have died or are missing, and nearly a hundred thousand have fled the town of Redding and nearby communities.

The worst is the story I hear at Bob's Ranch House diner in Etna this morning. A grandfather and grandmother were taking care of their grandkids for the weekend. Gramps goes to run an errand and soon receives a call from one of the children. The fire has suddenly burst all bounds. Flames are advancing on the house. Grandma doesn't know what to do. Can he come home, fast?

But he can't. Police have closed the roads, and ahead is a wall of fire. Gramps is still on the phone with the kids. He hears their rising hysteria. Then the flames come. His family dies in the fire as he is on the phone with them through those last terrible moments.

I felt so heartsick that I choked up and could scarcely eat my breakfast. Up top, the smoke we hikers walk through (or, if lucky, merely look down upon in the valleys) is not merely forest burning, bad as that may be. It's also the hopes and dreams and lives of many people. For me, going back to the mountains today is impossible. It confirms a decision I was considering yesterday, along with other hikers: to jump north to Oregon or beyond, wherever the air is clear.

My swing through the Big Bend has gone well until now. From the trailhead at tiny Castella, a one-shop hamlet just southwest of Dunsmuir at mile 1499, the trail rises several thousand feet into beautiful Castle Crags, then the next day gains another thousand feet across talus-covered slopes full of flying grasshoppers (sounding deceptively like rattlesnakes) into the Trinity Alps.

In the morning, these legendary mountains are swathed in smoke. The famed views of Mount Shasta to the east are lost in a white murk beyond a ridgeline or two. It's a bit like wandering through watery clouds of milk.

At first I expect it to be like this all the way to Oregon, since there are major fires to the north and south. But then, around sixty-six hundred feet, just below the tree line, a northwest wind begins to clear the skies and the upper reaches of distant peaks suddenly appear above the lower-lying haze choking the valleys.

This becomes a daily pattern. Each morning as the Carr Fire worsens, the smoke at lower elevations becomes notably heavier. Setting out on a stretch from Parks Creek Road at mile 1539 several days ago, my eyes began burning and I donned a medical mask. (I normally wear these on my hands to protect them from the sun.) But as the trail neared seven thousand feet, and as the late morning winds picked up, the air cleared. To the south and east, a heavy band of murk butted up against the mountains, with Mount Shasta and other peaks making only brief cameo appearances. But to the north, at high elevations, the skies were blue and pristine.

Deep into the Russian Wilderness, around mile 1585, I sit a spell with a pair of other hikers, Woodchuck and Gently Used. We look out at the sharp smoke line below us to the southwest. Woodchuck, the older of the two, with a resplendent long white beard like Father Time, fears the Carr Fire will grow so big that even here, around seven thousand feet, there will be no escape from the smoke. If so, he says, he'll just go somewhere else. "I'm old," he says. "I adjust." Besides, there are worse things. Like cancer. Over the winter, doctors removed the tip of one ear and a slice of his lower lip. "Skin grafts suck," he says in his soft mountain-man accent. "Feels like dead meat. Can't drink my coffee without spilling."

The Russian Wilderness is a day of sawtoothing—up a thousand feet, down again into a valley. Soft and fast trail through forest one moment, goat-walking along vertiginous rock cliffs the next. After one particularly hot and long climb, I look up at another ridge and think, "Wouldn't it be nice if we didn't have to climb that?" But the PCT offers no respite. Up and over she goes.

After Etna Summit, at mile 1599, a group of us hitchhike into little Etna, ten miles to the east. The skies are clear. Fifty or so tents are pitched in the town park. Etna is a foodie's heaven. The best place in town, the Denny Bar, distills its own gin and vodka and offers a menu and ambiance more typically found in Manhattan than a tiny hiker town in Northern California.

I could easily have zeroed here. But alas. Overnight, the Carr Fire has again substantially worsened, and in Etna you cannot see clearly to the end of the block. Hiker posts from the mountains to the north are not much better.

It's time to jump north, with fingers crossed.

THE KLAMATH MULES

BILL ROBERTS

Bill Roberts is a familiar figure in the Klamath National Forest. A Forest Service packer and cowboy poet, Bill has been around since the early 1970s when the PCT was being built from scratch. For more than four decades, he and his pack trains have hauled in countless loads of tools and supplies for dedicated trail crews all over Northern California and into Oregon. Mules are the offspring of a male donkey and a female horse and are prized pack animals because they combine the intelligence and stamina of the donkey with the greater size of the mare. They are typically tasked with carrying 150-pound loads.

Roberts remains an integral part of the efforts to keep and maintain the trail through the Klamath National Forest. Roberts's poems, like his trail work, have had a lasting impact. The PCT is part of him, and he is a vital part of the trail.

The mules of the Klamath pack in the crews
That work out on the trail
They have a will that comes from the soul
And a spirit that won't fail

And those crews are the future of America
Young, strong, and bright
They hike for miles to work all day
Then have class in camp at night

When lightning strikes the Klamath
But the smoke's too thick to fly
The call goes out for mules and packers
To bring in the supplies

They've brought people out of the mountains
Who alone couldn't get back
'Cause they were sick or injured
An equine medivac

We took a hundred loads of cement
Up the trail on sidehill ground
For a bridge upon the Crest Trail
Fifteen thousand pounds

The folks we meet out in the hills
Say their hearts fill up with pride
To see working mules on the trail
Like they have since Pinchot's time

And the mules like to work
It's bred into their blood
They can pack in the heat and in the snow
Or can work in the rain and the mud

Some people say they're stubborn
But they don't really know
They're cautious, cool, and calculating
With every step they go

The mules don't ask for much
Just some grain and hay
A drink of water now and then
And a place to roll each day

Wormers, vaccinations, salt
The total trust of a friend
With some iron shoes upon their feet
They'll give until the end

People come from around the world
To hike on the PCT
They stay in town to shop and wind down
And to get a bite to eat

The economy's the winner
They spread their wealth around
The pancake challenge is on the Travel Channel
From the café here in town

The mules are the ambassadors
Bringing joy to young and old
They've been seen on Facebook
Where their story has been told

So when you see a string of mules
Winding through the woods
Snowy mountains high above
While packing in the goods

With rivers flowing freely
From peaks down to the sea
Those mules have stood the test of time
It's the Klamath's legacy

From *Mountains Meadows And Mules*
by Bill Roberts (Blurb Books, 2014).
Reprinted with permission of the author.

THE OREGON CASCADES
FORESTS
FOREVER

COVERING OREGON
SECTION A—SECTION G

California Border • Fish Lake • Crater Lake •
Cascade Crest • Willamette Pass • McKenzie
Pass • Barlow Pass • Columbia River

GOING TO MEET THE DEVIL

BOB WELCH

There are parallels with the earlier story "Walking Thru" as Bob Welch describes his building anxiety about safely navigating the steep north face of Oregon's Devils Peak. In years to come, Welch would face mountains that made Devils Peak look like a molehill, but this was his first week on the trail. Thus, to Welch, Devils Peak might as well have been his personal Everest.

For many thru hikers, Oregon is built for speed, with long stretches of forest and relatively flat trail. Perhaps not surprisingly, some thru hikers have created the Oregon Challenge: complete the Oregon portion of the PCT in a mere two weeks. However, we consider Oregon to be a string of volcanic pearls, each with its own personality and beauty that deserve to be savored.

It was the sixth day since my brother-in-law and I had left the Oregon-California border in an attempt to hike the 452-mile Oregon portion of the Pacific Crest Trail. We had already put in nineteen miles and had four uphill miles to Freye Lake. I was dying.

Okay, not literally dying, but laterally dying, having propped my fresh-from-the-creek feet over a log while lying on my back to ease the swelling. I didn't want to move again. Ever. But the first lesson of long-distance hiking is to go even when your body says no.

For a year Glenn Petersen and I had trained and planned this trip. Fatigue would not stop us. Blisters would not stop us. Mountains would not.

The Messenger of Doom came walking toward me, obviously whipped. Her presence startled me because we'd seen only a handful of hikers, none going the opposite direction. Until now.

She had an ultralight pack, just like mine. She was a little younger than me and was walking slightly ahead of her husband.

"Hey, same packs," I said, stopping to chat.

"Yeah," she said. "Where you headed?"

"The Columbia River," I said.

"Do you have ice axes and crampons?"

The question furrowed my mental brow. I shook my head no. This, after all, was Oregon, the most benign of the three PCT states.

"We didn't either," she said. "Wish we had. We turned around at Devils Peak. Too much snow."

"Really?" I said.

"It was scary. We nearly died."

If the ice axe and crampon reference was a sucker punch to my gut, the "we nearly died" line froze me like a stun gun. With those three words, a year's worth of preparation, planning, and training seemed suddenly in jeopardy.

Okay, relax, I told myself. *Maybe she's overstating the danger.*

"We were doing Oregon too," she said. "We'd planned this for a year."

This, I realized, wasn't some willy-nilly decision. She and her husband had found the stretch so scary that they'd given up their entire trip and walked twenty-six miles back rather than risk pushing ahead. I couldn't dismiss her warning.

We each said "good luck," and I headed my way, she hers. I turned to see Glenn talking with her.

"Doesn't look good, Bob," he soon said to me.

I didn't want to hear that. I wanted to hear something optimistic, some reason why it made sense for them to turn back but not us. Instead, Glenn did what he always did when indecision arrived. He pulled out his maps.

"The challenge is the north face of Devils Peak," he said. "It falls off steeply."

I knew we were going to encounter lots of snow, but danger had never figured into my pre-hike equation. We'd talked about what-if-we-get-separated scenarios. Storms. Injuries. That kind of stuff.

"So, why do we have to stay high like this?" I said. "We have maps, GPS, compasses. Why not leave the trail and pick it up here?" I pointed to a spot northeast of Devil's Peak. "Stay low. Skirt around the mountain. Stay out of the snow."

"Bad idea to leave the trail," said Glenn.

Glenn was an Eagle Scout, the son of a Boy Scout leader. I had been kicked out of a Cub Scouts meeting by Kenny Clark's mom for getting too "rambunctious."

"We're just going to have to check it out for ourselves," said Glenn.

So that was that. We were going to walk twenty-six miles, mostly uphill, knowing that we might need to turn around and walk twenty-six miles back. In defeat.

Welcome to the Pacific Crest Trail. Sometimes it is your friend, sometimes your adversary, but always it is a mystery. I planted my trekking poles and, along with Glenn, headed up the hill, into the fading light, for Freye Lake. And for whatever lay beyond.

This was it. By day's end we would either be triumphantly past Devils Peak or in retreat, our trip in shambles. In 8.6 miles, we would know our fate.

The uncertainty gnawed at me. The more I tried to ignore it, the more it returned to pester me. I desperately wanted to complete this cross-state hike as we'd planned, border to border. On the other hand, Glenn and I weren't seasoned adventurers willing to risk all for a notch in the belt.

The morning's hike was a quiet one. The only revelry was muted recognition that we had hit the hundred-mile mark of our journey. About three miles from Devils Peak, patches of snow started dotting the trail.

The snow patches rose and fell like whale backs: perhaps two to five feet high, deeper in the well-shaded areas. Each foray over snow widened my imagination as to the challenges of what lay ahead. At one point, we stopped to look at our maps. The tightly spun brown-on-white contours etched a four-point challenge: Luther Mountain, Shale Butte, Lucifer, and finally Devils Peak.

When we reached the dicier spots, what I wanted was a clear sense that we were safe to proceed or foolhardy to do so. Cut-and-dried. Black-and-white. Head on or turn back.

As we reached timberline, Mount McLoughlin rose majestically behind us, its north face far whiter than the south face we'd seen while crossing the diabolical lava fields below Brown Mountain. Devils Peak's north face would be similarly chalked in white.

Wildflowers fronted jagged shale, a reminder of the Cascades' beauty-and-the-beast nature. At seven thousand feet, on the west flank of Luther Mountain, we reached our highest point since the trip started. What impressed me was the sheer bigness of the land beyond: massive mountains splashed with sheer walls of shale, craggy peaks here and there, rolling buttes of timber speckled with white-bleached snags. Geographical features that we'd never heard of and were small potatoes compared to, say, Mount Jefferson or Mount Hood, yet scattered 360 degrees around us in a display so large as to humble me, a mere ant amid God's sprawling grandeur.

"Mornin'."

I mentally lurched. The guy seemed to have materialized from nowhere. He was up a slight hill in front of two tents. He had a cup of coffee in his right hand and seemed no less casual than if he'd been my neighbor standing on his porch and seen me going to fetch the morning paper.

"Hello," I said.

"Acorn," he said, extending a hand.

Huh? Oh, of course, his trail name. He was, I realized, a PCT hiker. We hadn't seen many.

"Doing a section with my daughter, from Ashland to Crater Lake. Got turned back by Devils Peak. Too tough. Too much snow."

Exactly what I didn't want to hear. A glance north suggested that this was where the trail wound out of the woods for good and lay buried beneath deep snow shrouding ridges ending with Devils Peak.

"We didn't have ice axes or crampons so decided to hang out here for a while," he said. "See if it gets better. We didn't even make it to the back side."

Certainly he wasn't waiting for snowmelt; some of this stuff wouldn't be gone for a month. What he was actually waiting for, I assumed, was a fresh set of footprints from a couple of guinea pigs like us. We obliged. The Welch-Petersen unspoken plan was simply to go slowly, be cautious, and talk things through.

"One step at a time, Bob," said Glenn.

Trekking poles firmly anchored, Glenn planted each foot with caution, then moved forward. I followed suit, willing myself to look forward, to focus on each step, not on what would happen if I slipped. After a quick glance down, I'd already calculated that the result wouldn't be death but some broken bones and scrapes on a shale outcropping a few hundred feet down.

As we traversed the lip of Shale Butte, Glenn broke the cadence of boots punching into snow. "Great sled run," he said, then nodded to exposed shale at the bottom. "Tough ending."

I liked that. Humor was good. In a few minutes, we again hit a rocky trail. Pausing to rest, we could see Devils Peak a mile north-northeast: a craggy rock, lacking the aesthetics of so many other Cascade peaks. It was not the pile of sugar that, say, a wintry Mount Hood appears as. Instead, it was more like something a child on the beach would make with a bucket of wet sand. Only a few splotches of snow remained on the sun-facing south side, which was comforting and, we would soon find, deceptive.

We swung around to 7,474-foot Lucifer. Because the PCT ran through a fat swath of the ridge, there was little danger of slipping down a snowy slope. On the other hand, at one point the dirt-and-rock trail disappeared into a mass of snow that appeared to have been dumped by a semi truck's covered trailer. Huge.

Neither of us said anything. We just stared at a mass of snow a few feet taller than us. Glenn took his trekking poles in one hand and started chiseling steps straight up the block of snow. While he began his slow ascent, I mentally shook my head and headed downslope and around the mass of white. Better to stay out of the stuff even if it meant some cross-country trekking.

I was wrong. Within five minutes, I wasn't even within shouting distance of Glenn. I scrambled up the hill, duly chastened by my stupidity, and fell in behind Glenn. Soon we popped into the open, traversing the south face of Devils Peak as if on a freeway.

"Not bad at all," I said.

"No, we can deal with this," said Glenn.

Of course, just as music is really about the pauses between the notes, so is communication about what isn't said, not what *is*. Neither one of us was mentioning the north face.

Devils Peak towered above us, a remnant of some eons-old volcano. The trail snaked from the south side of the ridge to the north on the Devils Peak–Lee Peak Saddle. After two days of stewing about what lay beyond, it was time for us to peer over the edge and learn our fate.

The ridge fell dramatically off into a quarter-mile slope of white that ended with a peninsula of trees and a snow-fed lake. With an icy veneer to the drop-off, I realized how dangerous traversing down could be. But my spirits soared when I saw we didn't have ice. The mid-afternoon snow was sun-washed and soft. The marks left by others suggested a few had post-holed their way down, while others had thrown caution to the wind and glissaded on their butts or backs. Some, it appeared, had skied on their boots.

"Wow," said Glenn, a view suddenly opening up distant peaks to the north.

"This isn't bad, is it?" I said, looking for some assurance. "I mean people clearly got down this thing."

"Sure did," he said. "Looks like good sledding."

"The question is," I said, "can we stop once we get going?"

I already was thinking about technique. Whether we should be dragging our trekking poles to prevent us from getting out of control. And if we underestimated our speed, we'd wind up in the trees or the lake. Although reasonably certain we could get safely down, I was still nervous.

"We need to be careful about this," I said. "Should we take our hands out of our pole straps? Should we dig in our boo. . ."

Glenn apparently hadn't heard the questions. He'd already plunged down the slope, using his boots as skis in a sort of semi-controlled slide. Within a few moments, I saw he was already home free, having reached a gentler slope and stopped. "Hey, come on down!" he yelled.

Until now, I realized, I'd worried so much about the dangers of Devils Peak that I hadn't been able to let them go even when the empirical evidence screamed, "All safe!" I was *The Wizard of Oz*'s Cowardly Lion, still trembling even when realizing Oz the Great and Terrible was nothing but a little old man.

I launched forward, leaned back, and slalomed left and right, partly out of control but knowing the worst I could do was faceplant in soft snow. When the two of us reached the bottom, I surged with unbridled joy. It was as if two days of fear had melted into a lake of relief.

I looked back up at Devils Peak and pointed an accusing finger at it. "Is that all you got?" I screamed. "You couldn't stop us! Nothing can stop us!"

We'd gotten past Devils Peak. Never mind that we still had more than three-quarters of the state to go, including peaks far higher than this one. But I could practically see the Bridge of the Gods spanning the Columbia River.

From *Cascade Summer: My Adventure on Oregon's Pacific Crest Trail*, by Bob Welch (self-published, 2011). Reprinted by permission of the author.

SNOW JOKE

KATHRYN BARNES

Kathryn Barnes and her husband, Conrad, left comfortable positions in London to hike the PCT in the summer of 2015. Neither of them had ever taken on anything like this in their lives. While sunning on a beach in Dubai and under the influence of the book *Wild*, they decided to hike at least part of the PCT. Starting at the Oregon-California border they were coming to terms with the challenges the trail threw at them. Despite their growing confidence, they still weren't sure of their decision. In the following passage from Barnes's book describing the couple's PCT experience, *The Unlikeliest Backpacker: From Office Desk to Wilderness*, the couple is near Mount Thielsen and anticipating their next set of challenges.

Here they meet up with Dan, a fellow hiker they had encountered days earlier. Dan had been on the PCT before. Despite his experience, he did not enjoy snowy stretches. Barnes reminds us that facing one's fears can create a make-or-break moment for all concerned.

Funny things happen in the woods. A glance at the map showed the trail was about to steadily ascend to one of its highest points, cutting through the Mount Thielsen Wilderness. We knew this inevitably meant encountering snow. Imagine our delight when the initial miles began on a wide, clear, and mostly level forested track. We marched away, naively discussing how easy Oregon would be if it was all like this, until gradually the odd spot of compacted ice appeared.

They grew in coverage, shaded from the sun by the dense canopy of branches above. At around 6,800 feet we lost sight of the trail altogether, beginning to negotiate routes across slippery ice with hundreds of calculated decisions: Up and over? Straight across? Or down and rock scramble? Whenever visible, we followed other footprints. Our progress dramatically fell to little over a mile an hour.

After a couple of painful hours, we found Dan sitting on a rock, eating a lunch of champions: crackers and peanut butter. "You enjoying the snow?" I asked him with a smile, knowing how much he dreaded it. You see, up until then he had managed to deliberately avoid getting himself into snowy situations, but that morning he set out with cautious optimism to see if he could manage it. "Oh yeah! Those online people that said Oregon was good to go are talking a bunch of shit! They've got no idea what they're talking about from their armchairs back home!" It was obvious from the irritated tone in his voice that he wasn't enjoying his day.

Conrad was staring at Dan's footwear, which contained metal chains over his boots. "I see you've got spikes. Are they helping much on the ice?" "Well, they give some traction; I'd slip and land on my behind if it weren't for them, but it's so damn icy I'm all over the place!" I inwardly smiled at the butt slip I had experienced not ten minutes ago. "Yeah, what is it about snow that makes it selectively pile up on the trail?! There's been some really sketchy bits with *massive* drop-offs," I quipped. Conrad then pulled out the camera and started searching through it. "I took a great picture of Kathryn fairy-stepping along a steep snowbank. You can see the mountain falling away at the edge!" Finding the referenced picture, he flashed it around. "Nice one! Thanks for your support," I joked. But I had to give it to him, it was a remarkably tense shot!

Dan was weary. "I'm glad I've got my beacon, 'cause this is dangerous! I wouldn't call what we're doin' 'hiking' right now!" He was referring to the emergency GPS Spot beacon he carried, which he used to send generic "I'm safe" messages back to relatives each night and could be activated to alert search and rescue if he got into trouble. With safety in numbers, we joined forces. After all, Dan's emergency signal provided a glimmer of reassurance if the worst was to happen.

On a high outcrop, where the trail intersected with another, we came across three day hikers. They were sitting on rocks, munching giant bags of crisps [chips] while carving doorstop [large] sandwiches using an army knife and a block of cheese. The men were in fine spirits, happily chatting away, informing us of their plans to rock-climb the jagged shark-fin–resembling glacier above. But Conrad and I were distracted, completely mesmerized by their food. You see, we had started experiencing what's known in the hiking business as hiker hunger. With our miles generally increasing, and having spent the morning negotiating the snowy approach to Mount Thielsen, I was so low on energy that my stomach grumbled with appetite. Conrad focused on the crisps—his personal version of crack—salivating.

While we all made small talk, I tried subtly complaining about living on dehydrated food, sadly to no avail.

The day reached a heart-thumping climax high up on a steep, frozen ledge. Dan stopped dead in his tracks, letting out a resigned "Aww, heck," as we eyeballed the tall, mogul-ridden ice field swallowing up the trail. Conrad stepped up at this point, walking to the perilous edge to size up a possible route down. Meanwhile I turned my attention toward Dan. "Throbbing Thrill Hammer," the very tongue-in-cheek trail name he had self-ordained the previous year, had already hiked two thousand miles of the California trail, so I was surprised by his hesitance and anxious demeanor. My outlook lay somewhere in the middle of the two. Yes, I was scared, but fortunately, thanks to Devils Peak, this wasn't the Brits' first brush with human tobogganing.

Dan had road-walked that section, so while I nervously watched Conrad climb onto the chest-height ledge, I comforted myself in the knowledge that I was becoming particularly adept at taking tumbles in snow without breaking anything. More importantly though, and unbeknown to me at the time, I actually was getting a smidge braver by the day, with sporadic spikes in blood pressure becoming somewhat routine. Our second butt slide down a steep ice chute involved a shorter, tamer slope compared to Devils Peak but also contained many more trees to potentially crash into. Conrad went first, with Dan standing somewhere in the background filming the event for his popular Captain Dan YouTube channel. Maybe that video would have gone viral if Conrad had suffered a gruesome crash, but thankfully we all eventually followed down without casualty. It was amusing—once I was safe, of course—to turn around and see Dan's rigid frame following warily behind my own. From his fearful expression I realized I was doing pretty well. I have to say, I had handled this challenge with far greater confidence than the last—and would even go as far as to say I kind of enjoyed it. Who knew that facing fear head-on before giving it a chance to develop would prove so simple?

As the three of us arrived at the much-anticipated Thielsen Creek there was no sign of water. I froze, confused. We needed water. Anxiously, we left the trail and began trekking downhill while listening for clues. It took a few tense minutes before we registered a flowing sound echoing beneath our feet; yes, we had been walking over a fragile snow bridge. Looking ahead about a hundred meters from where it should have been, a melted break in the ice exposed a narrow stream of water. Relief poured over me.

Thielsen Creek was a prized break spot. In a small clearing beside the fast-flowing stream we settled onto a clear patch of dirt, removing our shoes and socks to bask in the sunshine.

From *The Unlikeliest Backpacker: From Office Desk to Wilderness: A hike along America's Pacific Crest Trail*, by Kathryn Barnes (Hornet Books, 2019). Reprinted by permission of the author.

Barnes and her husband eventually made it to Canada. Her ultimate reflection once back home was to realize that she had spent too much time fixated on the difficulties they encountered. Looking back, her appreciation of the opportunity they had to experience so much breathtaking wilderness is what remains.

FACING MY FEARS ON THREE-FINGERED JACK

RUSSELL "MORRISSEY" MEASE

I love heights, but I hate edges. The very thought of grasping crumbling rock to prevent myself from falling the hundreds of feet that I can see yawning below is enough to tighten my stomach. Russ "Morrissey" Mease's evocative account of his detour to the top of Three-Fingered Jack, the remnant sentinel of an ancient volcano in central Oregon, elevated my blood pressure several times. You are right there with him as he conquers his own fears "finding a perch atop Three-Fingered Jack."

Although the PCT is designed as a crest-walk along a series of mountain ranges, the trail itself does not summit any major peaks. As it follows the spine of the Oregon Cascades, it brings hikers tantalizingly close to most of the prominent peaks. Mease observes, "For those who seek these greater thrills, peak-bagging along the way can provide a challenge and reward unparalleled on any other long-distance trail. The pull of a summit is, to some, very hard to resist."

—RH

I cross Highway 20 at Santiam Pass on the morning of August 31, 2012, before making my way up the trail toward Three-Fingered Jack, six miles ahead, distinguishable by its many jutting peaks. At 7,481 feet, Three-Fingered Jack is not the tallest volcano in the Cascades, but it is nevertheless a very dramatic form visible for miles, whether one is heading northbound or southbound on the PCT.

The PCT passes west of the summit where it connects to a spur trail that leads to the base of the mountain, and there I find a piece of Day's Inn stationery swiped from a room in Bend, our last town stop, placed under a rock.

"Totally addicted to getting high on rock . . . climbing Three-Fingered Jack," Siddhartha's scribbles shout to Washout, Threshold, and me. Looking up from the note toward the peak I can barely make out the jagged top of the mountain through trees lining the short trail to its base.

Pulling out my journaling pen, I scratch out a response below Siddhartha's message:

"I can't let him have ALL the fun!" Carefully placing the note back underneath the rock for the others, I head up the trail.

Siddhartha had been bragging about his climbing exploits throughout the hike. It is not that I need to compete with Siddhartha, for we all hike our own hike, and my journey is not Siddhartha's journey. But I do have something to prove to myself—that I can step off the well-worn path and be a risk-taker and experience what few experience. I am on this quest to challenge myself, push my limits, see what is possible.

Past the initial jog through the trees, the trail quickly disintegrates into several paths up a steep, sandy slope. I choose my route and begin the climb, all gear on my back, my feet slipping a half step down the mountain with each forward step. The route is not a trail, as it turns out, but a wash of sand, scree, and rocks, and it takes substantial effort. The only solid footholds are infrequent large boulders buried deep enough to support my weight without sliding. Making frustrating progress in the scree, I decide to make my way over to the tree line to use the buried roots and branches of the small trees as footholds and slowly make my way up. At the tree line I leave my pack along with one trekking pole in a conspicuous place.

Soon I approach what I believe to be the summit on a rocky embankment only to see another much taller rock tower to my left. Straining to see the top, I catch a glimpse of Siddhartha, unmistakable in his neon-orange cap. He's sitting like a bodhisattva, silently surveying the view. In a world of his own, unaware of my presence, he is in that place where a hiker merges his identity with the natural world. I feel like I am intruding on a personal moment, so I relax and take a short break.

I call, and he perks up and looks around.

"Cueeeeee!"

"Cueeeeee!" His voice reverberates down to me.

"Where are you?" he calls out.

"Turn to your right."

"I see you!" he shouts, followed by, "this could very well be the stupidest thing I have ever done!"

This last response is an apparent attempt to discourage me from following him. It gave me pause and should have stopped my ascent. It doesn't. It takes me two more hours to climb to the pinnacle.

At one point, I have to decide between two equally disturbing routes. I take what looks like the safest route, only to find myself, after twenty minutes of white-knuckle climbing, clinging to a crumbling, thousand-foot vertical wall with nothing but gravity and terror below me. This "safe" route takes me to a precarious place with no way forward, and I backtrack across a traverse, one of the most dangerous spots in which I have ever found myself.

Rock is crumbling beneath every other handhold, falling with eerie silence to the chasm below, finally echoing as it crashes and breaks hundreds of feet down. I make my way slowly back to safety, take a few breaths, and close my eyes with gratitude that I have escaped a horrible fate. The only other route to the top, the route I had earlier deemed too risky, is now my only way forward.

The route requires a tricky move of leaning my center of gravity away from the wall while ducking under an overhanging ledge before reaching the safety of the rock slope on the other side. I rehearse the move in my head several times, take a firm grip and lean back, nothing but my fingers clutching baseball-sized knobs of crumbling rock to keep me from plunging down the mountain. I make my moves only after testing each hold for stability and emerge safely on the other side.

I have climbed to a saddle beneath the peak forty to fifty feet above me. Close to my goal, I have only one way to the top: a sheer vertical wall. Siddhartha has already descended to meet me here at the base of the tower.

As I sit down to survey the challenge and work up my confidence, Siddhartha ascends and descends the wall again as if to say: "If I can do it twice, what's your excuse?" While he is on the wall, a shadow moves by me, and looking to my left I see a large juvenile bald eagle circling the spire. Soon another eagle comes into view, and both soar around us several times. I am in the company of eagles!

Rushing with adrenaline and pride, I climb the wall, moving deliberately and with deep concentration, and finally sit at the top on a spot approximately four feet by four feet, the true summit. A wash of something indescribable flows through me as I survey the landscape. Mounts Washington and Thielsen and the Three Sisters are visible to the south, Mount Jefferson's conical snow-covered peak to the north.

Fear begins to wash away, and a flood of emotion comes over me as my eyes well up and tears stream down my cheeks. Courageous or foolish, it didn't matter. I realize how precious these experiences are. The feeling is amazing and one that will stay with me for a long time.

Later, back among the trees, Siddhartha and I rest and eat lunch. He pulls out a box of red wine he has carried from Bend, and I share my aged Asiago cheese. It's a fitting celebration for a memorable morning.

As I continue north on the PCT that afternoon, I tingle with satisfaction at the recent experience. I know that I am hooked—"addicted to rock," as Siddhartha put it.

There is something about climbing a mountain that is distinct from hiking a trail. The pull of the summit somehow gives a purpose and energy to every step that is sometimes lost in a long-distance hike. The energy is focused. The goal is not months away but only hours, and the reward is often out of this world. I know this will not be my last summit attempt on this trip.

COLD GOING

SHAWN FORRY

Any hike has its challenges, no matter one's intent. Walking from Campo north in a typical year on the PCT means a hiker will encounter some snow and, at the very least, unpredictable weather. In the autumn of 2014 two seasoned hikers and longtime friends, Shawn "Pepper" Forry and Justin "Trauma" Lichter, set out from the northern terminus of the PCT on October 21 and headed south with the intent of finishing in early spring. There is no record that anyone had undertaken let alone completed a winter thru hike before or since. Forry estimated the probability of success at a meager 17 percent. But, using a combination of skis, snowshoes, and trail running shoes they made their way to Campo, arriving on a rainy, blustery March 1, 2015.

While Forry and Lichter may have benefited from the record low snowpack and unusually high temperatures that affected the western United States that winter, winter is still winter. Days are short, alpine temperatures are bitterly cold, and conditions are difficult. After the pair completed Washington in just twenty days, Oregon required a month to traverse. They were blasted by sixty-mile-per-hour winds near Mount Hood just before being blanketed by two to three feet of snow. In an interview about halfway through their journey, Forry commented, "When it comes down to it, it's just one foot in front of the other, managing the risk, and dealing with the weather and whatever comes your way." We found Forry's account so unruffled and subdued, given the magnitude of their achievement, that I spoke with him for more detail (see the accompanying sidebar). It remains difficult to fully appreciate the cold, the isolation and solitude, and the danger.

Of all the PCT stories from the past decade, this one stands out as a feat of endurance that many would call crazy and others would see as amazingly heroic. Bundle up and read on.

—HS

I hear the timid, persistent beep of my watch alarm cutting through the chill of the predawn air. I groan; it is time to emerge from our warm, insulating cocoons yet again.

Justin "Trauma" Lichter and I settle into our morning routine with military-like precision. We don puffy jackets as our headlamps illuminate the inner walls of our shelter. We prepare breakfast from the safe harbor of our sleeping bags. Rule number one of winter travel: an object at rest will remain at rest unless acted on by an unbalanced force. Winter's chill is our ever-present unbalanced force, along with the steadily stronger call of the south. So we push on.

This reality has greeted us nearly every morning for the past 106 days. Three and a half months ago, we stood at the northern terminus of the Pacific Crest Trail, marked only by a clear-cut swath of land and a few commemorative wooden posts. Our backs to Canada, we faced the great unknown of the wintery North Cascades. A beautiful ribbon of uncertainty stretched for nearly 2,650 miles in front of us, a trail both Trauma and I had fallen in love with nearly a decade prior. Yet here we were again, this time attempting to experience the entirety of the PCT in a new season, a new direction, and a new light.

The whys have been discussed many times over: Why the PCT in the winter? Why attempt such foolery? What should my tax dollars go toward your rescue? This account is about the what, which in turn may explain the why.

Draw a line 2,650 miles long anywhere in the world, follow it, and what will you see? Who will you encounter? What will you experience? For many of us familiar with the Pacific Crest Trail, or any long-distance pursuit for that matter, even these questions are hard to resolve. Therein lies an answer of sorts: adventure. With the PCT's recent rise in familiarity, people are discovering that true adventure can still be had in this postmodern age of exploration.

Months of tumultuous travel and less than ideal conditions lay behind us to the north. We had already overcome a month of persistent rain, sleet, snow, and slush through Washington. Oregon greeted us with record-setting lows punctuated by frostbitten toes for both of us. We found ourselves living Northern California's headlines announcing the Storm of the Century, complete with winds of over one hundred miles per hour and double-digit precipitation records, then the unskiable Drought of the Century snowpack through the High Sierra. When immersed in these types of conditions, tenacity is hard to distinguish from stubbornness.

Day 107 had us figuring we had about three hours to reach Walker Pass, a destination we had been looking forward to for many months. Walker Pass meant endless possibilities for recovery and sanity in the form of civilization. Town meant hot showers, a warm meal (or three), and being able to hold a conversation without the wind carrying off every other word. Town meant emotional recharge. Binge-watching *Project Runway* can do that.

Only days earlier, we had been climbing up Forester Pass, the highest and most elusive pass of the entire trail. That day shrouded us in whiteout conditions. Our opinions fragmented on the route we should follow, and then there was the notorious chute. The jittery excitement of skiing one of only a few passable options through the Great Western Divide left us ecstatic and relieved.

Lower elevations ahead meant less of a chance for deep snow and avalanches to impede our progress. For us, it was the closing of a trail chapter we had dubbed the Scary Miles, a sigh of relief of sorts. From here on out we had only seven hundred miles of desert hiking, which we knew we could cover. The enticement of challenge had become a constant companion, but now we had lost that old friend.

Rounding a corner on the trail, I saw it. Perched atop a saddle was a simple green tent and the silhouette of a man. This is a common sight along the trail during summer, but this was February. This was the first person we had seen on the trail in seventeen hundred miles. Trauma, perhaps out of habit or disbelief, nearly walked right by. The man stared. "Are you the two crazy guys attempting the trail this winter?"

Kevin Henson was training for his own PCT hike slated for later in the spring, and we couldn't have been happier to meet him. Rusty in conversing, we discussed the requisite hiker topics: gear, water, weather. We found out about the sad and shocking closing of the Saufleys' Hiker Heaven, a reminder that the world continues to turn regardless of such things. Abruptly we wished each other the best along our respective journeys. It was a simple encounter, but when you're immersed in the experience day in and day out, it's easy to forget how odd it is to not see another soul on the trail for seventeen hundred miles. In hindsight, we could have chatted for hours if only we hadn't been so out of practice conversing with others.

There are two types of solitude: one that is daunting and one that is enriching. Both have equal merit, but, as a whole, solitude is something most of us avoid. Too much and it will fester out of control, reaching recluse-like status. In our darkest moments, we truly felt alone.

After post-holing for two days to self-evacuate for frostbite, we sat in a diner, feet throbbing and swollen, and that daunting solitude came to light. We had to face the reality that our trip might be over. We had literally been blown to the ground by the persistent gales atop Gabbot Pass in one the most remote sections of the High Sierra. I'd felt the slow seep of icy rain, day after day, through all of my layers. Together all of this felt not only uncomfortable but also defeating. And humbling. In responding to such challenges one has a choice. I chose to focus on that which I could control. I don't dwell on what is out of my control; I focus on the present.

We were two men traveling through an empty canvas of snow and possibility. We were without distraction and without excuse. We were living with the reality of our own choices, actions, and consequences, stripped of all fat. Life in its simplest form, distilled to its basic elements.

People say they are inspired by our efforts, but I think the same inspiration was paid back tenfold to us. Trail angels such as Karen Grossjan in Chester invited us in to celebrate New Year's with her family, when otherwise we would have been in a dingy motel for the night. Being interviewed by the youthful classmates of Christy Rosander's Think Outside was awe-inspiring and humbling. And to have twenty-odd folks come out to witness our finish on a cold and drizzly day in March was unexpected and heartfelt. These experiences could easily have been taken for granted, if not for our months of sensible self-denial out in the wilderness.

Life is what we make it. What I am taking away from this experience is to embrace most what we fear often: failure, uncertainty, and the isolation of wilderness. I marvel that a ribbon of trail can far exceed our greatest expectations and that it's out there for any of us who simply dare enough.

THE EPIC WINTER HIKE OF FORRY AND LICHTER

When Shawn Forry and Jason Lichter decided to walk the PCT south in winter all the way to Campo they knew there would be adjustments to make if they were to be successful. They prioritized speed and kept a watchful eye on forecasts. Weather conditions could change quickly, and moving south as efficiently as possible would combine to keep the two hikers focused.

Winter means short days and long nights. It was imperative to make the most of every sliver of daylight. Getting up early so they could meet the trail at first light was a daily goal. If navigating the trail was straightforward, they sometimes began their day's hike guided by headlamps.

Beyond the short days and long nights, they were faced with the wet, rainy conditions in Washington, followed by colder and snowier conditions farther south. Having dry clothes and sleeping bags was a very prominent concern. Switching into the one dry change of clothes was essential as those wet items joined them in their sleeping bags at night to dry from the hiker's body heat. Because they used a floorless tent, Forry commented that their insulated sleeping pads were the most indispensable equipment they carried. As soon as the tent was up, Forry and Lichter got into their sleeping bags. While in their bags they made their only hot meal of the day, melted snow for the next day's water (they relied on an alcohol stove that had the advantage of simplicity but took too long to provide sufficient heat to melt snow quickly), and then slept. In the morning, after much multitasking, getting out of those warm bags was the last thing they would do.

With a cold breakfast to start their day and each with a liter of water to carry, they journeyed daily southward. The men were guided by the longer intervals between resupplies and the need to travel as lightly as possible, factoring in the weight of snowshoes or skis. Travel was slow but steady. After a few hours of walking Forry and Lichter would stuff their faces with bars, granola, or cheese for their first real meal of the day. In rainy and frigid Washington, the desire to stop to eat was diminished considerably. After ten to twelve hours of hiking the routine would start all over.

Experiencing consistent thirty-three-degree temperatures and rain were some of the worst conditions they experienced, both physically and mentally.

To keep the ever-present chill in check, it was vitally important to maximize the efficiency of breaks and keep moving. Despite their efforts to stay dry, they were consistently soaked through. Ultimately the two resorted to ponchos as the most waterproof barrier. Their preference, looking back, was hiking in dry snow rather than slogging through the slush they experienced in Washington.

Given the PCT's dramatic gains and losses in elevation, deciding whether to wear snowshoes or skis remained a constant dilemma. If there was consistent snow, then skis were the obvious choice. If the snow was sporadic, the prospect of walking in ski boots was not as attractive as putting on snowshoes. Snowshoes became the lesser of two evils. It wasn't until they reached the Tahoe area that they could consistently use their skis. This decision-making process was not foolproof. The hikers experienced superficial frostbite after getting caught in a record-breaking snowstorm in Oregon. They would feel this for the rest of the trip. Nursing the frostbite and preventing infection was a constant reminder of the calculated risk that didn't work out as hoped. However this mistake helped prevent future missteps.

That Forry and Lichter had previously walked the PCT was motivating. Each step forward contributed to their confidence. Knowing what was ahead and wondering what that might be like in the winter was encouraging. This walk was like revisiting old friends. Even though they had to stick close due to safety concerns and the need to switch roles breaking trail, each still had time for his own introspection. The exhilaration of ascending and descending Forester Pass combined to signal to the two men that they were going to complete their trip.

An ever-present risk was snow conditions. Their combined experience in the backcountry certainly helped them stay safe in managing the inherent challenges of winter snow travel. The low snow depths reduced the avalanche concerns but increased the chance of hazards just below the snow surface. Vigilance was a distinct key to their success.

In terms of navigation, the two are strong believers in map and compass skills. Complete reliance on technology is not something to which they subscribe. During this thru hike, they used a GPS device only a few times. They felt that what makes navigation sense in the summer doesn't always make sense in the winter. Winter presents a blank canvas of sorts that for some can be intimidating. However, the confidence in each other and their combined navigation abilities proved to be a great advantage. One example of this was the choice to stay high in the Sierra and out of the PCT and Muir Trail corridor in an effort to keep their skis on and maintain the momentum that eventually took them to the southern terminus.

I expected Forry to have a preference for heat after this experience, but I was wrong. "You can always get warm," he observed with a slight smile. But, not surprisingly, there is no desire to repeat the adventure. Forry and Lichter have moved on to pursue other endurance hikes in the United States and around the world, aided by the same compatibility that helped them succeed on their winter hike of the PCT.

—Howard Shapiro

GROWING UP ON THE PCT

NICHOLAS KRISTOF

In the original article published in *Backpacker*, Caroline Kristof was given the opportunity to include a number of "corrections" to her father's reflections on their seven summers on the PCT. Our format and length restrictions made it difficult to incorporate Caroline's comments. Alas. However, to give you a feel for the repartee, we have included a couple of samples. Nick, for much of their time together on the trail, was usually, according to him, "the one to choose a good campsite." Caroline observed, "Dad's idea of 'a good campsite' doesn't always align with mine. Dad will point to a vaguely level site dotted with rocks and elk feces and exclaim, 'Caroline, this is perfect. All those weeds and roots will serve as nature's mattress.' I relent, and then Dad whips out the air mattress he needs for his 'sensitive back,' even though I couldn't bring extra underwear because we're 'ultralight.' I have a fun night being jabbed by sticks and Dad wakes up perfectly rested from 'nature's mattress.'" Since Nick never carries a stove, Caroline contends that she introduced her father to tuna packets so he could at least "switch off between tuna and his cardboard chocolate protein bars for breakfast, lunch, dinner, and every snack in between. Worse, this is not far from how he eats at home."

Having also hiked with our daughters on the PCT, we too have learned that one's progeny will call you out on all of your follies, foibles, and hypocrisies in a way other hiking companions would not. However, in the end, we suspect that Nick would agree that we would not have it any other way.

My daughter, Caroline, was striding far ahead of me as dusk settled on the Pacific Crest Trail in Southern California. After hiking twenty-five miles that day, over a rocky, hilly desert, I was exhausted and felt the weight of my pack—but Caroline, seventeen, kept charging into the horizon, with a load just as heavy.

"Hey, Caroline, wait up!" I called. "Don't get too far ahead!"

No response. She couldn't hear me.

"Caroline!" I shouted, louder this time. "Slow down for the elderly!"

She was now even farther ahead. My mind conjured cougars pouncing on her, rattlesnakes biting her. I noted that Caroline had now completely disappeared into the distance. The first stars were coming out, and I began to worry. Would she have the sense to stop before it became pitch black? What if she set up camp seventy-five feet off the trail and I walked right by her? Would we find a decent camp spot this late? I grumpily reflected that there were significant disadvantages to her growing strong and leaving her dad in the dust.

I tried to speed up to catch Caroline, but my legs wouldn't have it. The trail wound over hills and I couldn't see far ahead. Soon I would need to pull out my headlamp. *Damn teenagers.*

And now I had a bigger concern: What if she decided to hike the rest of the PCT without me?

My trail name is Scribbler and Caroline is Tumbler, because she's a gymnast, not because she's always falling. Scribbler and Tumbler decided in 2012 to section-hike the PCT. Caroline was fourteen that summer, and I was fifty-three, and we both had backpacking in our blood. I grew up in Oregon, hiking chunks of the PCT, and wanted to transmit the experience to my own kids a generation later. The paradox, of course, was that an essential element of my own youthful treks was that there were no grown-ups along, while I selfishly wanted to participate as my kids enjoyed similar experiences.

At first, our hike was intended to traverse only the 455 miles of the PCT in Oregon. Very quickly, we decided to add Washington as well— but I had some doubts about whether we would manage this. Our sons were becoming busy with college and summer jobs, and I worried that Caroline would fall prey to the real world as well. Anyway, what teenager wants to spend quality time with her dad, year after year, getting bitten by mosquitoes?

Our hiking window that first year was early in July in what turned out to be a big snow year, and we hadn't appreciated how much of it there would be. We completely lost the trail under three feet of snow in the Three Sisters Wilderness and headed north by map and compass. Back then, we didn't have apps like Guthook and Halfmile to locate the trail, so it was the most difficult hiking I've ever done. On top of that, it poured so much that at one point we were hiking up a mountain and not entirely sure if we were on the trail or in the stream that descended beside it. When it wasn't raining, the mosquitoes were on the hunt and particularly targeted Caroline. She wore DEET repellent and a head net—and they didn't help much.

"Dad!" she exclaimed excitedly as we passed Elk Lake. "I just counted—I have forty-nine mosquito bites on my forehead alone!"

Despite the bugs, rain, and snow, we were hooked.

Early on in our hiking relationship, I was the insufferable sage, taking advantage of my half-century of hiking experience to guide my youthful apprentice. When we were lost in the snow, I instructed Tumbler to look for blazes and old footprints. At one point, I triumphantly showed her some tracks ahead, and we eagerly followed them, thrilled that we had found the trail again. Sometime later, Caroline noticed that the footprints had toes. And claws.

"Dad," she said, "I think that's a bear you're following."

My most important wisdom concerned the weather. Nothing is more critical, I advised Caroline, than being prepared for the elements. Not only that, you must be ready for the worst rainstorm, the deepest snowfall, the coldest freeze. And above all, never let your sleeping bag get wet! Once we were hiking on a forested ridge in the Oregon Cascades. It was a chilly, breezy evening, a bit overcast, but I assessed what I could see of the sky and pronounced us safe without the tarp.

"Are you sure it's not going to rain, Dad?" Tumbler asked. Surprised by this challenge to my authority, I point out that the wind was coming from the west, where the sky looked clear. She said nothing.

Nothing, that is, until 3:00 a.m., when she shook me. "Dad, it's raining," she said.

Grrrr. I jumped out of my sleeping bag, grabbed my headlamp, and scrambled to set up the tarp by myself in the pelting rain.

We finished up Oregon and Washington over three years. In 2015 we set off from the Mexican border, winding north through the desert. It was 140 miles into our first California desert hike that I saw Caroline disappearing into the gloaming and shouted ahead for her to slow down and wait. Just as I was working out how to break the news to my wife about Caroline being eaten by a cougar while tending her rattlesnake bite, I rounded a bend—and there she was. Tumbler had set up camp in a lovely sandy cove thirty feet off the trail. Boulders shielded the spot from the wind, and the sand looked soft and inviting. She was lying on her sleeping bag, doctoring her toes and waiting for me.

I looked around for something to complain about. In our hikes, I was usually the one to choose a good campsite. Alas, the spot looked annoyingly perfect. Quiet, aching, my pride as battered as my knees, I glumly complimented her on the site and rolled out my sleeping bag.

Caroline was now seventeen, and there was upheaval in our hiking relationship. Since I no longer set the pace, my own hiking idiosyncrasies began to show. I tend to hike more slowly than many other hikers but for longer hours and at a consistent pace. Tortoise-like, I prefer to get up at dawn and hike until dark, tottering slowly but with few stops and covering twenty-eight to thirty miles a day. This made little sense to Caroline, who was now inclined to get up later and then hike faster.

Still, we relished these father-daughter days, even if we each contended that the other was a bit crazy. Normally at home I'm on email and cell phone, and Caroline is buried in her phone, but the wilderness imposed quality time on us and cemented a powerful bond. Like all backpackers, we treasured the benefits of unplugging, the glorious scenery, the sense of accomplishment that comes from seeing a crag far in the distance in the morning, rounding it in the afternoon, and seeing it far behind in the evening.

The rattlesnakes brought us together. So did the sunsets, the glacier-fed mountain streams, and the exhilaration of sliding down snowfields from Forester Pass. There was a thrilling sense of accomplishment in fording snow-swollen rivers or in scoring our first thirty-mile day together, and something of a spiritual reverence in passing through alpine meadows or seeing a herd of mountain goats.

Our bond deepened as the years passed and I became increasingly reliant on Tumbler. If I was in denial about our role reversal, it became abundantly clear one day in year five of our project. We were in the High Sierra, which was full of snow when we passed through in early July. It was bright and sunny, but my sunglasses didn't fit well, so I didn't use them.

Muir Pass was gorgeous, with a gentle slope, a blanket of snow, a stone mountaineers' hut, and peaks as far as the eye could see, speckled with alpine lakes. As we began to descend, both my eyes abruptly exploded with fiery pain. It felt as if grit were in my corneas, no matter how often I bathed them with snowmelt. There was some relief when I closed my eyes, but that didn't help my hiking.

I realized immediately that I had snow blindness—basically sunburn of the corneas—because of my failure to wear sunglasses. As I staggered down from Muir Pass, pained, frustrated, slow, and blind, I was almost completely dependent on Tumbler. She wasn't just guiding me down the trail; she was now the team leader. Which made me wonder: what was I?

I had worried that Caroline would lose interest in the trail as she grew older, leaving me without a hiking partner. Instead, the opposite happened. She grew more interested, leaving me without a hiking partner. Let me explain.

After graduating from high school in 2015, Caroline decided to take a gap year before college, and after a weeklong hike together she insisted on continuing on her own for another month.

Disaster!

On her second day by herself, Caroline joined a "trail family" of thru hikers—and they quickly sabotaged all my years of careful indoctrination. I'm a believer in packing ultralight, so we don't even carry a stove. Likewise, given that my constraint is usually time away from work, we never take zero days. Alas, Tumbler discovered what she was missing. "Child abuse" is how she dryly termed my previous approach to hiking.

"Who knew?" she explained. "Hiking can be fun."

Ouch.

On the phone from the trail that summer, she recounted with excitement that one of her new hiking buddies carried baby wipes and let her use them each evening to clean up after a day on the trail.

"What!" I sputtered. "Think of the weight!"

"Dad! They're wipes—they weigh nothing!"

On our next hike, the insidious effect of Tumbler's experience hiking with others became even more evident. She suggested that a half-day in a trail town, to get a shower and a nice meal, might not ruin our hike. She argued that occasionally setting up camp in the late afternoon to cherish a sunset, rather than frantically looking for a camp spot as night fell, might not be evidence of insanity.

This evolution of our hiking pattern was bittersweet. I was thrilled to see that Tumbler's love for hiking continued as she moved into adulthood. But hot meals? Really?

In August 2018 we set off on the final leg of our PCT odyssey, traversing the northernmost part of the trail's California section. For our last two hundred miles, we had fine weather, and the tarp stayed at the bottom of the pack. But forest fire smoke blanketed the trail, obscuring scenery like the jutting crags of the Trinity Alps and offering a reminder of a changing climate and environment. When I began backpacking in the 1960s and 1970s, trails were rarely closed because of forest fires, while now this happens all the time.

It was late in the season for thru hikers, so the PCT was mostly empty. One day we didn't see any other hikers at all. We talked—about music and politics, friends and history and books.

We had managed this joint project together, seeing so much wilderness, enduring so much cold and rain, feeling so much exhilaration and awe. As we completed the last few miles of our seven-year section hike, it hit me that just when you think you've figured your kid out, it's time to let go. I wanted to savor the memories and chat about all our adventures together—but then I buckled down, because I saw that Tumbler was waiting for "one-speed old dad" to catch up.

And the most gratifying part of that last section? We spent a good deal of it talking about what to hike next, together.

From "Growing Up on the PCT," by Nicholas Kristof, *Backpacker* (August 21, 2019). Reprinted by permission of the author.

THIRST

HEATHER ANDERSON

There are a number of legendary hikers who have staked a claim to their fame by walking the entirety of the PCT in the least time, twice in one year, and the most times. At last count, Scott Williamson had thru-hiked the PCT an incredible thirteen times and was the first to "yo-yo" the PCT (walk the trail northbound and southbound in the same year). Belgian hiker Karel Sabbe completed the trail in a little more than fifty-two days but had a team helping him. Heather Anderson joined that PCT pantheon in 2013 when she completed the PCT in an incredible sixty days, seventeen hours, and twelve minutes on her own as a self-supported hiker. I remember following the news of her last days as she approached the Canadian border and feeling a sense of awe that anyone could average over forty-four miles every day for two months facing the challenges of the PCT.

It was no fluke. Anderson has walked a "Double Triple Crown" (finishing the PCT, Appalachian Trail, and Continental Divide Trail twice) and holds several speed records, including the Arizona Trail (2016) and the women's self-supported record for the Appalachian Trail (2015). In this glimpse into her 2013 hike, Anderson describes resupplying at Timberline Lodge and continuing north, crossing the torrent of the Sandy River and heading on into the night where she would confront an even greater challenge.

I walked into the zoo-like chaos of Timberline Lodge's parking lot and made my way to the store inside the Wy'East building—thirty minutes before they closed. I'd spent the previous couple of hours climbing from the highway in the valley up to the tree line on 11,250-foot Mount Hood, where the eponymous lodge stood. Although Timberline Lodge and the surrounding area was popular with tourists and day hikers, Wy'East was clearly designed with skiers in mind. I hurried past the empty ski racks and closed-up rental closets to the small gift shop. Once again, I'd eaten all of my food. The addition of tuna for dinner and the extra calories of the last few days had stopped the dizzy spells, aching arms, and buckling legs—even my swollen toe seemed better. I collected my box and bought a few extra snacks. Back at the parking lot, in full view of the towering white summit of the strato-volcano, I dumped my food into my backpack and threw away the battered shipping box. *It's only a day to Cascade Locks . . . and Washington. You're almost home.*

Three hours later, I arrived at the alluvial destruction zone of the Sandy River. Two men were camped a short distance away, their tent tucked into a flattish, sandy area clear of the many rocks and uprooted trees that littered the glacial river's wide floodplain. They waved me down and cautioned me not to cross until the morning.

"You can camp here with us. It's too dangerous tonight."

I glanced at their roaring campfire. It was 9:15 p.m., and dusk was gathering. I picked up a sturdy looking stick from their stockpile of firewood.

"I've gotta give it a try."

At the bank, I stood with my stomach knotted as I watched the roiling, frigid glacial silt, fifteen feet wide. For a second, I was eighteen again and looking down at deep, vast Lake Powell from the edge of a thirty-foot cliff. Others were jumping in, and I intended to as well. My stomach was in knots, but then—as now—I tried to be brave.

I thrust the stick into the chocolate milk torrent and nearly toppled over. *It's nearly four feet deep!* I tried again and again, up and downstream, seeking smoother water without deep holes. Finally, I found a spot where it was only up to my mid-thigh, although whitewater broke around partially submerged boulders along my path.

After walking to the edge of the cliff and looking down at Lake Powell, I had known it was time to take back control of my fear of heights. *There is a normal level of fear when confronted with falling into space. There is also irrational fear that can take you over.* Deep breath. Three strides and I had been plummeting.

I stepped into the Sandy River.

Methodically, I worked my way across ten feet of river, plunging the stick as I probed blindly for firm footing. It was nearly dark, and the racing water made my eyes swim with vertigo. Reaching the strongest channel of the current, I lifted my right foot to take a step and felt the water grab hold and slowly spin me to face downstream. There—in the never-ending tumult of pounding water disappearing down the flume—I glimpsed my demise. *This is how it ends.*

The water of Lake Powell had been dark and heavy, leaving me oddly suspended in time and space until I located an emerald glimmer above me. Reflexively, my limbs had grasped spasmodically for purchase to take me toward it.

It took everything I had to bring my foot back down to the bottom of the Sandy River in a controlled manner and regain my equilibrium.

I lifted my eyes from the churning and focused on reaching the rocks on the opposite bank, now only five feet away. *Stab, step, stab, step.* I breathed slowly and deeply to keep from shivering as the icy water stripped all my warmth away. *How long have I been in this river? Ten minutes? Three? An hour?* I could no longer feel my legs and feet, but the other side was still just beyond my reach.

Seconds after plunging into Lake Powell, my arms and legs had fallen into synch, every fiber and all my focus on the beckoning shimmer. Arid desert air filled my empty, burning lungs as I burst from the darkness into the light. I was free—exhilarated. With unexpected clarity I understood baptism, the way it felt to conquer fear, and the words: "Take up your mat and walk."

At last, on numb, frozen stubs, I stumbled clumsily up the loose soil on the other side of the Sandy River. Turning, I lifted my arms in triumph. The men on the other side cheered. I threw down my stick, exhausted, and hobbled away.

My feet hurt as though they had been asleep for an eon. The grit in my shoes ground into my feet with such painful intensity that I wasn't sure I could handle it. A half mile later, I stopped, sat on a log, and pulled them off. After changing socks, I scraped as much gravel out of my shoes as I could. Then I hiked at maximum speed to rebuild warmth and circulation that my body had lost in the river. Adrenaline from my brush with death spurred me forward. I knew that it was three miles—including a long climb up Bald Mountain—to my camp.

A few yards up the trail I pulled out my treat for the evening—a caffeinated gel. I swallowed it and began to power up the climb, head down. Switchback, switchback, switchback. As I neared a turn, I glanced up to see cougar eyes illuminated just feet from my face. Unlike my other encounters, I did not recoil or bark defensively. Instead, I lunged forward, arms over my head and I ROARED.

The lion did not pause for a second investigation. It turned tail and fled up the trail, disappearing into the night. Caffeine and adrenaline coursed through my body. I could literally feel the chemicals throbbing in my veins, and I shook with the visceral urge to physically lay hands on the opponent and fight it. I was done being afraid of the night, of lions, of failure—of anything. Chest heaving, I stood and stared in the direction it had gone.

I roared again.

When I had stepped away from the southern terminus fifty days before, it had been the biggest jump of my life. Since then, I'd felt as though I'd been falling the entire time—until that moment when I flung myself into the face of my greatest fear, ready to fight. After fifty days in freefall, I'd landed. I was the lioness now, roaming the day and night fearlessly. Willing to fight anything in my path. To take anything on, whether it be lions in the night or raging glacial rivers or the self-defeating voices that lived in the dark recesses of my own mind. I was now a living incarnation of courage.

I shattered the silent forest with my voice: NOTHING. WILL STOP ME. FROM GETTING. TO CANADA!"

From *Thirst: 2600 Miles to Home*,
by Heather Anderson (Mountaineers Books, 2019).
Reprinted by permission of the publisher.

IT SEEMS THAT EVERY YEAR IS THE YEAR OF FIRE

MARK LARABEE

The anecdotal accounts about the impact of fires that have increasingly typified the PCT experience are, alas, supported by data. The kinds of disruptions shared by Michael Mayer in "Fire!" and Mark Larabee's visceral response to the human-caused destruction of his (and our) beloved Eagle Creek PCT bypass are becoming the new normal. In 2021, the Congressional Research Service reported that the average annual acreage burned in the twenty years since 2000 more than doubled that burned yearly in the 1990s. Since 1960, three of the five most devastating wildfire years have occurred in the last five years, and in California six of the twenty largest wildfires in recorded history happened in 2020. As Larabee notes, the fire season along the PCT is beginning earlier and lasting longer, and the fires tend to be more intense, hotter and larger. This dystopian future does not have to be. Larabee concludes with a passionate plea for us all to play a part in changing course.

After a careless teenager tossed a firework into the tinder-dry beauty of Eagle Creek in the Columbia River Gorge, it changed my worldview. Admittedly, that view was myopic.

Eagle Creek and many other spots I've visited across the West have always been my places of respite, reflection, and regeneration. They are places I love, where I find peace and see hope in every shimmer of green. They have always felt eternal and solid because they have been there for eons and will be there long after I became dust. Or so I thought.

The fire that swept Eagle Creek and the gorge shifted my perspective. Hope and joy continue, but I should never have fallen into complacency that even well-protected places such as Eagle Creek were safe from humankind's ravages. That perspective should have been there all along.

It was September 2017 when Eagle Creek was ignited. From Portland we watched the billowing smoke column with dread as gorge winds pushed the fire across the steep forested hillsides that held our favorite trails. The fire trapped 140 hikers in the woods that first night and then threatened to level entire communities for days on end. Imagine the wildlife scattering. The fire was so intense that it jumped the mighty Columbia River.

I always knew that this could happen even in the most iconic places. Remember Yellowstone? But that reality lived in the back of my consciousness somehow, a distant worry rather than an in-your-face certainty. But at that moment, I felt helpless. All I could do was sweep the ashes off my porch and hope that this very special place would survive.

My first hike in Oregon was with a new friend up the Eagle Creek Trail. She couldn't wait for me to see it. I had moved here from Southern California in the wet spring of 1995 and quickly learned I had to hike in the rain or remain indoors for much of the year. I never thought I'd find something locally that rivaled the magnificence of the High Sierra, where I'd cut my teeth as a hiker and climber. But there it was, forty minutes from the house. Grand, barren granite peaks? No. But deep clear pools, towering firs and cedars, lush ferns, and dripping, moss-covered walls of basalt towers. I was hooked.

Three-plus years after the fire, I'm planning another backpacking trip to the High Sierra with friends. I'm thinking about Eagle Creek again. Really, my thoughts are about fire. August has always been Sierra time. It doesn't get any better than scouring the Ansel Adams Wilderness or rock climbing in Tuolumne Meadows as summer wanes.

Rather than August, we're thinking about a June hike this year. Late summer days are now more often than not choked with wildfire smoke. It's uncomfortable breathing in that dirty air, and hiking into smoke is plain frightening. I was hiking the Pacific Crest Trail across Oregon in 2005, on assignment for the *Oregonian*, when we walked into the thick smoke of a fire. We felt so far out on a limb and had no idea where the fire was burning. It was late in the day, and we had few options but to nervously bed down and spend a sleepless night waiting it out.

In September 2020, thick wildfire smoke again blanketed Portland, trapping people indoors for more than a week as air quality sank to dangerous levels. At the time, fires ripped through the Oregon towns of Talent, Phoenix, Detroit, Blue River, and Vida. People died, homes vanished, and countless lives drastically changed overnight. More than five million acres burned in California, Oregon, and Washington alone that year. At one point, eighteen hundred Pacific Crest Trail miles were off-limits to people, as every national forest in California and most in Oregon closed.

Years of well-intended but misguided fire suppression, development pushing into open spaces, and unusually hot and dry conditions mix year after year to create an explosive situation. Much of the West has been experiencing drought for the last two decades. Millions of trees in California, weakened by the lack of moisture, have succumbed to invasive bark beetles. Many of those areas, quite predictably, have burned.

We are living in a new era of megafires in the West. The past decade was the hottest ever recorded on the planet. It seems that this is the new normal. Our climate is rapidly changing and putting pressure on ecosystems and species to adapt or whither. Across the world unimaginable difficulties await as communities face extreme weather events, wildfires, and floods. Think of the biting cold that knocked out the Texas power grid in 2021. Basic services will fail. Economies will be disrupted. Food and water sources will be ravaged and could disappear. The poorest people likely will be the most affected. For the PCT hiking community, that means our favored places are in jeopardy and our favorite times of the year to go to them may have to shift.

After the Eagle Creek Fire I wrote that we should put our emotions aside and focus on the fact that there has always been and always will be fire. Western forests are fire-dependent ecosystems. Certain species thrive in burn areas and help the forests regenerate. It's nature's balance, and it happens in geological time. Consider that in 2017, only 25 percent of the gorge was in the burn area and less than a quarter of that burned at high severity. Many trails and special landscapes were unscathed.

That's all true. Almost. Today's fires are happening more frequently and are often more severe. But I certainly was wrong about putting aside our emotions. Our emotions, like fire, are a force of nature. Emotion drove hundreds of people to volunteer to restore trails in the gorge after the Eagle Creek Fire. Emotion guided many others to open their checkbooks and support the communities damaged by fires. That's the right response.

During the COVID-19 pandemic, Americans flocked to hiking trails for the first time just for a chance to get out of the house, for something different. Not surprisingly, they found joy and a sense of wonder. I'm sure a high percentage are converts for life. While many of us who have always lived the outdoor life may lament the fact that the trailhead is more crowded, these newcomers are an opportunity in the making.

We should harness this wide-eyed force of humanity while they are high on big sky and beauty. As a community, we must tap into our emotions—our dread, our anger, our sadness, and especially our joy—to counter the forces that are changing our planet. If humans are finally going to stop dithering and work hard to save our only home, we must let our emotions rule.

Be selfish. How does it feel to watch your favorite places burn? Let's work harder to take care of them. Let's protect more of our undeveloped land for future generations. Let's take better care of ourselves and one another. Let's protect other species before they disappear. It's time to put our backs into it.

I used to think all this and feel somewhat helpless because this is a problem that nations cannot seem to figure out. After Eagle Creek, I realized that it's my responsibility to do what I can. There are small things I can do—that each of us must do—to protect the places we love and make the planet more sustainable. It's about choices. We make them at the grocery store, in the way we get around, in the food we eat, the energy we consume, and in the causes we support with our time and donations. All these actions can seem like drops of water, but millions of drops create a stream and a river and an ocean. Every little bit helps. It's really about standing up for what you believe in. It's about living your values. I know I can do better.

Fairly early into that 2005 hike across Oregon, I met up with Tim Stone, then the PCT administrator for the US Forest Service. We talked a lot during that year about the trail, protecting large landscapes, the limitations of governments, engaging volunteers, and the mostly human-caused pressures that make this work more difficult. He said something then that sticks with me today. He meant it as a warning.

Wilderness areas can be undone just as easily as they can be done, he said. Without a constituency to support them, they can go away.

That's where we come in.

GIDGET DOES SECTION G

BEN DAKE

When we read Ben Dake's self-deprecating and humorous essay, it reminded us of Patrick F. McManus's "A Fine and Pleasant Misery: The Backpacker" that we included in *The Pacific Crest Trailside Reader: Oregon and Washington* volume ten years ago. Both stories find the sweet spot in the intersection of old-school sensibilities, the generation gap, and hyperbole to recount a backpacking trip that does not play out as planned.

We can all use a reminder to never take ourselves too seriously. While we may have cringed at some of the gender stereotypes in Dake's tale, it seems fitting that the ultimate joke is on the seasoned veteran.

I've spent the past forty-five years hiking the Pacific Crest Trail, and I've seen changes. The trail is busier, the gear is lighter, and I'm older. A couple of knee surgeries, a paunch (my resolve to diet is strong after a fat-laden meal but seems to dissipate before the next feeding frenzy), reduced padding on the bottoms of my feet, and more meds have slowed me. Still, I'm out there every summer.

In early 2015, I visited my mother in the presence of her friend and housekeeper, yard maintenance person, and personal assistant, Gidget. She is a youngish woman of enormous energy and good humor.

I had my hiking equipment spread over the patio and house preparing for another PCT adventure: Timberline Lodge north to Cascade Locks. Exciting as the prospect was to me, Gidget overheard me grousing to my mother about how I needed a goat, llama, mule, or beefy teenager to carry my pack. Amazingly, Gidget chirped: "I could help carry your stuff."

I was momentarily taken aback. Isn't it amazing how quickly the mind can begin to systematize information? The conversation went this way:

"So, Gidget, have you ever backpacked?"

"No, but I'm on my feet all day."

"Have you ever carried a pack?"

"Well, not really, but I carry forty pounds of liquid fertilizer in a back-pack sprayer all day."

"Hmmm. Have you ever slept on the ground, eaten dehydrated food, pumped water or cooked and, uh, gone to the bathroom in the woods?"

"Huh?"

I thought that pretty much took care of any emerging prospects. Not so. She kept asking about dates and mileage. I noticed she wore decent hiking boots all day while she worked. The chauvinist in me asked her to Google "porter." The next day she addressed me as "Sahib." Oh my!

A picture began to form in my feeble imagination. It involved me pleasantly strolling along the trail with fifteen pounds on my back painlessly enjoying myself and chatting with thru hikers. Gidget would be ahead of me scoping out campsites and having them set up in time for an early cocktail hour. I pictured Gidget cooking, doing dishes, and pumping water while I napped and read my book, which she carried. Gidget would make morning coffee and bring it to my tent. She could probably learn to scrub up my dentures and give foot massages too!

I easily outfitted Gidget with gear from years of leading newbies on hikes and rearing two daughters. In early August, friends dropped us at Timberline Lodge. We camped nearby, and I did my best imitation of Norman Dyhrenfurth leading the 1963 American Everest expedition as I directed my new porter. (Did I just date myself?)

An early start would be essential because even in the mountains temperatures were expected to be in the upper nineties by afternoon. So I suggested that perhaps she could have coffee ready at six in the morning, breakfast by six thirty. We could be hiking by seven fifteen. I spent the evening watching Gidget drink most of my bourbon and congratulating myself on otherwise having put together a promising team. I spent the night listening to Gidget moan and snore and talk to herself in her tent.

One always expects a few glitches at the start of a hike. I woke at dawn. No coffee. Gidget was still in her tent. I made coffee and took it to her. Gidget had her oatmeal in bed too. She was nursing a little headache, she said. Couldn't have anything to do with a pint of whiskey. I broke camp and packed our packs. Since she was clearly not feeling well, I decided to take the tent and a few other small things I had hoped she would be carrying.

Gidget was in the bathroom at the lodge until about nine. It was already seventy-five degrees outside. I was the epitome of patience waiting in the parking lot. She emerged from the bathroom in full make-up, with jewelry and clothing I had never seen when we were packing. She was ready for a *Vogue* magazine photoshoot. I didn't know they made hiking shorts that short. She was glistening with suntan oil.

We walked to the PCT behind the lodge and were about to take obligatory initial photos by the sign indicating mileage to Mexico and Canada when Gidget announced she couldn't find her phone. I waited while she searched the parking lot, our camping spot, and the bathroom. She found it on the floor next to the toilet.

Finally, we were off at the crack of eleven. It was eighty degrees and rising. I took an extra blood pressure pill.

Things seemed to go well for the first hundred yards. Then a series of a thousand pack adjustments, pole adjustments, potty stops, and starvation abatements began. We lunched at noon and were already a good quarter-mile into our trip. This section is mostly downhill except for a few canyons one must hike out of. Gidget didn't like the downhill portions and was glacial on the uphill. Being old and terribly gallant, I offered to take a few more items from her pack. I took the stove and fuel and my smashed and bent beautiful new Teflon pot. I was wondering what happened to it when she explained she'd had to push to get her "new outfits" into the pack. "Oh, I see," I said, reaching into my pocket for another blood pressure pill.

While on the final descent into Zigzag Canyon, with steep ground on either side of the trail, Gidget announced that she needed to make an emergency potty stop. I told her I'd meet her near the creek. Three young guys were walking toward me. I engaged them in conversation as long as possible to give Gidget some privacy. Judging from the screams it wasn't long enough. But looking up the canyon, she oohed and aahed and forgot about her recent exposure.

We had planned to spend the first night at Ramona Falls. Not a chance. It was probably better to cross the Sandy River in the cool of the morning anyway. I found a lovely flat spot on Rushing Water Creek and waited for Gidget. Finally, I decided we could go over setting up camp another night. So I set up the tents and got dinner started and waited for Gidget and the water pump to arrive. She ate and went right into her tent. I pumped our water.

I didn't see her again until morning. It was barely light. I had one eyelid lethargically opened enough to spot Gidget in her fluorescent lime-green fleece sweatsuit, orange stocking cap, and matching flip flops. She was humming "Kum-ba-yah." Her sleeping bag was stuffed, her pad was stuffed, her tent was collapsed, the coffee was in the filter, and the stove was ready to be lit. Embarrassed, I crawled out of my bag. I taught my new hiking companion how to light the stove and pack the tent. My body hurt, and all I could think about was more sleep.

The sun was up and the air warm, given the hour. Soon we were crossing the Sandy River. This is one of the more hazardous crossings on the Timberline Trail, which circumnavigates Mount Hood and shares a portion of the PCT. Gidget insisted on wearing her bathing suit in case she needed to swim despite my assurances to the contrary. The four square inches of material it was made of certainly didn't take up much room in her pack. Every time I cross these torrents it takes me a few minutes to figure out the best place to cross. It took Gidget a nanosecond. Three young guys fell all over themselves to piggyback her across. I got wet; she got ferried. I carried my pack, despite an offer to help her "father." She had hers handed across. I hiked alone to Ramona Falls behind the youngsters' laughter. I spent the time computing whether I really was old enough to be her father.

We had a tearful parting at Ramona Falls as the young men continued on the Timberline Trail and we headed down the stunning PCT. It was cool under a canopy of old growth alongside impressive rock formations. Gidget was back in lime green. She scampered across the fallen logs that made the crossing of the Muddy Fork easy and then took off up the mile-long hill on the other side. She was coming into her own as a PCT hiker. I was lagging under the weight of my pack, my sore feet, and a general delicate male ego-related malaise.

Scampering along the trail, Gidget loved the mountain views and Lost Lake, the breezes and conversations with other hikers. Thru hikers passed but were happy to slow down and chat for a few moments. It was just our second day, and I knew what she was thinking: Mexico to Canada! I could do that!

I was thinking about slipping the food and some rocks into Gidget's pack and finding a camping spot at Salvation Creek. I wondered if that creek was named by some old wheezing geezer whose feet hurt but couldn't stop until he found water.

This hiker barely found it, and it barely had water. Our spot was spacious, even luxurious. It was the last time Gidget needed help setting up her tent or pumping water. I knew it wouldn't be long now and she would have both tents in her pack, be a mile or two ahead of me and have camp set up when I arrived. Things were looking good.

Gidget had worked in fine restaurants, and so I knew it was only a matter of time before she mastered preparing the various meals of dehydrated glop I had put together. My plan for a porter was working even better than I'd imagined. She took the toiletry bag and disappeared into the woods. She didn't return until dinner was ready.

We were off at the crack of 10:00 a.m. Everyone we had seen for the past three days had already passed our campsite, while Sahib hobbled around and Gidget practiced packing and repacking while trying to choke down some oatmeal. We debated whether to stay on the PCT and hike to Wahtum Lake or break off at Indian Springs and connect to the Eagle Creek Trail. I was leaning toward staying on the PCT because I had been up and down Eagle Creek a few times already. Anyone we talked with vetoed my thinking.

We met dozens of thru hikers on our steep descent to Eagle Creek. Gidget loved hearing all the trail names. She imagined what hers might be. As I painfully waddled down the two miles I couldn't help but compare myself to Stephen Katz in Bill Bryson's *A Walk in the Woods*. I was probably imagining my trail name.

By the time we made camp for a final night and were relaxing with a liquid sedative, I found myself whining about how painful the day had been. Gidget was full of vigor and excited about the beautiful day. She said she felt profoundly alive and full of energy. She loved all the views and the "green tunnel" of trees and the streams and decided she should take the trail name Wild or Reese or Cheryl. I suggested we move some gear from my pack to hers so that we could call her pack Monster. I also silently vowed that later that night I would throw away one of her boots.

I dozed off thinking she had become too enthusiastic and self-sufficient. I probably should have told her about recent Sasquatch or bear sightings. Nah.

The last day was smooth. We had the glitches worked out and assumed our proper roles. Our friends picked us up, complimenting Gidget on how good she looked and fawning over her for being a "good sport."

One thing won't change: I can hardly wait to be Memsahib's porter next summer.

Dake says, "The real Gidget knows me well and is actually a fabulous hiker, and the author is actually not the sexist pig he presents in the story."

THE COLUMBIA AND VOLCANIC WASHINGTON LAVA, MOSS, AND LICHENS

COVERING WASHINGTON
SECTION H–SECTION I

Columbia River • Bridge of the Gods •
White Pass • Mount Rainier • Snoqualmie Pass

A WANDERING MINSTREL

MARK VOTAPEK

A good friend of mine retired to Honolulu. An ophthalmologist by training but a cellist at heart, Dave has been playing for many years. A while back he sent me the flyer from a concert he had attended featuring Mark Votapek. "He played the Brahms Double Concerto brilliantly," was Dave's assessment. It wasn't my affinity for music that inspired Dave to send me the flyer but my interest in all things PCT. Mark, it seems, has a history of combining his music performances with outdoor adventures. Play a concert, climb Mount Rainier. Raft the Colorado River and play concerts along the way (including on a raft). Walk the Pacific Crest Trail for the second time and add a series of concerts to it.

"The first time I did it, I liked it well enough to do it a second time but to combine it as a concert tour," he told Steven Mark of the *Honolulu Star-Advertiser*. His audiences were not your typical symphony crowd. He played in open-air venues (like parks and the southern terminus), a biker bar, people's homes, churches, and community centers along the way. Mark did not strap his cello on his backpack but, with a few exceptions, arranged for the next sponsor to pick up the cello from the prior host. Since the concerts were regularly spaced, the distances were never far.

I walked on the PCT for three weeks with my nephew some years back. He plays concert bassoon. He brought reeds and a mouthpiece on our journey, and I was forever looking back to see him fingering an imaginary bassoon through a piece of music. Even when Mark did not have his cello with him on the trail, he noted, there was "almost always music going in my head," and sometimes a tune would get stuck there. There was a two-week stretch when he could not dump "That's Amore." There were other times when it was Mahler or even "Happy Birthday" that got lodged in his head.

I've seen hikers backpack with various musical instruments. Even ultralight hikers will bring a harmonica. Guitars and ukuleles are not uncommon. I have shaken my head to see someone packing a hefty didg-eridoo. And there was once an annoying, piercing pennywhistle nearby. But a cello concert on the PCT would be an amazing experience. I'm hoping that Mark will do another thru hike and give me a chance to be in the audience.

—RH

I've hiked the PCT twice, and in most ways my hike was probably just like countless others' hikes. I loved being out there in the wilderness full-time, being in top shape, and getting all the excess city life out of my head—"getting in tune" as The Who would say. I loved the people and friendships dotted across five thousand miles, sometimes disappearing and then popping back up two thousand miles later as if they had been nearby all along. But maybe my 2013 PCT hike was a teensy bit different. That was the year I performed twenty-seven cello concerts along the way from Mexico to Canada.

Two of those shows, and what happened between them, could be camp-fire story material. (Please have that fire in town or at a campground where fires are allowed. Three hundred miles of the trail were closed in 2008 because of wildfires, and it's only gotten worse since then. No campfire story is worth any wildfire risk!)

Monday, September 2, 2013
The Timberline Lodge staff has a beautifully set amphitheater that they use for the outdoor Americana Music Festival. The audience can see Mount Jefferson behind the stage. From the stage, one can see the looming south side of Mount Hood. It was around noon when I was the opening act, which allowed me to be on the trail by 1:30. With the entirety of Washington ahead of me and it already being September, good weather meant "keep moving northward," even on a concert day.

I performed in my cleanest clothes (those used in town and for sleeping), basically looking like a hiker but smelling a little less like a sewage plant than hikers often do. Several old Oregon Symphony audience members from my days as Principal Cellist there drove up for the event, but what really made this Timberline stop great was that it gave me the chance to reunite with the hiker Fun Size from Portland. Fun Size and I had hiked the first thousand miles from the Mexican border together, only getting separated when I had too many concerts to keep up. So when he arrived at Timberline a week or so ahead of me, he decided to take a break and just wait for me to catch up. I might have asked him to wait for me a couple (hundred) times since we'd begun at the southern border.

These concerts, when I often had little time to practice or make my best professional presentation, really taught me that music is primarily about reaching people. Nearly no one who heard me was going to care what notes I missed or scratched, or even if I stopped in the middle to explain something. There wasn't that same constant pressure for precision that classical musicians usually live with. These shows were about conveying the big picture, making people like and be moved by music they typically wouldn't ever hear performed live.

That shift in priority certainly changed how I played. I won't pretend that those performances would have sounded good on a concert stage, but it made me realize that the concert stage performances wouldn't reach these people nearly as well as playing informally, at their place, in their comfort zone. I got used to talking more while playing, seeing if I could get kids to laugh at the funnier parts of the music, even getting some audience participation. More than once, before I could even put the cello away, audience members would be handing me a beer. And several of the people in each town who sponsored concerts became lasting friends. I came away sometimes feeling "This is how it's really supposed to be."

Yet when the shows were over, all thoughts turned to being like every other thru hiker. North, miles, water sources, weather, feet.

Fun Size and I walked west from the lodge, passing all the Labor Day weekend recreationists. Not hiking so fast to miss the flowers and views of that side of Hood, but fast. Then, at about 4:30 while walking, I got stung by a hornet, in the back of a leg, through my sock. This was my third sting of the year. What was up with the bees? I used to get stings all the time as a kid but hadn't since then.

I walked on, and in about fifteen minutes I started to feel queasy and then light-headed. I sat down, took a Benadryl, and then took a puff of my inhaler for the first time in months. In the next twenty minutes I went through the following symptoms, some of which I remember, some of which Fun Size later told me. I had a hard time breathing, my throat swelled, and at one point I turned white and was gasping and convulsing while my eyes rolled back. But what I remember most clearly was not being able to see except for vague spots like some bad Impressionist painting viewed through a shower curtain. Apparently this was anaphylactic shock. It passed in what was probably no more than twenty minutes but felt like hours. Then I sort of "came to" and moved on to having sweats, chills, and shakes.

I hope that I thanked Fun Size enough for being there. It's not like there was much of anything he could have done other than keep asking me what I needed, only to get berated ("I don't need anything, shut up!"). It was just great to not be alone through it.

I wrote in my journal that night, "Basically I felt better after that, other than feeling a little weak and having pain where the sting was, plus a cramp in my hip and pain in my feet."

That writing was not me trying to be funny. That's how one gets after hiking twenty-two hundred miles in four months. The discomforts are merely one's transportation northward toward your next big meal. So we up and continued to the Sandy River, a careful but easy water crossing, and found a good campsite on a flat bench on the north side.

Tuesday, September 3

I didn't mind that this day was less eventful. I was still a little gimpy, and my leg was swollen from the sting. But we finished off the north side of Mount Hood with some stunning, dramatic views of its glaciers.

I've always liked taking alternate trails and extra side trips (summits, lakes, off-trail rambling, etc.), so when there's an alternate that is both more scenic and surprisingly not longer than the PCT, it's a must-walk. We split off from the PCT at the Indian Springs Camp to the top of the Eagle Creek Trail. Eagle Creek must be seen to be believed, with one stunning waterfall after another draped in greenery.

Wednesday, September 4

In April, Fun Size and I had started at the Mexican border on the same day with twenty or so other hikers, and we had kept moving northward in fairly close symmetry. We all started calling ourselves the Mexican Train. Motto #1: It's not a race. It's a competition to see who can eat the most. Motto #2: There's always room for one more on the Mexican Train, as long as you bring Cheetos or Oreos to share. Motto #3: A pound in the pack is like five pounds in the (insert absurd location). We had many other mottos and colorful alternate trail names, but if you're not laughing at those three you probably won't find the rest any funnier. And if you are laughing at those, hmmm. I'm not sure what people thought of us. Annoying with our bantering and odd comedy? It kept me happy nonetheless. Since gradually after those first two months the group had become more spread out along the trail, it was great to be walking with Fun Size again.

We arrived in Cascade Locks and picked up our resupply box at Shrek's Swamp early enough to spend a lot of town time (and beer money) and still get in big miles. It was on this day that we learned that the forecast called for a legit pre-autumn storm. We'd already made it through some surprisingly wet California and Oregon weather up to this point, so we weren't overly concerned with the forecast. We knew that the host for my next concert in Trout Lake was picking us up on Friday, and figured we'd be fine being wet for a day and a half.

We pushed across the Bridge of the Gods into Washington optimistically, watching the skies, but relaxed about our prospects.

Thursday, September 5
We hiked past fairly normal forestland, packed with huckleberries, on past Panther Creek Campground. The rain held off until the late afternoon but made up for its late arrival by becoming very heavy very quickly. We arrived at Crest Campground in a deluge. My only interest was in getting my tarp tent set up while keeping critical items and the inside of the shelter as dry as possible.

The night was restless, up every few minutes doing paranoid checks for drips, wiping down the ceiling and sides of the shelter with a spare sock. Some moisture soaked in through the tent floor, but otherwise I managed to stay dry.

Friday, September 6
The previous night's heavy rain didn't stop. We sloshed through it for seventeen miles that morning with the temperature hovering a few degrees above freezing. The majority of the trail had turned into a creek, really at least a couple of inches deep of water. I was scheduled for a performance at seven that evening at a church, and I couldn't imagine how it was going to happen. My hands had gone numb, and I fumbled to do the simplest things like button my jacket. If I couldn't move my fingers enough to unzip my fly, how was I going to play cello?

Fun Size and I reached a road crossing south of our planned rendezvous with our Trout Lake host, Doug Anderson. We spotted an unoccupied camper van with an awning that provided some shelter from the elements. Loitering at this refuge, we called Doug, who came to our rescue. In the mid-afternoon I got dry clothes, a shower, was fed stew and hot cocoa, and gradually felt just fine. I hadn't seen my wife, Emma, in the last five hundred miles, but she had picked up the cello from Timberline and arrived with it in Trout Lake in the late afternoon. Previously, for the six or seven shows that summer when she had been in town with me, we had a few numbers we performed together, her playing violin. In Trout Lake, for the first time, we didn't rehearse at all.

Now that performing was looking possible, I asked Doug if the show would still go on with this weather. He was calm and confident.

To my surprise, the church was nearly packed. Word had spread throughout the community that this storm would create all manner of marooned PCT hikers. Many townspeople drove to the trailheads to offer rides and opened their homes to distressed hikers. It was heartwarming and hand-warming to see a whole town act as guardian angels.

Both hikers and residents converged on my concert. The audience felt like a large family reunion. There were hikers with whom I had walked for a hundred miles but hadn't seen for months. I usually joked about inviting heckling as part of the audience participation, and this was one time when some friends took me up on it. It ranged from a silent attention to being a little raucous (by classical standards anyway).

I can't remember exactly how well I actually played, or even what music I chose for that night. Maybe I'm forgetful, or maybe those things aren't what's most worth remembering. I just remember it as one of my favorite concerts along the way.

CROSSING PATHS

ALICE TULLOCH

Alice Tulloch has a rich PCT history. Tulloch is a retired civil engineer, wilderness primitive skills instructor, and widow of "No Way" Ray Echols who tragically died in a fall near Deep Creek on the PCT in May 2006. As Tulloch strides across Bridge of the Gods she contemplates those who have come before her. Namely she is imagining Lewis and Clark and the Corps of Discovery two hundred years earlier. How might they comprehend the twenty-first-century hiker-adventurer? Would they even be able to comprehend the world we know and so often take for granted?

Tulloch raises some thoughtful and provocative questions. As we come more and more to terms with the fate of our world due to the effects of climate change and our reliance on non-renewables we will have to find suitable answers. The views and solutions Tulloch articulates in "Crossing Paths" and the accompanying sidebar, "Leave No Trace: From Ultralight to Post-Carbon Hiking," are sobering and force us to contemplate both the near and not too distant future.

We loved Tulloch's metaphor of crossing paths—the connections we make on the PCT with flora, fauna, and people of such diversity of age, background, nationality, and, increasingly race—so much that we have used it in titling this anthology.

Stepping out to cross the Bridge of the Gods, I look down through the grating to the massive Columbia River coursing darkly below me. Dawn squints from the east. Looking up and down the river, I think of the Lewis and Clark expedition descending by canoe in late October 1805, after crossing seventeen months of the unknown, with just the brute force and ingenuity of the company's hands.

My tiny pack is twelve pounds of ultramodern gear and a couple of days' worth of highly processed food. Their gear was packed in barrels, boxes, oilcloth, canvas, and hides. They were living off the land to supplement the dwindling dried foods they had brought from St. Louis, some two thousand miles away. Many of their original wool and linen clothes had surely been ripped or rotted off their backs, replaced with buckskins by then. I was struck by how different our experiences of this place were. My belly was full from the "char burger" in Cascade Locks. Their bellies were lean but recently restored by the salmon and roots given them by the Columbia River people.

The difference is the age of oil. Almost every article of gear in my pack is made of and transported by fossil fuels. Here's what I learned from a wander through the internet: The fabric and silnylon on my pack are made largely from natural gas, through many complex steps. The soles and synthetic uppers of my trail runners are from the plastic family. The Esbit tablets that fuel my stove are hexamine, made from formaldehyde and ammonia, synthesized from ethanol, usually as a petroleum distillate. My titanium cook pot comes from mines in Australia, South Africa, the Middle East, or Norway, smelted and refined with large amounts of electricity and shipped by ocean vessels powered by fossil fuels.

My polyester and polypropylene clothes come from coal and petroleum, manufactured on some other continent. The down in the sleeping bag is natural goose feathers, raised in eastern Europe or Asia, shipped in container ships as well. Plastic ziplock baggies are essential now. Even the paper of my maps is made by using massive amounts of electricity and chemicals to extract the cellulose from trees. Rare earth metals, mined in China, shipped across the Pacific, make my electronics work. Virtually every object I brought on my long hike depends on oil, natural gas, or coal.

I traveled to the trailhead in a car, manufactured from steel and rubber from far countries. The road was asphalt. Around here most of the gasoline comes from far away. I stayed in a motel and ate at restaurants whose furnishings and supplies all came from elsewhere, largely made from synthetic materials. The oranges for the fresh orange juice at Thelma's in Big Bear traveled, thanks to oil, from southern California or Florida. My mind staggers to think of the tangled trails that produced the amazing and reviving breakfast buffet at Timberline Lodge.

We live in a special time, when our extraction of the stored sunlight of the eons before humans has provided such a favorable window for long-distance hiking. This is a rare time. Lewis and Clark traveled far but not light. The Indigenous first peoples of North America also traveled far, but in deep relationship with their environment, in advantageous seasons for serious reasons. Now we travel afoot, hell-bent for the border, perhaps not quite appreciating how unique this form of travel is in human history.

I am among those who have concluded that the amount of carbon that our civilization has released from those fossil fuels is now impacting our climate. I am among those who conclude that 80 percent of the known reserves of oil, gas, and coal must stay in the earth to avoid serious consequences. I anticipate that those effects will impact our civilization in disruptive ways within the next ten to twenty years. Very soon. When fossil fuels are not available for all this, how shall we hike?

I am among those who are committed to respecting and repairing the great gift of life that has been given to us. I write this note to begin a conversation about how we can protect the long trails that we love. Let us begin to reimagine how the treasure that is a long trail will be trod.

Only two hundred years ago, Lewis and Clark came this way. Would they look up at me now on this soaring steel bridge and puzzle over my choices for wilderness travel? Is it marvel, or is it challenge we feel? Is all that we have learned about perseverance and transformation on the PCT available as we plot our route to the future?

FROM WHERE I STAND

LEAVE NO TRACE—FROM ULTRALIGHT TO POST-CARBON HIKING

So how do we reduce our carbon footprint while hiking the long hike? I'm assuming you already know that simply changing out light bulbs and recycling aluminum cans will not address the predicament of climate destabilization, mass extinction, resource depletion, economic inequality, unsustainable global debt, and overpopulation. Long-distance hiking needs to reconfigure itself for the long emergency that already is the predominant theme of the twenty-first century. Ignore what the pols and chattering class like to talk about; this is the real deal.

Overall, the major contributors to climate change are food production, transportation, manufacturing, and building heating. Our biggest impact as hikers is travel to and from the trail. This includes all those hitchhikes into trail towns like Julian, Kennedy Meadows, Tahoe, Sisters, and Skykomish. For long-distance hikers, greenhouse gas sources are represented by the food we eat along the way, how we travel to and from the trail, and the gear we take with us. Depletion of key resources will impact our favorite ultralight materials, such as silnylon and titanium.

To begin this experiment in reducing our hiker eco-footprint, we could find inspiration from camping in the old way, as represented by Horace Kephardt, Nessmuk, and Robert Baden-Powell. This was the 1880–1930s era of roughing it. Their equipment included wood and canvas pack frames and rucksacks, wool clothing, wool blanket bedrolls, leather boots, and pack mules to carry the weight. I have learned from direct experience that humans are lousy pack animals.

I'm not advocating a return to hobnail boots, but can we think creatively about reducing our carbon and environmental footprint while still loving the long trail? What will long-distance hiking look like by 2050? Preparing our own trail foods, using solar dryers, rather than buying plastic-sealed MREs. Using foods without animal products. Using foods and materials grown local to our home places. Traveling to and from the trail on energy-efficient transportation. Using packs, tents, and clothing that do not include silnylon, Cuben Fiber, titanium, hexamine, or plastics. This demands that we get just as creative in our gear as I've seen the community be for the last twenty years. This also means supporting local manufacturers of lightweight materials and clothing. For example, couldn't those amazing merino wool T-shirts be produced from local sheep in local mills, reducing the clothing-miles of the garment? Couldn't we be buying shares in community-supported regional geese farms for down clothing? You get the idea. These are radical ideas, but I don't figure the hiking community for being hidebound.

An important calculation has not yet been made regarding the trade-offs between fossil-fuel-based materials and natural materials from cattle and sheep who are methane greenhouse-gas contributors. Shoe leather and wool clothing and bedding have served humanity for millennia. We'll each use our own best judgment, now and after fossil fuels are no longer available.

My personal plea is to let go of the electronics. Save pack weight. Reduce our dependence on geopolitically volatile rare earth metals from far away. Be here now. Learn the real skill of land navigation. Get the lay of the land through all the amazing ecosystems a long trail traverses. Love the trail through direct acquaintance with its rocks, waters, critters, and flora. Feel the freedom of the hills in the old ways, in a totally new way.

Once you've walked from Mexico to Canada, you will know of what I speak. Let's take "leave no trace" to a new level. The trail is not about nifty gear and uploading self-centered videos. It is not about speed or glory. You don't do the trail, the trail does you. You will instinctively know what it means to tread lightly as a shadow on the mountains.

—*Alice Tulloch*

BREAKING THE PCT SPEED RECORD

REES HUGHES

There have been numerous debates on the relative advantages of thru-hiking and section-hiking long trails. As section-hiking advocate Jeff Vreeland observes, section-hiking is easier on jobs and families, involves less upfront cost, reduces pressure to make daily miles, and allows you to pick when and where you hike. Others add that section-hiking minimizes hiker burnout. Korrin Bishop boils down the pluses to "flexibility." The disadvantages include the constant reconditioning that a section-hiker faces, the logistical challenge of getting to and from distant trailheads, finding suitable hiking partners, and missing that "thru-hiker family" experience.

In our section-hiking, we felt that each segment of the PCT was special. We did not have to walk the Hat Creek Rim when it was blistering hot or battle snow in the North Cascades. We were able to round Mount Hood when flowers were at their peak, avoid fire closures, and minimize daunting water crossings. And, unlike some thru hikers who "endure" the thousand miles of trail between the High Sierra and the Washington Cascades, we have never experienced scenery fatigue.

This is where the notion of "hike your own hike" makes the most sense to us. However you approach the PCT, it has to fit with your life.

> *"Of all the paths you take in life, make sure a few of them are dirt."*
> —*John Muir (written on a stone at Casa de Luna)*

My wife, Amy, our oldest daughter, Chisa, and my long-time hiking partner and coeditor of this anthology, Howard Shapiro, were making our way south along the Pacific Crest Trail toward Brown Mountain

Shelter in southern Oregon in late July 2014. It was our sixth day out, and by this time it had become clear that Oregon's legendary mosquito population preferred Amy and Chisa when given the choice. As a result, Chisa, swollen from bites, had earned the moniker Trail Bait and Amy had been christened Sock Monkey for her use of socks as hand protection, a snappy accessory to her backcountry clothing ensemble. The voracious mosquitoes of the Sky Lakes had served as ample incentive for Trail Bait and Sock Monkey to walk far beyond their usual range the day before in order to reach drier country. This day we had dialed it back and were enjoying the abundant huckleberry crop as we proceeded just ten miles to Brown Mountain. About mid-morning, striding toward us was lanky Joe "Stringbean" McConaughy, in lightweight shorts, with a small daypack. Joe was en route to establishing the PCT speed record for supported hikers, a blistering fifty-three days, six hours, and thirty-seven minutes (since broken). It was not lost on us that this translated to nearly two marathons each day for almost eight weeks through snow, across rivers, up and down. He graciously allocated some fifteen minutes of his total to our questions that day.

My own story is a little different, as is the PCT speed record for which I am in contention.

When I walked the PCT through Washington State, my first section of the trail, the first flight of the space shuttle occurred (spaces shuttles are now retired), IBM released its first PC (they don't make them any more), Lady Diana married the prince of Wales, and Ronald Reagan had just become president of the United States. It was 1981.

I can't precisely identify the time when a decision was made to undertake this adventure. Howard recollects that we hatched a plan to spend thirty days on the PCT when flying from our new lives in the Pacific Northwest to our native Kansas during the winter holidays of 1980. When we floated the adventure more publicly in our friendship circle it was enthusiastically embraced by our mutual friend Jim Peacock, who quickly became the third in our party.

I arranged to take a leave from my position at Seattle University, and Jim, who was headed to grad school in the fall, quit his job. Howard, as a teacher, had summers off. We outfitted ourselves with military surplus wool pants, heavy leather boots, and way too much of everything. We sent resupply boxes to the ski resorts at White, Snoqualmie, and Stevens Passes. We negotiated with a friend to drive us in his little Chevette with our bloated backpacks to Panther Creek Campground, a few miles north of the Columbia Gorge.

We made it to the rounded top of Big Huckleberry Mountain on that first day. Just barely. Upon cresting that three-thousand-foot climb, we collapsed, content to lie splayed out across the summit. The warm sun slowly revived us, providing just enough energy to appreciate the expansive view and eventually set up our first camp. That campsite, I wrote at the time, "captured it all . . . We had a panorama of the Gorge, mountains, and the awesome spire of Mt. Hood, while being surrounded by a carpet of flowers. However, all the beauty could not mask the ache of my muscles and my total exhaustion." We were surrounded by heaven but felt like hell.

Our soft bodies protested loudly the next morning when the packs were returned to our backs. But each day we suffered less until it was no longer even a consideration.

We talked about our life dreams, worries, and challenges in a way that can only happen when you have unlimited time. We laughed to the point of falling down as we became Rocky, Boris, and Pierre, alter egos born from our evening games of hearts. As a trio we became a well-oiled machine when making or breaking camp. As we pushed our way north, our confidence grew as we passed each test along the way: lightning storms, gnarly water crossings, long days of hiking, soaking rains, and bears. We cherished our in-depth exposure to wilderness, and, as we approached the end of thirty days, there germinated the seed of an idea. Why not take on the entire PCT? Our world was rich with possibilities and short on obligations in those days. We were recently minted young professionals without families. Yes, why not?

On our final night, camped aside the exuberant Bridge Creek, we met three vigorous, gray-haired men who shared the primitive Hideaway Camp with us. Through our lenses as twentysomethings, these three were defying the laws of nature by still backpacking in their sixties. They exuded such an infectious radiance and positive spirit. We were even more impressed when they explained to us that they converged every summer for a week in the backcountry. "We want to be those guys," we concluded.

We walked a couple more sections in 1982, but life was quickly becoming more complicated. Marriage. Career moves took me to California and Jim to Maine. Years passed. It was proving difficult to make the PCT a priority. As a new decade began, we renewed our vow not to let this dream slip away.

Since now we each had small children, negotiations with our wives began well in advance, with diplomacy continuing to the hour of departure. We had been granted a precious ten days to walk from McKenzie Pass north to Timberline Lodge in 1991. For three sleep-deprived, out-of-shape fathers yet to embrace the "go light" revolution, on that first day back on the PCT we struggled up through the lava fields surrounding Belknap Crater to the southwest slopes of Mount Washington. My journal entry that day was reminiscent of our climb up Big Huckleberry a decade earlier: "Anyone seeing us as we trudged the final mile of the day would have assumed we were suffering through a lengthy forced march. We were tired, hungry, and experiencing the aches and pains of our adjustment to carrying heavy loads." This was to become a first-day ritual for most of our long walks together.

"Despite the challenges," I concluded that day's entry, "we were thrilled to be together. We barely missed a beat in picking up where we left off when we emerged at Rainy Pass." We talked, we laughed, we marveled at the beauty of the landscape, and our bodies strengthened. We encountered but a handful of other hikers. The Pacific Crest Trail Association was still two years from hiring its first staff person, and the book and movie *Wild* were more than two decades from elevating the profile of the PCT experience, so we were still exotics on the trail. While waiting for our ride at Timberline Lodge, one wag asked to take a photo of us to show his wife what three fellows who had been in the woods for ten days looked like.

It wasn't until 1997 that we could resume our quest by hiking south from McKenzie Pass to Crater Lake. In the intervening years, my position at the university had changed, we had adopted a daughter from China, we had sold a home and bought another one, and my in-laws had retired to our community. Howard and Jim had their own life complexities. But, most importantly, we were back.

Eight more times over the years, some combination of Howard, Jim, and I walked sections of the trail, slowly chipping away at the total length of the PCT. From Rocky, Boris, and Pierre we had evolved into Team Geezer as we edged from our fifties to our sixties. The speckled gray in our beards gave way to mostly gray and was well on its way to all gray. When I retired in 2008, a daunting half of the trail remained unwalked. Yet I never doubted that I would finish.

In retirement I was able to accelerate my progress. In addition to Jim and Howard, other family and friends joined me for sections. My new schedule opened up times of the year previously off-limits because of work. The high deserts of Southern California really must be walked in the spring. And the northern Sierra and southern Cascades were often still warm and sunny in September. Most of my days and nights on the trail were gloriously beautiful. And while not all stretches of the PCT are spectacular, I came to appreciate the stark landscapes of the desert as much as the ice-sculpted North Cascades, the volcanic string of pearls along the Cascades as much as the deep forests that seem to extend forever, the dramatic High Sierra as it shouts its glory as much as the tarns and creeks that humbly whisper their presence. When I am out on the crest it is a rare day that I am not up early. There is nothing more sublime than to emerge from my bag and gaze out over a broad valley with distant layers of mountains rimmed with a crimson glow. The sun reaches out, warming me as it peeks over the horizon. Who wouldn't be pulled back to the trail year after year?

With the arrival of 2016, two sections in my quest to complete the PCT remained, totaling less than two hundred miles. Jim had agreed to fly out from Maine in April to walk from Tehachapi to Agua Dulce. We walked through unimaginably brilliant expanses of California poppies, yellow coreopsis, and purple lupine as we crossed the Mojave. And Howard and Bruce Johnston, my partner on several sections, joined me for the last leg in July, ninety-six miles. On the final night, I was surprised at the power of the emotion that welled up, overpowering my normal reserve. The PCT had been a thread constant through my adult years. When we had climbed Big Huckleberry Mountain on that first night with overloaded packs and soft bodies, we were looking at the world as one of infinite possibility. Now, thirty-five years later, I was a much older man who saw the world differently, who saw a wonderful and delightful world but no longer one of infinite possibility. Since starting the trail, I had gotten married and had a family and a career. Now I was retired, my children were grown, and my body had aged. The trail had been a part of all of that.

Over two dozen different section hikes spanning thirty-five years, benefiting from countless acts of kindness and support, got me to August 1, 2016. It was then that I walked out of the woods to reach Highway 36 west of Chester, California, to complete the final link in the journey I had started as a young man. My pilgrimage was in great contrast to the thru hiker who finishes in six months or conquers the trail in fifty-three days, six hours, and thirty-seven minutes. Sure the trail changes them too. But, for me, my thirty-five years bring together the wisdom of the trail with the joys, sorrows, and realities of life. The PCT has been the path of my life.

In the end, I walked nearly eighteen hundred miles with Howard and Jim, spent nearly a half-year of nights with them in a tent, and shared challenges and witnessed miracles. They accepted my weaknesses and nourished my strengths. They added humor and joy to every day on the trail. They had grown old with me. And, above all, we processed and celebrated the progress of our lives much as we have the miles on the trail. These have been precious times on the PCT. Each journey together has been its own miracle, something you only realize from the perspective that age provides. Now I understand the quiet joy and ease with which those three guys shared their story with us forty years ago.

We are those guys.

TENDER IS THE NIGHT

KASEY KOOPMANS

Kasey Koopmans was born in Seattle and raised, as she puts it, "between the ferny undergrowth and strip malls of its suburbs." She studied in New York City for four years and left with a bachelor's degree and "a trunk full of cocktail dresses." Her blog, *The Importance of Elsewhere*, is inspired by a Philip Larkin poem with the same title. "Elsewhere," as Koopmans describes it, is "a wonky fairground for displacement. Weird and embarrassing things happen out there in Elsewhere, and such dissonance is compelling; it sharpens awareness of ourselves, our certainties and our possibilities. It confirms our existence."

A smile forms as we are easily drawn into imagining the meadows and lake-dotted landscape just south of Chinook Pass in Mount Rainier National Park. We are reminded that, around every bend in the trail, magic may await us. With humor and reflection she helps us take it all in.

The morning is chilled, but there's a holdover of tenderness (I don't know how else to describe it) from the evening before. I tread lightly, taking it easy on the morning—and, in return, Washington takes it easy on me. The trail unspools on even grade along a series of lakes with surfaces so still and clear that I can count the pine needles in their reflections of the trees. I take a break by one of these lakes and eat the peaches from Naches. Peaches are the sexiest fruit alive. Am I right, or am I right?

Half a day of hiking later, I stop again for a long snack. I don't notice it until I am fully unpacked and having removed my shoes, but the creek bed I've settled in is thick with yellowjackets. For the first time since I was five years old, I get stung. *Goddamn it.* I squeeze a glob of hand sanitizer over the welt. I'm not sure if that's something you do for stings, but it gives me the illusion of agency, and I reckon that killing "99.9% of most common germs" can't hurt. Sanitized or not, the welt will fester for days.

Today the trail is edged with dead wildflowers—premature casualties of Washington's dry year. I could mourn the end of summer, but how about an ode to autumn instead:

Where are the songs of Spring? Ay, where are they?
Think not of them, thou hast thy music too,—
While barred clouds bloom the soft-dying day,
And touch the stubble-plains with rosy hue.

—John Keats

There may not be bounties of wildflowers, but the change of seasons means I still get my color kicks. Belts of red and orange grow thicker all the time.

At the top of a small pass, I look back from whence I came and get a wide-angle view of Old Snowy and Knife's Edge. The hikers up there today have sunshine and 100 percent visibility. Those bastards. I'm already scheming how I'll have to get back to Goat Rocks next season to see it in all its goaty splendor, when I turn the corner and suddenly: Rainier.

In all its unobstructed glory. Incredibly clear and incredibly close. I start shouting when I see it, I suppose from joy. Weekend backtracks when he hears me shriek, to make sure I'm okay. I sit, study the mountain, and eat brownies. I am more than okay.

With the golden hour upon me and espresso fudge coursing through me, I cross over into Mount Rainier National Park in high spirits. I start switch-backing down, taking my sweet time with every turn. As I do, I run into three teenage boys. They all have dreads, and their Pink Floyd phrases shine round about them.

"Where's the, uh, lake?" One of them asks me. Dude. *There are so many lakes,* I think but don't say out loud. "Do you know the name of the lake?" I ask. A long confused silence follows. "I can check my maps?" I offer. "Naw, we don't need maps." Another long confused silence. "Is there a trail junction up ahead?" the blonde one finally asks. "Yes!" A question I can answer. "There are a few junctions about a quarter mile back." They nod to each other smugly. "Yeeeah, we could sense it." I tell them to keep that trail sense.

I continue the mellow descent until the trail levels and wraps around Dewey Lake. Lord, it is beautiful. Word must be out about Dewey's beauty because campsite after campsite is filled beyond capacity. I find Weekend sitting on the edge of the lake. The world is in a state of supreme dusky peace—isolated fish jumps the only blips of disturbance. I find an empty campsite next to a few other PCT hikers and unfold my Tyvek. Darkness falls and settles softly over the lake and my sleeping bag. The tender night returns.

"PASTOR MARY, I DON'T THINK WE SHOULD TAKE THE REST OF THE CHURCH ON THIS HIKE"

MARY E. DAVISON

At the age of seventy-six, despite having had three joint replacements, Pastor Mary Davison completed her fourteen-year quest to complete hiking's Triple Crown in 2017. That alone is extraordinary. However, Davison, a mother of two and grandmother of ten, was not yet ready to take off her walking shoes and subsequently walked the American Discovery Trail from the Atlantic Coast to Nebraska. These two short accounts describe Davison's first section hikes on the PCT in 2003 and 2004 just as her trail adventures and addiction to walking begins.

As of 2020, the American Long Distance Hikers Association had recognized 482 Triple Crowners, more than double the number recognized just seven years earlier. This elite subset of PCT hikers is joined by those who have completed the PCT "yo-yo" (walking the entire trail in both directions in a single season) and those who have finished the PCT multiple times. In the decade to come, who knows what new threshold hikers will pursue.

So I discovered I like multiday backpack trips. Did I then say, "Oh, I think I'll work on the Triple Crown?" Of course not. I'd not yet heard of the Triple Crown. I knew there was something called the Pacific Crest Trail

(PCT) that went through Washington State, where I lived. I knew of the Appalachian Trail in the eastern part of the United States. I'd never heard of a thru hiker. I'd never heard of the Continental Divide Trail. The only Triple Crown I knew of was a horse race.

A parishioner was working on completing the Washington part of the trail. Interesting. It sounded like a fun project. When I began, I wasn't thinking beyond Washington State.

The section I chose to do first wasn't the best, the most scenic section of the PCT or the beginning or the end of the trail. It was the most convenient. My first PCT section began at Chinook Pass and ended at Snoqualmie Pass. Mike, a young, red-haired parishioner who had walked part of the Wonderland Trail [a trail that circles Mount Rainier], was game to go too. A pastoral colleague dropped us off at Chinook Pass, and my son picked us up after work six days later at Snoqualmie Pass.

I set out with my old REI external frame pack, a five-pound sleeping bag, and a six-pound tent for the two of us. In those days I thought three pounds per person for a tent was the lightest possibility. I would never consider carrying such a heavy tent or sleeping bag now.

From my days in the Mountaineers, I remember there was a great view from a short climb above Sourdough Gap. Mike dutifully followed his pastor on a scramble up the rocky crag with a sheer drop on the other side even though he wasn't particularly comfortable with heights. Mike could have hiked much faster than his pastor but always let me lead, inexplicably saying that going at my pace would keep him from hurting himself.

The most memorable part of the trip was the elk. We saw a herd of elk from a distance in Big Crow Basin, and the next night we heard more, although we didn't realize at the time what we were hearing were elk. It wasn't until we reached the Ulrich Cabin on the third night that we definitely identified the strange sounds as elk. We woke up the next morning in the cabin and found thirty to forty elk outside. We crept as quietly as we could down a creaky wooden ladder from the sleeping loft, carefully opened the squeaky door, and took many pictures of quiet elk life as the herd, mostly cows and calves, grazed around us.

I have been amazed ever since at the sounds elk make. Male bugling in the fall rutting season is entirely different. In domestic bliss as they grazed around us in the meadow surrounding the Ulrich Cabin, elk made high-pitched sounds very much resembling the sounds E.T. made in the Spielberg movie.

Leaving Ulrich Cabin, we hiked in clear-cuts most of the way to Snoqualmie Pass at the same time that an unusual ninety-plus-degree heat wave hit the Pacific Northwest. Our packs were heavy. I was still carrying a sun shower, a book, a lot of cooking equipment, and heavy food for three-course dinners, as well as a heavy tent and bag. I have never done well in heat. At one point, Mike and I struggled upward to an old logging landing and collapsed. There was no shade, and we were really spent.

Mike said, "Pastor Mary, I don't think we should bring the rest of the church on this hike."

I laughed almost hysterically as I thought it the funniest statement ever, right when I was wondering why we had ever come on this hike.

We survived the heat and the hike and at the end of our six days arrived at Snoqualmie Pass. I'd completed 69.5 miles of the Pacific Crest Trail.

In August a year later, it was time for my second section of the PCT. I wrote about my plans in the church newsletter and asked if anyone wanted to come along. Two people were interested in coming with me for two different sections. Wonderful

Gary, a younger man from my congregation, and I set out from Panther Lake Campground as a storm system moved into Washington. It poured. All day. Gary pulled out a yellow poncho from his pack and found it was his small daughter's and didn't cover much of a full-sized man. At lunch, I rigged the rain fly with some cord, a good thing as Gary was almost hypothermic by then. He found something dry to wear and also found his own poncho, the right-sized one. Life was better then, even in the rain. It rained the next day too. We walked through wet foliage in the Indian Heaven Wilderness, which left us even wetter. When the sun finally came out and we could dry out, we were overjoyed. In spite of the rain, we enjoyed walking by lakes and peeking through the trees at Mount St. Helens. Gary's family picked him up at Big Mosquito Lake. My son wondered why in the world I chose to camp at something named Big Mosquito anything. Yes, there were mosquitoes.

The rain had stopped, and I braved a night alone at Big Mosquito. I hadn't camped alone before, but I thought I could manage one night. After a day of solo hiking, I met my second companion, Kathy, near Mount Adams. Her dog, Tasha, came with us. We loved the Mount Adams area and later the Goat Rocks. Kathy was a kindred spirit who loved the mountains as much as I did and also had hiking and climbing experience, making us a good team.

The flowers were in full bloom near Mount Adams and the Goat Rocks. The views were spectacular, some of the best the PCT has to offer, with high mountain crags and glaciated Mount Adams and Mount Rainier. We camped by one of my favorite waterfalls in the Mount Adams area, not seeing (until the next morning as we left) the sign telling us not to camp in the overused area. Fields of lupine accented with Indian paintbrush were abundant and filled the air with perfume.

Kathy's husband, David, brought us a food drop at a road halfway through, and Kathy took a break as I walked an uninteresting section. She wanted to walk only the pretty parts; I wanted to walk it all.

Before we reached Sheep Lake we crossed Walupt Creek on an incredibly hot day. We were so glad to see water, and it was so hot that we shed all our clothes and sat in the creek. All went well until Kathy sat on my glasses, which I'd placed on the bank, her bare butt popping the lenses out. I repaired them with duct tape and looked like Mr. Magoo for the rest of the trip.

I took a short Therm-a-Rest air mattress, having learned that old bones don't do well with just a foam pad. I borrowed a two-pound down sleeping bag. I was still thinking a three-pound tent was lightweight. I also wore heavy boots that gave me blisters and continued to use my ancient external frame pack. One hiker said he hiked without a stove to save weight and tried to cut a pound of weight from his pack for each year he hiked past sixty years of age. I took note of stoveless hiking and lightweight goals. Hmm. I was sixty-three. How could I cut three pounds? Or did my down sleeping bag mean I'd shed three pounds already? But I'd added the air mattress. I plan to go lighter next year.

Mountain goats grazed below us as we went over the side of Old Snowy Mountain and Packwood Glacier. Mount Rainier stuck its lofty head above a sea of clouds before us from the knife-edge ridge. Near our highest campsite were banks of bright pink monkey flowers. From our tents tucked behind trees we had an incredible view.

Descending from Goat Rocks, we reach our campsite on a very hot day. It was so hot Kathy took off all her clothes and sat leaning against a downed log. I thought she was the funniest sight I ever saw, casually walking around stark naked except for her hiking boots. After a while, she put a shirt and shorts on, and almost immediately four guys walked into the camp. Her timing was impeccable.

It rained again the last half-mile into White Pass, where we met Kathy's husband. I'd walked another 110 miles of the PCT. Little did I know that before thirteen more years passed, I would complete the Triple Crown.

From *Old Lady on the Trail*,
by Mary E. Davison (Vandeleigh Publishing, 2018).
Reprinted by permission of the author.

WANTED: SITE WITH A LAKE VIEW

BARBARA WIEDEMANN

The most perfect spot
and I almost passed it up
just to go another few miles.
Perfect was the little lake
with reflections of the mountains
with snow on the far bank
with very green grasses on the near
with the sounds of water flowing and frogs calling.
And there were Jeffrey pines and white fir
and pushing through the soil
bright red snow plants.
Sometimes one shouldn't be so organized,
so driven.

And then there was the day
very windy and heavy cumulus clouds
thirty miles left to Echo Lake,
I wished for a campsite out of the wind
with no possibility of falling trees or limbs.
I wished for the sun in the morning for warmth.
I got it all—
large boulders to obstruct the wind
a clear, flat area for my tent,
and even a view of a lake.
The trail provides as they say.
And there was that August day
smoky from one of the Washington fires
either Mount Adams or Stehekin.

But the wind shifted
and the smoke left
so I went off trail to Basin Lake.
Alone and semi-nude
I swam in the cool waters
enjoying the solitude
until a lost boy scout appeared
and then wandered off.
Above the lake
twenty mountain goats gamboled,
their bright white a contrast to the grays and greens.
Photos can't capture this.

WEATHERING THE STORM

HEATHER "MAMA BEAR" BURROR

A mother and daughter together on the Pacific Crest Trail. That doesn't seem unusual until you learn the daughter recently turned nine. She is about to be one of the youngest people to thru-hike the PCT as the pair close in on the Canadian border. Just a few weeks from finishing, the weather throws a wet and thunderous wrench at them.

The descriptions of the damp and rainy trail accompanied by lightning and loud thunder remind us of our own experiences in this section, when overriding gloom shrank the surrounding world and made us appreciate not being alone. In their case, the Burrors call on the same determination that has brought them this far.

Heather Burror seems to use "tent" and "tarp" interchangeably in her story. Trail shelter has evolved from the traditional tent with enclosed sides and bottom and rain fly. Extremely lightweight tarps are increasingly popular, with hiking poles often incorporated for support. They can be tied to trees and staked down. A blend of the two, the tarp tent, offers the lightweight features of the tarp with some of the greater protection of the tent (e.g., netting and rain fly), and innovation has resulted in additional hybrid designs.

I had the opportunity to speak with both Heather and Sierra Burror and was impressed by Heather's devotion to her daughter and a child's willingness to spend that much time with a parent. The strength of their love and respect was crystal clear, and the two have continued to inspire each other in various pursuits, including long-distance trail running and hiking the Colorado Trail and the Continental Divide Trail. Sierra was the California Interscholastic Federation Valley Championship 3,200 meter champ as a high school senior in 2021 and went on to run cross country and track for Cornell University.

I was struck by Heather's commitment to support Sierra's independence and foster her self-confidence, supporting her daughter's interests without directing them. Decisions on the trail were made together. "Let the interests flow naturally," Heather concluded. This approach has contributed to Sierra's successes in learning, walking, and running. Through all of their achievements and time together, they agree that there has been one constant. Sierra is still always ready to eat.

—HS

Thunder rumbled in the distance. "Mommy, I think we should set up the tent," Sierra suggested. "Are you sure?" I queried as I glanced from the blue sky above down to the postage-stamp sized patch of level ground in the bushes next to the trail. "I'm not sure our tent will fit here." "I want the tent tonight," Sierra insisted. Reluctantly, I pulled out the tent and began finding ways to squeeze it into the limited space.

At age nine, Sierra "Monkey" Burror was just a few hundred trail miles from becoming the youngest on record [since broken] to thru-hike the Pacific Crest Trail. An experienced hiker, Sierra had already spent more time in the backcountry than many adults do in a lifetime. Sierra had hiked through rain, snow, hail, and sleet, climbed many snowy passes, waded through icy rushing creeks filled with freshly melted snow, and slept countless nights under the stars. If Sierra wanted the tent, I would set up the tent without question. I was soon glad I did.

From the comfort of our soft, down sleeping bags, we listened as the storm approached with increasingly gusty winds. Rumbling thunder grew louder and louder. Soon the storm was directly overhead. Blinding flashes of lightning illuminated the inside of our tent. Ear-splitting crashes of thunder immediately followed. Then, as the thunder and lightning seemed to drift off into the distance, rhythmic splashes of rain began. Soon torrents of rain poured down on our tent like water from a fire hose. The downpour eased only when another series of brilliant flashes and shattering booms commenced. Then a volley of pea-sized hailstones pelted our tent. Although the hail did not penetrate the tent, it left pockmarks on the tent fabric, while hailstones bouncing under the tarp accumulated on the floor. We lay awake through seemingly endless rounds of lightning, thunder, and driving rain. Finally, in the wee hours of the morning, the storm's fury waned and we fell asleep, exhausted.

We woke to the sound of a more gentle rain steadily dripping on our tent. Huddled inside, we packed up quickly and donned rain gear before heading out into the elements.

A thick, heavy fog engulfed our camp, and a fine rain continued to fall. Water clung to the huckleberry bushes that lined the trail, soaking our legs as we pushed through the undergrowth. More water seeped into our shoes as we squished down the soggy trail.

"The sun will come out tomorrow," may be a common adage, but this isn't true along the PCT in Washington. Trail legends abound of hikers who quit just short of the border, unable to tolerate another day of cold, Washington drizzle. Trudging down the trail, fingers and toes numb from the damp cold, I tried to imagine spending our remaining weeks on the trail plodding through the likes of this.

"When's lunch?" Like any thru hiker, Sierra was always ready to eat, and after several hours of slogging in the rain her stomach growled loudly. But the prospect of munching our lunch while shivering to keep warm, sitting on a damp log or huddling under a dripping tree did not appeal. So we marched on, hoping for some kind of miracle.

Our miracle soon came in the form of a brightly colored sign proclaiming "TRAIL MAGIC! Hot Food! Cold Drinks!" at Tacoma Pass. Our pace quickened at the promise of trail magic ahead. With no expectations, we could not be disappointed! Reaching Tacoma Pass, we followed signs leading down a narrow side-trail through the bushes to two large pop-up tents sheltering an amazing trail magic operation. Under one tent, "Not Phil's Dad" manned two Coleman stoves, heating water for hot drinks while cooking up two pots of chili. The other tent sheltered five cloth chairs set up in a semicircle around coolers full of cold refreshments and boxes full of delicious snacks.

Dropping our packs, we each grabbed a blueberry muffin and melted into a chair. Together with section hikers Matt, Jennifer, and Rachel, we sipped hot drinks, devoured bowls of steaming chili, wolfed down chili dogs, and nibbled on candy bars, fruit, and other snacks. Although the drizzle continued, underneath the shelter our clothes and shoes partially dried, and warmth slowly returned to our extremities. Refueled, refreshed, and rejuvenated, we hiked on after almost two magical hours.

Matt, Jennifer, and Rachel soon caught up, and the five of us continued together. An expert in fungi, Matt (also known as Mush) spent the afternoon identifying mushrooms and telling us more about them. The miles passed quickly as we swapped stories.

Reaching a small creek, we finally parted ways. Matt, Jennifer, and Rachel decided to make an early camp in a nearby meadow, hoping to beat the rain. Sierra and I planned to continue on and camp at Stirrup

Creek, where we hoped to meet our Finnish friend Piia, with whom we had recently camped. Reaching Stirrup Creek, we found a perfect flat site just across the water. But Piia was nowhere around. Knowing we were behind her and would arrive later in the day, Piia had undoubtedly saved the site for us and hiked on. Reluctantly, we set up our tent, grateful for Piia's kindness but disappointed we would not camp with her.

Snuggled in our warm sleeping bags, listening to the rain pinging against the tent walls, we settled in to read. Sensing movement at the foot of the tent, I sat up suddenly, straining my eyes in the dimming light. Two small, beady eyes stared back at me. "A mouse!" I gasped, as the tiny gray body slipped back under the tent flap. Unzipping the tent, I poked my head out of the narrow opening, shining my headlamp in the direction the mouse had scampered. Multiple small mice scattered, dashing away from the headlamp beam. As I swiveled my head, mice continued to scurry away from the light wherever I pointed it. We were surrounded, outnumbered, and unnerved.

Sighing heavily, we slowly began packing up our gear. Mice, with insatiable curiosity, can be destructive little vermin. One had chewed through the eyelets and shoelaces of my hiking shoes near Belden. Hikers told stories of mice chewing through rain jackets and backpacks. One friend even told of being awakened by a mouse scampering through her hair! Sharing our camp with hungry, inquisitive mice simply was not an option.

Wet gear packed, we stepped into the pitch-black night. Dark, angry clouds obscured the moon and stars. A fine mist continued. My dim headlamp, long overdue for a battery change, cast only a faint glow onto the trail directly in front of me, more shadow than light. I tripped over tree roots and stumbled over rocks as we slogged up the trail. But with no camping in sight, we had no choice but to continue on.

By the time we found a suitable spot to camp, we were several miles up the trail, and drizzle had become a heavy, driving rain. It was almost 11:00 p.m. Fumbling in the dark, I set up the tent, and we scrambled in. Once inside, we peeled off wet clothing and gear and piled it in a corner before again crawling into our dry sleeping bags. I slept for a while but awakened to the sound of rain as it continued to beat the outside of our tarp. Looking over at Sierra, I noticed the bottom of her sleeping bag protruding out from under the corner of the tarp, exposed to the rain. Pulling her feet back inside, I assessed the damage. The bottom of Sierra's down sleeping bag was now sopping wet. Further, by pushing her feet beyond the tent wall, she had allowed a steady stream of water to pour into the tent. Our sleeping pads and gear now floated in a large pool.

I glanced at my watch: 4:00 a.m. Attempting to bail the water seemed futile, and it was too early to start hiking with our fading headlamps. Checking to make sure our electronics were still dry, I rolled over and went back to sleep. Two hours later, I woke again, and so Sierra woke too. The rain continued to pound the outside of the tent. Inside, the tent resembled a shallow swimming pool, with almost an inch of water lapping up against our sleeping pads. Maple, Sierra's stuffed spider monkey trail mascot, lay face down in a puddle. Sierra pulled Maple out of the water, and we both laughed as water dripped from Maple's sodden fur.

But getting packed was no laughing matter. Both of us were cold and tired, and even pulling on warm layers seemed a Herculean chore. Turning our shoes upside down, I watched water drain out and splash into a puddle. Sierra squished into her wet shoes and began hiking. I stayed behind, trying to cram our soggy tent, weighed down by at least a pound of water, into a tiny stuff sack.

By mid-morning, we had sufficiently warmed, and we began to notice the beauty of our surroundings in the Mount Baker–Snoqualmie National Forest. Brightly colored fungi, including orange-and-yellow, fan-shaped, chicken of the woods mushrooms grew from mossy fallen logs. Tall, stately trees guarded the trail. Sierra put her arms around one immense trunk that would have taken several more hikers to completely encircle. Then nature added her own trail magic to the moment as the sun finally broke through the clouds, lighting the forest with a soft golden hue. As the clouds began to slowly drift apart, we caught our first glimpse of the tall mountains surrounding us and the Alpine Lakes Wilderness ahead. The day suddenly filled with promise. No, the sun might not always come out tomorrow. But sometimes it does.

SERENITY NOW

AER PARRIS

The PCT can be a social or a solitary experience. We all find our own balance. Some days seem longer than others, while occasional restless nights can be quiet agony. I prefer hiking with a friend but appreciate the opportunity to periodically walk alone and then come together when we take a break. Aer Parris shares some of their day with another hiker, and that proves the perfect adjustment, one that allows them to enjoy the trail experience again.

—HS

Hiking with another person changes my brain chemistry. It is bizarre. I can't explain it. But it is lovely.

Felix Felicis hiked with me again, starting at the delectably late hour of 9:00 a.m. until the beautifully twilit 9:30 p.m. We took three luxurious hour-long breaks, each time chatting our heads off.

During our hike we were mostly silent, with me reveling in the joy of following someone and the safety of not being alone. My mind, it seems, does not go to those ugly places with someone else there.

Instead I wondered at the bursts of white fireworks of the spent dandelions, the play of golden light dancing in the long grass, the matchstick dead trees outlined against the setting sun.

The sun lowered red and burning into the distance, and orange, blue, pink, and purple all blurred together—making the separation between them all impossible to comprehend—creating a new color in their union. We looked toward the long, thin clouds that gave further definition to the magic show, and I felt happy, silently sharing the splendor with another person. Silently loving the trail side by side.

Today it felt like my adoration was renewed, and I am overwhelmed with gratitude. Today I remembered what I love about this place, this journey. Today I found the time to revel in the minutiae, the stuff I am out here to explore. Today I found love again.

THE NORTH CASCADES: THE GREAT WHITE NORTH

COVERING WASHINGTON
SECTION J—SECTION L

Snoqualmie Pass • Stevens Pass • Glacier Peak •
Rainy Pass • Manning Provincial Pass

THE TRAIL PROVIDES

DAVID SMART

Years ago, on a walk over Hannegan Pass in the North Cascades, my three fellow backpackers and I were dogged by torrential rains. Water gushed down and across the trail. Moisture, driven by persistent wind, penetrated every protective layer. There was no escape. It was when we recognized the impossibility of getting more than 100 percent wet that the experience was transformed. Overgrown trail. Trail a mud pit. River ahead. No problem. Charge through. We had been released! Free from the fruitless worry of trying to stay dry.

As with the mechanics of laughter yoga, the unabashed joy of jumping in a puddle is catching. Soon the warmth and lightness spreads until you cannot help but smile. That is the moral of this story as David Smart, Bucky, and Bradley conquer a typical North Cascade "rainaggedon."

—RH

We were less than two hundred miles from Canada when thick, dark clouds covered the morning sky, and sheets of rain spread across the mountains. Cold, wet, and miserable, Bucky, Bradley, and I marched uphill in our rain jackets and rain pants through ankle-high water. The freezing water flooded down the trail, flowing over my feet and turning them to prickling blocks of ice. Without adequate tree cover, rest spots were few and far between, and we were forced to walk exposed to the elements.

Each of us had donned two heavy-duty trash bags, one for pack coverage and one to wear as makeshift poncho since our rain jackets hardly kept us from getting wet, serving more as a protective layer. Even though it was cold and the freezing water chilled my feet, everything from my ankles up heated quickly while walking. Sweat ran down my back beneath my soaked jacket.

The rain fell ceaselessly in this way for three days straight. We had not expected it but should have seen it coming, knowing Washington's reputation. We'd hardly dealt with any rain on the trail, and, although other hikers had dealt with longer stretches of rain, it was a miserable and unexpected challenge for our troika.

A misty haze shrouded the trail, and the thickening clouds made sunlight a distant memory. Unable to sun-dry our soaked gear and clothes, the miles stretched long, cold, and miserable. I thought back on the desert with fond memories. I would have given anything to see the sun.

Finally fed up with the situation, I muttered, to no one in particular, "This is insane!"

Bradley stopped and turned to me with a mad look in his eyes and a wide, toothy grin.

"Are you okay, Shake?" Bucky asked as he stopped behind us.

I glanced at Bradley. "Yeah. Was it something I said?" He seriously looked like he was going crazy.

Bradley cocked his head back and laughed maniacally. "That's the answer! You said it yourself. Only insane people would do this, right?"

And with that he leapt into a puddle, splashing and stomping, dancing in the rain.

"Shake?" I said. "What are you doing?"

Bucky and I glanced at each other with eyebrows raised. "Trust me!" he yelled. "Just try it!"

It took a moment for me as I considered his strange behavior to understand what he was doing. He seemed lighter, free from the misery he had been feeling moments ago. Was he actually on to something here?

Finally it made sense. If only insane people would choose to walk such a path, we would have to adopt insanity to make it out.

The playful attitude was infectious. After initial hesitation, I jumped into a puddle, kicked the water, and feigned laughter. While the cold itself hadn't dissipated, my relationship to the cold faded nearly instantly. The strategy was working. My eyes widened, and a huge grin spread across my face. This was the way out.

"Try it, Buck!" I yelled.

Before long, Bucky joined in, and we were splashing, kicking, and laughing up the trail. We'd gone insane, but madness lifted our spirits.

That night we found the best camp we could: a sad, soggy, treeless bog where we had no choice but to try to sleep. We attempted to pitch the tarp using trekking poles as support, but the poles couldn't stick firmly in the ground. Pools of water flooded into the space. After many collapses and failed attempts, we finally found a spot devoid of pools and strong enough to stand the rain. Thankful to be out of the rain for the first time that day, we crowded inside and immediately shed our soaked clothes, peeling our clothing from our skin and setting them at the foot of our sleeping bags just out of the rain's reach beneath the tarp's overhang. We changed into our thermals. Slipping into our sleeping bags with dried clothes was like escaping into a whole new world, one I had craved the entire day.

I turned my head when Bradley cussed. His eyes had sunk, and he let loose a deep sigh, holding up his sleeping bag. It was soaked, a shriveled, dripping blob.

I gritted my teeth as Bradley examined his bag for failures. Sleeping wet on a cold night seemed both miserable and a real danger at this point. Bradley looked at us sidelong. "Looks like we're sleeping close tonight, boys."

We nodded. It was his only option for surviving the night. The cold temperature arrived with the darkness, and we huddled close to him as he slid inside his wet sleeping bag.

That night I could hear Bradley breathing loudly as if forcing his breath to warm his body. It wasn't a good sign considering how easily he usually fell asleep. Before long he was shivering furiously between Bucky and me, and we nudged a bit closer hoping he would make it through the night. Eventually his body settled. We hoped everything was alright.

We woke the next morning to the sound of raindrops against our tarp. A pool of water had gathered by my head, moistening the hood of my sleeping bag, and I scrunched up to avoid the nearing moat.

"You sleep okay last night, Shake?" I asked.

He didn't respond.

"Shake?" Bucky asked. "You okay?"

Bradley shook his head. "Not good," he said. "Thanks for your body heat, though. I'm not sure I would have survived otherwise."

We lay motionless beneath the tarp for a few long minutes, hoping the rain would pass. The next town was still a day and a half away. The looming thought of another wet day was dreadful.

The limited food rations were our only motivating factor. We changed back into our wet clothes, slid our feet into cold, damp socks, then shoved those into our frozen shoes. After the tarp was packed away, it felt twice as heavy in my backpack with the extra water weight.

Immediately facing us was an uphill climb over the next ridge. That same gutter of cold, rushing water waited for us as we began to ascend. The energy to muster up our carefree insanity was gone. All that was left was dread, pain, and misery.

Suddenly, as we marched through the flooded trail, I felt a penetrating cold pierce the tips of my toes of my left foot. *Are they freezing?*

The sensation crawled higher and turned to a hot burning flow. It was a shocking pain greater than any I'd felt before.

Stories rushed into my mind of snow-seasoned hikers with missing fingers and toes.

Could that happen to me? The thought made my heart race, and my breath turned irregular. The feeling crawled higher up my ankle.

I couldn't hike any longer. I leapt off the path and began to untie my shoe to see what damage had occurred. Just as I felt the pain was at its highest point, I felt a warm light touch the back of my neck. The rain stopped. We looked back into the sky as rays of sunlight fanned down into the basin. The clouds vanished, and warm sunlight filled the world. The pain left me at the first sight of the sun.

Standing in disbelief, we rejoiced with hands to the sky, then immediately got to work. Not knowing how long the sun would stay, we rushed to unpack our belongings, spreading them atop bushes and shrubs to dry.

I smiled at Bradley as he threw his sleeping bag onto some bushes. He nodded. We soaked up as much sun as we could while the warmth briefly poked through the clouds. We really had embraced the insanity of this journey, but now it was almost over. As our gear began to dry, the sunlight brought us strength and the will to go on.

The sun stayed long enough for us to dry our belongings and not a moment longer. The clouds returned, and the rain fell once again. But it didn't matter. We'd been granted a reset, similar to the feeling after a restful zero day in town. We were off once again to Canada, closer than we'd ever been before.

From *The Trail Provides: A Boy's Memoir of Thru-Hiking the Pacific Crest Trail* by David Smart (self-published, 2018). Reprinted with permission by the author.

THE PCT FAMILY

BARBARA WIEDEMANN

So it was chance that I missed the side trail
at the ninth switchback that led to Five Lakes.
It was chance that I didn't stay at a creek
and walked two more miles
to a spacious site with water in a nearby meadow.
It was chance that Colonel Tom Parker and his dog
were camping there.
Colonel Parker,
an original mountain man,
with clothes from Goodwill,
with no high-tech tent or sleeping bag,
carries canned food for his dog.
Colonel Parker hiked the Appalachian Trail,
rowed 1,000 miles down a river,
and does better outside than inside.
So it happened that he and I talked
through the evening and much of the next day.
But since he was southbound and I north we parted.

I remember Larb,
born in Bosnia,
lived in Denmark, Germany,
and now in San Diego,
an engineer at GoPro.
I said, "I can't detect an accent."
He said, "You learn to assimilate fast when you're a refugee,"

I remember Beth,
a forensic veterinary investigator
who uses DNA to solve crimes,
identifying a murderer
from traces of dog feces on shoes,
tracing a knife used in killing

the dog of Otis Redding's son
to the offender—
she travels the world.

I celebrate the chance meetings with my PCT family,
but I mourn terribly the good-byes.

A SOUTHBOUND ADVENTURE

CHRISTINE "DORMOUSE" MARTENS

It was July 2014, and Christine "Dormouse" Martens and her partner, John "Dirt Stew" Haffner, chose to do something that only one in ten thru hikers do. They decided to walk north-to-south on the Pacific Crest Trail. Those familiar with the North Cascades know that spring often pays little attention to the calendar and hikers can still encounter a substantial snowpack in July. Not to be deterred, Martens and Haffner conquered initial fears and came to terms with the demands of the trail.

Martens observes that the continuous line that is formed by northbound and southbound hikers intersecting on the trail is a unique form of thru hike. When they meet, hikers have yet to share any of the same experiences but eventually will share all the same trail. Often it is not until we look back that we can fully view both where we have been and where we go next.

Martens references Hiker Haven and Andrea and Jerry Dinsmore in her story. In 2003, the Dinsmores first took in three PCT hikers, and they have hosted hundreds since. Although Andrea passed away in 2017, as of this writing Jerry still welcomes hikers to Hiker Haven.

"John!" I screamed. "I can't do it! I can't—I can't move." I was shaking, and tears were rolling down my cheeks. We were approaching Park Creek Pass, which at sixty-one hundred feet was completely covered in snow. Glancing down from my feet into the valley I felt as though I would fall for a thousand feet if I so much as breathed wrong. We weren't even on the PCT yet.

It was July 6, 2014, and we decided a few days before we started our southbound thru hike that we would take a low-elevation alternate route for the first sixty miles. Park Creek Pass was the highest point before we joined the PCT. We picked an alternate route after we heard how bad the conditions had been on the PCT for the first few south-bounders. They reported that one hiker had slipped in the snow and fallen several hundred feet. Trees broke his fall—and several of his ribs.

I had already been nervous about the first part of our hike. Until I heard about the person falling, my biggest fear had been getting lost. John "Dirt Stew" Haffner and I had hiked the Appalachian Trail together four years earlier, and we realized that the experience did not prepare us for this. Nobody in his or her right mind takes on the higher-elevation portions of the northern Cascades of Washington this early in the season—nobody except hopeful southbound PCT thru hikers.

They say you carry your fears with you, and we certainly did. We carried ice axes, crampons, an emergency beacon, a GPS device, a compass, and extra batteries for the GPS. We wound up using all of it except for the beacon.

John looked back at me and yelled, "Just step in my steps!"

"Your steps are too far apart! I'm tiny compared to you!" I yelled back. Adrenaline pumped through my veins, pushed by my fear of heights. Every time I looked down, the whole world started to spin and my stomach jumped into my throat. Luckily, my husband has no fear of heights. He came back to help me. Together we inched our way to the top of the pass, where I raised my ice axe in triumph.

Once we joined the PCT, the next section through Glacier Peak Wilderness was far more challenging and beautiful than I could have imagined. For up to thirty miles at a time through this section of a hundred or more miles, we were above the snow line. The mountains were unforgiving. Crampons weighed down my feet. Each step on the steep snow was either like walking on sand or walking on ice. My energy quickly got depleted.

For every mountain we climbed, we were rewarded with spectacular views of jagged mountains covered in snow. We met our first other southbounders in Stehekin, and, after following a pair of footprints we falsely assumed were pointing us in the right direction, we ran into another southbound thru hiker. We decided to tackle the section together. Each of us took turns kicking steps and we hiked long days, hoping every day to make more progress than the day before. More than halfway through the section, we began rationing our food. The miles were going by too slowly, and it was hard to know how many more days the section would take.

We vowed to burn section K, page 8, of Halfmile's maps the moment we got to civilization. When we reached the Dinsmores, the trail angels near Stevens Pass, we did just that.

"We get about twenty or thirty south-bounders each year, and only a handful make it," Andrea Dinsmore said. I looked in the mirror at my sunburned face and the gashes on my body from bushwhacking through avalanche chutes in the snow. I wondered if I would be one of them.

We parted ways with our newfound friends. Every south-bounder ahead of us was on our radar. We knew each one by name. Although we met only seven south-bounders on our whole journey, we knew of many more, both behind and in front of us. The times when we met another south-bounder were times of pure excitement. Invariably we'd wind up talking about beginning in the snowy Shangri-La of Washington.

Once we hit Oregon, waves of north-bounders passed us, some arrogant from having walked many times the distance we had but most completely oblivious to our existence. Since John shaved at each town when we got a shower, he could easily have been mistaken for a day hiker or weekender. We preferred it that way. We counted seventy-eight north-bounders who passed us one day. To them, we were a rare sighting, but to us, they seemed like an endless parade.

There is something funny about the moment when north-bounders and south-bounders cross paths. Altogether we have walked the entire Pacific Crest Trail, yet we do not have a single shared experience of the trail. It makes for both helpful and frustrating conversations. I think hikers have selective memories, and a lot of the information we got from northbound hikers was false. I can only hope that what we shared was more reliable. When in Northern California the last stragglers finally pushed past us, we were happy to have the wilderness to ourselves again.

Northern California delighted us with a crescendo of mountains. As they got bigger, so did our appetites for the Sierra. We had left the mosquitoes behind in Washington and Oregon and were able to enjoy the scenery, especially the lakes and waterfalls. As we stopped in towns along the way, locals asked us if we were going to make it to Canada in time. We were constantly explaining that the trail can be done southbound as well and that we were actually on schedule for arrival at the terminus. We started learning about the ongoing drought and the effect the water shortage and wildfires was having on small towns along the PCT. Wildfires had chased us off the trail in parts of Oregon. We struggled with long road walks where there was no water, and we even had to bypass a section where there was no alternative route around a fire.

I was acutely aware of every liter of water we consumed. As we approached the Sierra, water slowly became abundant again. We climbed what felt like a staircase of mountains leading up to the High Sierra. At each high point, John would proclaim: "Now this is the highest I've ever been!" Each day the scenery became more jaw-droppingly gorgeous. We felt the constant push to make miles as September progressed. Our goal was to make it out of the Sierra by October. As we gained elevation, it got cold, particularly at night. I was happy to have an extra down jacket as well as my ten-degree sleeping bag. We camped at lower elevations when possible.

Although many thunderstorms chased us over the passes, we were overjoyed when we had the perfect day for a climb up Mount Whitney. We were low on food during this section. While we conversed with other hikers on the way up, several John Muir Trail hikers gave us their extra food, since they would be finishing their hikes at Mount Whitney. In the end, we got through the High Sierra just before the first snowstorm of the season.

By the time we were hiking in the desert, we were lean, mean, hiking machines, and the prospect of twenty-to-thirty-mile stretches without water didn't intimidate us. With the water report in hand, we had our water consumption down to a science.

Besides the lack of water, we didn't know what to expect from the desert in October since there had been little information online before we started our trip. I had assumed it would be outrageously hot during the day and freakishly cold at night. It was neither. There were hot spells, yes, but nothing like what north-bounders experienced earlier.

What hit me the most about hiking through the desert was the solitude. We went weeks without encountering another hiker. We knew there were a few other south-bounders in front of us, and although they were days or even weeks ahead of us, their footprints were perfectly preserved in the sand. From those footprints we could see where they had stopped for a break, where they had gotten water, and where they had gotten lost. It gave us a strange sense of camaraderie.

On our last night on the trail it rained. It was the first rain in weeks. The rain-packed sand was hard and the footprints we had been following for hundreds of miles disappeared overnight. That made me realize that all those people had finished their hike. Mother nature was reminding us that our journey was almost over, and soon the land would forget us as well.

But I will never forget the trail. I have been forever changed by my thru hike. I realized that this journey had made me a better person. I could see the impact people were having on the land, and I felt responsible. I appreciate water more than ever. The kindness of strangers restored my faith in humanity.

At the southern terminus of the PCT, I pulled out the trail register. After reading the entries from the two or three friends who finished before us, I wrote: "Congratulations, south-bounders!" We were elated to be two of the few who succeeded in reaching the southern terminus.

ORDEAL BY ICE AND SNOW

IAN SARMENTO

Ian Sarmento's story illustrates what can happen without the right equipment and experience in navigating the winter PCT. Ryan Forsythe, author of "Sometimes They Come Back," in *The Pacific Crest Trailside Reader: California*, observes, "There are two types of stories of lost hikers. First are those the hikers themselves tell of being stuck or stranded, perhaps due to injury or horrific weather, before somehow miraculously finding their way out. And then there are those stories that others must tell, of friends or loved ones lost forever." Sarmento, thanks to a blend of determination, stamina, and luck, lived to tell his tale from the wintry north. While there will be some second-guessing of Ian's decisions along the way, there can be no question about his courage, his fight, and his unwillingness to give up.

October 19–November 11, 2012

I was hiking in the rain south of Glacier Peak when I passed two other thru hikers midday waiting out the weather in their tents. After a few hours of hiking, rain turned to sleet, and eventually sleet turned to snow. I crossed Red Pass and was soaked to the bone and freezing, so, after descending a thousand feet to a small patch of trees, I decided to set up camp as it started to get dark. When I awoke in the morning, the snow was knee-deep to mid-thigh-deep, with some waist-high drifts, and it was still coming down. I packed up and decided to make a move for lower elevations but soon lost the trail. As I cut downhill, the side of the ridge was covered with snow nearly waist-deep. I aimed for a creek with the intention of following running water to lower elevation and, I hoped, eventually exiting the wilderness. After following the creek for an hour or so, I noticed a saw-cut stump and soon three small logs with saw-cut ends lying across the creek. There was a noticeable indentation in the snow on the other side that further suggested a trail. I crossed the logs and followed this trail the best I could, eventually coming to a nice human-made bridge. I next came to a side trail with a sign that read "Trail Abandoned—Use New Side Trail .25 Mile North of Sitkum Creek on PCT." I continued on until I reached that side trail, where there was another sign posted: "White Chuck Road and Trail Washed Out." Fuck!

I continued north on the PCT until I reached a sign reading "White Chuck Road, and Kennedy Hot Springs." Scratched into the sign were some comments from other hikers including "Both Destroyed!!!" and "Not an exit!!!" Fuck!

I stayed on the PCT, intending to cross Fire Creek Pass and camp by Milk Creek, hoping that the Milk Creek Trail would offer an exit. But by nightfall I had lost the PCT just north of where it crossed Glacier Creek. (Not realizing that the trail required fording the creek there, I continued straight instead.) I dug in next to a boulder, set up camp, and hoped to find the trail in the morning. By morning a fresh three or four inches of snow had fallen.

I crested the ridge. I saw no sign of any trail. The ridge dropped steeply down in front of me. To my left was a steep, treacherous pass, complete with sheer cliffs and glaciers, and to my right the ridge gradually descended until there were trees on it. I couldn't cross the pass, I didn't want to slide down into the canyon ahead (this eventually happened anyway), and I didn't want to backtrack, so I followed the ridge to my right, hoping to find a sign of the trail once I got into the trees. Branches cut off, blazes, anything.

However, the ridge grew steeper and steeper until I started sliding out in long sections, stopping myself on trees, until I reached a small cliff. I lowered myself, holding on to small trees and branches. Eventually the route I had chosen became nearly vertical, offering me no other options other than to continue forward until encountering a similar drop-off of about twenty feet. I maneuvered horizontally holding on to trees until I found a more manageable section of cliff. I dropped my pack and trekking poles first, then urinated on my hands to warm them enough to gain enough grip strength to lower myself by grasping exposed roots or rock. When I got to my pack, which had rolled about twenty feet in the snow I noticed that my camera had fallen out of my hip belt pocket. I dug all around in the snow, went downhill, went back uphill: nothing. I had lost the only thing making me feel somewhat connected to the outside world and other people. My video diaries of this whole misadventure were lost. I felt more alone.

I continued on until the terrain flattened and stumbled through a patch of small trees bent over under the weight of the snow. I reached another sheer drop but was able to descend and navigate scree slopes to the canyon below. I followed the creek at the bottom downstream until it dropped off steeply into a section of canyon with twenty-foot vertical walls. Then I backtracked until I reached another waterfall. Each side of the canyon was too steep to ascend, so on the floor of the canyon, between two branches of the creek, I stomped down and scooped out as much snow as I could on the flattest spot for my tent.

And I waited. And waited. And waited. And starved. And froze. And waited.

On day two, for some reason, I had a premonition that after nine nights in my tent I would be rescued. I spent the next nine days rationing food at three hundred to five hundred calories per day. The first five or six nights were very cold. During this period the snow would melt a little during the day but be replenished at night with new snow. After that it warmed up enough to rain, and even the nights were only slightly below freezing. After night nine, the snow had mostly melted. During this period I spent each day crazy with hunger pangs, hoping, and thinking. There were times I was extremely anxious. Sometimes I felt good about my decision to wait for help and other times I contemplated trying anything I could to escape. I would drift back and forth between feeling relatively calm and sedated to helpless and anxious. At times I was confident that I would survive, and other times I was less hopeful. By the fifth or sixth day I began imagining airplane sounds from the noise of the creek. Two days later I began imagining helicopter noises, and by day nine or ten I would constantly hear both airplanes and helicopters. I wore earplugs the last two days to protect my sanity the best I could.

After the ninth night the snow had melted enough that I should have made a break for it then, but I decided to wait the day out to honor my premonition. If I wasn't rescued I would go for it the next day. This was my first full day with zero calorie intake. The day came and went, and when I woke up the next morning I decided that if I were going to die in the wilderness, I wasn't going to die lying in a nylon coffin in that godforsaken canyon I had grown to detest.

I packed and headed for the upstream waterfall, carefully climbing hand over hand beside it, then following the creek to a low spot in the cliff above the steep canyon wall. This was the only possible chance I had to climb out. I crawled up the scree slope on my hands and knees, then grabbed onto rocks and roots to climb the canyon wall. I fought through thick undergrowth and trees until I was able to climb a small knoll to view the surrounding area. I spotted a route for getting up the canyon wall and back onto the ridge from which I had descended ten days ago. I crossed a steep, unstable scree slope very carefully with each ill-placed step sliding out. Once across the scree, I had to attempt a climb. I started up, and, grabbing on to the frigid rock face for dear life, I made it. Thinking back, I cringe at the thought of how narrowly I had made it and just what would have happened if I'd made a mistake. I re-surveyed my surroundings on the ridge, hiking around the area for a couple hours. I eventually traced my steps back to Glacier Creek, found the trail where it crossed, and followed it up to Fire Creek Pass, which was still completely covered in enough snow to make navigating very difficult. The north side of the pass still had deep snow drifts, but the way became clearer as I lost elevation going back into pine forest.

It started raining lightly, and by nightfall I was pretty wet. I camped on the trail north of Milk Creek. The next two passes were pretty much the same—difficult to maneuver, covered in snow, and sometimes frightening. I made it to Stehekin on a Friday. My last meal, if you can call it that, had been on Monday. Hiking without any food, after already barely eating for nine days previously, was very difficult. Sometimes I could hardly keep moving when going uphill or through the snow. Having to lift my feet to step over logs or rocks felt like I was lifting blocks of concrete. I ended up consuming massive amounts of water in spite of hardly sweating. When I arrived in Stehekin, I had lost eighteen pounds. I was ecstatic to have found my way out and to eat again but also extremely sore and a little disoriented.

After I decided to continue north to the border (with a GPS this time), my backpack was unbearably heavy as I carried an abundance of extra food. It was at least sixty pounds. The first twenty miles to Rainy Pass were smooth sailing. Then it started snowing again, and by the time I reached Cutthroat Pass a fresh three to five inches had fallen. The higher I climbed, the more snow remained from the last storm. It was frozen to a hard shell and very slippery and made for difficult walking. The north side of the pass was worse, and, wherever there was a steep ridge, the trail was completely snowed over, then frozen solid, making it nearly impossible and completely terrifying to traverse. This treachery continued north of Harts Pass. I had to traverse a section on one ridge on my knees, facing the mountain, and stabbing my trekking poles a foot into the snow to anchor myself. North of Rock Pass I slid about one hundred feet down the ridge until stopping myself by digging my elbows and poles into the snow. Then, using a pole as a break, I slid down to the next switchback. Several times it took everything I had to keep going. The last day it never got above thirteen degrees Fahrenheit. My nose was bleeding all morning from the cold dry air. By nightfall, before the sun had even finished setting, my thermometer read zero degrees. Ice had formed in my inflatable sleeping pad the night before and ruptured it, so I set up a bed of pine branches under my tent for extra warmth.

I finished my thru hike on November 11.

SASQUATCH AND SPIRITS

TAMI ASARS

As was noted in the introduction to Monte Dodge's "My Close Encounter with Bigfoot" in *The Pacific Crest Trailside Reader: California*, few legends have transcended cultures, eras, and regions like that of Sasquatch, Bigfoot, Yeti, or Ts'emekwes. Common to all is the notion of a species of shy, wild, hairy giants living in the remote wilderness. Despite the absence of fossil records, the mythology continues thanks to periodic sightings, footprints, even stomping noises. However, maybe it is time to consider other explanations for unexplainable phenomena deep in the forests.

Thump. Thump. Thump. "Did you hear that?" my husband calmly asked as I looked around wondering the same thing. We listened for breaking sticks, for rustling, for other indications of animals, but the forest was silent. The thumps repeated and sounded as if something large was repeatedly stomping. I'd heard this sound many times before when hiking, the result of an elk crashing through the forest. In those cases, more noise had followed. What could the powerful stomping possibly be, we wondered? We were on the new stretch of PCT near the ancient grove of trees by the Suiattle River. Suddenly, a pinecone hit me in the head. "Ouch!" I shouted. Then another one landed nearby. I looked up, trying to find the Douglas squirrel responsible, but there was no sign of one. Two more pinecones came flying before we decided to move on and get away from the eeriness of whatever was happening in the forest. The large trees and mossy undergrowth gave off an unearthly feeling, and we were interested in finding out what might be lurking nearby.

Let the record show that, in all my miles of boots on trails, I've never seen a Sasquatch. When people talk about the beast's existence, I land somewhere in the middle, usually sliding back and forth between those who know Sasquatches exist and those who know they are mythical. But since my husband and I couldn't explain the unsettling feeling we'd had or the pinecones to the noggin or the loud thumping, I went on a quest to resolve the mystery after I returned home. The most logical explanation, I was told by local rangers, was a Douglas squirrel gathering fruit and nuts for the winter, just as I had suspected. During late summer, the squirrels store bounty for cold-weather nourishment, and it's commonplace for them to drop many cones at once. Could the thumping have been from dropping pinecones? Perhaps, even likely. Although my husband and I both agreed that the thumping was very heavy and sounded bigger than a careening pinecone. The trees were tall, so it's possible we didn't see or hear the squirrels as they busily worked.

Part of me believed the Douglas squirrel answer, but another part wasn't convinced. Then, some months later, I happened to be talking to a fellow outdoorsman who had spent a great deal of time in the Darrington area nearby. When I told him our story, without missing a beat he calmly said, "Oh, those were the spirits." I questioned him further, and he told me that years ago the ancestors of local tribes hunted and fished in that area, and rumor had it that their souls still inhabited those forests and rivers. My husband and I were not, he said, the first to hear strange rumblings in that area. As I listened to more stories he shared, about others who had encountered similar happenings along the Suiattle River, I began to shudder. To this day, I have no idea what my husband and I felt and heard as we walked along the river, and I suppose I'll never know. Whether the answer is logical or mythical, as you wander through the large trees and mossy green forest of the new stretch of the PCT, keep your eyes peeled, your ears open, and your cameras ready.

From *Hiking the Pacific Crest Trail: Washington,*
by Tami Asars (Mountaineers Books, 2016).
Reprinted by permission from Mountaineers Books.

TRAIL AND DISTANCE ON THE PCT

ROBERT BIRKBY

In Robert Birkby's homage to trail building, "The Art of the Trail: An Aesthetic Appreciation of What's Underfoot," in *The Pacific Crest Trailside Reader: Oregon and Washington*, he rightly observes that the PCT is "a graceful ribbon three feet wide and 2,650 miles long." It is "a fusion of engineering, architecture, and artistry" that negotiates jagged mountains, dense forests, vigorous rivers, and shifting sands. As Robert "Pace" Caldwell noted in "Anatomy of a Trail Crew" (Pacific Crest Trail Association *Communicator*, Fall 2017), "You may not think about it when [you are hiking], but good trails don't happen by accident. They take skilled care and commitment." Birkby, in this piece, goes a step further and suggests that the best trails are those we "barely notice." So true. Yet, as we glide along on a well-crafted trail, we cannot forget our debt to the countless trail crew members who have made it possible by building and maintaining it. We must walk with gratitude.

> *"Time passes slowly up here in the mountains."*
>
> —*Bob Dylan*

I was booking it down the Pacific Crest Trail a week south of the Canadian border when I crossed paths with Ed Kuni. Grizzled and windblown from thousands of northbound miles, he looked really old to me.

I knew who Ed was from "The King of the Trails," a recent *Sports Illustrated* article that described his devotion to hiking. He had walked the length of the Appalachian Trail twice. Now age sixty-six, he was nearing the end of a two-year quest to complete the PCT.

I was a spry young guy at the time who had hiked the Appalachian Trail the previous year, setting off from Maine in a cloud of black flies and springtime chill. Five months later, as I neared Springer Mountain in Georgia, I had watched for a sign of what I should do next. It seemed the least the trail gods could offer after I had walked two thousand miles. When the universe finally spoke, the message was simple. I just wanted to stay on the trail.

Soon I boarded a Greyhound in Atlanta with a one-way ticket to Puget Sound. There was a girl in Seattle I was eager to see. Friends were assuring me that the Pacific Northwest was a backpacker's paradise of big forests and huge mountains. The Pacific Crest Trail was right there too. That's where I met Ed Kuni.

We didn't talk long. He was impatient to be on his way, and so was I. Miles won't hike themselves. We adjusted our packs, shook hands, and went in opposite directions, Ed toward Canada, me with Mexico twenty-five hundred miles away.

That was 1980. As I write this more than forty years later, I am older than Ed was when I met him, an age that no longer seems very old. I have no idea where the time has gone.

I do have a better sense of the accumulation of trail distances, especially early in long treks when, like most hikers, my internal odometer cannot stop spinning. How much trail can I cover in a day? How far to the next camp? The next resupply? The next state line? Our bodies are tuning up for the rigors of covering the miles. Feet toughen. Shoulders become accustomed to the weight of a pack. Legs build strength. Lungs and heart gain endurance.

Calmed by routine, the mind is getting into shape too. Wake up early to make breakfast and break camp, then spend the day paced by the mantra of footsteps. Make camp, fix supper, sleep, and do it all again. And again and again. And again.

We lighten our loads by tossing the unused pair of socks, the paper-back novel, that extra cook pot. As the miles go by, we gradually loosen the burden of time too. What we need to know about its passage begins to come to us by the days of provisions left in the pack, by the slosh of fuel still in the stove, by the gradual wearing away of boot soles. We know from first light on the horizon when to start the day and by evening glow when to wrap it up. If we are lucky, time disappears and we are one with the moment and the trail.

There are no rules governing trail time and distance. Hikers can take decades to patch together the sections of the PCT to say they have covered it all. Others bust along the full length so quickly that I assume they are pausing barely long enough to clean the bugs off their teeth and let their trail runners cool. Too much sugar in their breakfast food, I suspect.

The thing is, the faster you finish, the sooner you have to find something else to do. What if the trail gods tempt you to seek more of being on a trail, not less? You could, like Ed Kuni, turn around and hike the Appalachian Trail a second time, followed by the Pacific Crest Trail, but then what?

In my own eagerness to stay on the trail, I've had plenty of long-distance treks. I've also discovered the satisfaction of what might be called "slowest known time"—making the trail better while not moving very far at all.

First was the Beyond Macho Trail Crew, formed soon after I got to the Northwest. There were three of us—my friends Jay and his wife, Janice, and me. Five, if you included Mollie and Lizzy the mules. Six with Moon, a big loose-limbed goofball of a Labrador retriever whose chief talents were exuding boundless joy and helping with kitchen cleanup by eating all the leftovers. Every trail crew needs a member like that.

Jay and I had worked together on trails in the mountains of northern New Mexico at Philmont Scout Ranch, the national high adventure base of the Boy Scouts of America. We had enough confidence in our skills to bid on a Forest Service contract to maintain a long stretch of the Pacific Crest Trail in Oregon. Having never pursued a government project, we soon discovered we had underbid our nearest competitor by more than half. That would net us barely enough to pay for supplies, but it meant we could be on the trail for six weeks, and what's not to like about that?

Each morning we shook the frost off our tents and lashed everything onto the mules. I would lead them a quarter-mile down the trail and tie their halter lines to a tree, then start cutting brush encroaching on the trail corridor and shoveling slough off the tread. Jay and Janice would work the trail up to the mules and then lead them past me and a quarter-mile farther. Leapfrogging through the day (leap-muling? mule-frogging?) we would stop late in the afternoon and make camp. Most evenings we sat by a fire beneath the open sky. Time slowed, and it felt as though the world that was not the trail was very far away.

For starters, trails are the oldest marks made on the planet by humans. People left trails of footprints across the plains of Africa millions of years ago. You can see them today.

Study the PCT and you'll realize the countless person-hours required to sculpt a 2,650-mile pathway, one foot at a time. Sierra rock. Cascade timber. Desert, forest, tundra, and plain. The trail unrolls lightly across the terrain thanks to thousands of people investing years of labor. The Beyond Macho Trail Crew felt connected to them all, both present and past.

Our trail specifications matched those followed by teams in 1915 constructing early sections of what would become the PCT. They were the same specs the Civilian Conservation Corps used in the 1930s to put in hundreds of miles more, and by crews all the way to ours. Our tools were the same, too. Pulaskis for clearing slough and cleaning water bars. Mattocks and rock bars for leveraging stone. Shovels, axes, loppers, and handsaws for the rest.

Trail work toys with distance as well as with time. Hitting a rock with a mattock sends a vibration all the way to Mexico in one direction and to Canada in the other, like the spiccato bounce of a bow on a violin string. The pulse combines with those of other crews up and down the route, people we might never see or even know are there, but they are swinging tools too, adding to the harmonics and making the trail sing.

Gary Snyder got it when he wrote poetry about the trail crew experience after working in Yosemite in 1955. He understood the revelation of being in the backcountry long enough for the world to revolve around the point of the hand drill he was driving into a boulder, one hammer blow at a time. He got it about walking back to camp after a long day working under the Sierra sun and finding a bowl of stew in the cook tent and a cup of coffee from a big can kept warm over a pinewood fire.

And he got that for all the effort it requires, good trail work is labor meant to disappear. A trail crew wants hikers to embrace the sky, the forests, and the shape of the land but barely notice the tread flowing beneath their feet. The trail is a medium to encourage contemplation, a linear ritual of repetition and discovery that leaves no trace of ourselves as it transcends distance and time. It's not surprising that soon after leaving the Yosemite trail crew, Gary Snyder was steaming to Japan to become a Zen Buddhist.

I lost track of Ed Kuni, the aging king of the trails I met so many years and miles ago. Perhaps when he reached the end of the PCT, the universe told him it was okay to keep hiking and he continued deep into Canada, or he wheeled around to the Rockies and headed south on the Continental Divide. Maybe he went home to Pennsylvania, sharpened a Pulaski, and started tuning up a bit of the Appalachian Trail until his little section hummed in harmony with all the other lengths of all the other trails.

As for me, I'm fine with becoming a grizzled old guy staying on the trail as long as the trail gods will allow. Hike and do good work and be with friends. Coffee in the morning and a pot of stew at night. Campfire embers drifting, as time stands still, toward the stars.

THE NEW NOMAD'S LIST OF 101 TRULY COMPELLING REASONS TO GO ON A VERY LONG-DISTANCE HIKE

KIMBERLIE DAME

With a wink and a smile, Kimberlie Dame had no trouble coming up with five score plus one reasons to walk the PCT. Amazingly she missed some. Here are a few she neglected to include: You may make some of the best friends of your life; you will appreciate the radiance of dark skies like never before; you will gain a deep love and awe for the natural world; you will gain humility as you become increasingly self-reliant; you will laugh until your sides hurt along the way; it will change your life. When you spend time on the PCT you will have some of your own to add.

1. See a bear
2. See a mountain lion
3. See full-grown men carrying parasols to protect themselves from the sun
4. Hear silence
5. Finally hear what the nonstop thoughts in your head have been saying to you about yourself and others your whole life
6. Get all of your aging over with in one season
7. Give you something other than food as subject for your social media updates

8. Get crazy fit
9. Wear socks with sandals without appearing geeky
10. Have only one task per day for five whole months
11. Explore the exciting realm of sexting or phone sex (or both) with a partner left at home
12. Determine if your facial hair really would eat your head if left ungroomed for five months
13. Learn how to get lost
14. Become very adept at knowing exactly what time it is, based on the sun's position in the sky and what the bugs are doing
15. Forget what day and time it is
16. Learn how to help other people
17. Instantly belong to a community of giddy, like-minded people
18. Forget what your real name is
19. Forget why you ever became a career person
20. Forget what you look like with mascara on
21. Watch your feet grow
22. Watch your hair grow
23. Watch your patience with discomfort grow
24. Finally get through the entire library of "The Great Courses"
25. Finally understand what an empty mind feels like
26. Quit smoking
27. Quit drinking
28. Quit caring what you look like
29. Quit waking up late
30. Learn twenty-five uses for duct tape
31. Learn twenty-five uses for an umbrella
32. Learn twenty-five uses for trekking poles
33. Accrue daily skills at manipulating your partner to do what you want
34. Learn how to be submissive to your partner
35. Leave your partner
36. Get a new partner
37. Feel bad-ass
38. Be actually weird, instead of poser weird
39. Earn a tattoo
40. Have an accomplishment that absolutely no one can relate to
41. Meet other tourists in Canada and be able to respond no matter what they say with "yeah, but I walked here"
42. Experience pain that might actually trump the pain of giving birth

43. Become an excellent map reader
44. Become an excellent hitchhiker
45. Become psychic about where there are car campers with food
46. Finally "get" that "one day at a time" mantra you've heard others spout all your life
47. Sit gleefully around a campfire drinking beer with strangers and laughing till your body hurts
48. Get free pie [a tradition of Mom's Pie House in Julian, California, is to honor PCT hikers—those with a permit—with a slice of their famous apple pie and coffee]
49. Witness firsthand the intensity of a forest fire
50. Behold trees that are hundreds of years old
51. See beauty you couldn't possibly describe
52. Figure out that your skin is waterproof
53. Realize that debt collectors and solicitors can't reach you by phone anymore
54. Realize that you don't have to worry about drinking "too much" coffee
55. Don't pay car insurance for five months
56. Get over fear of heights
57. Get over fear of pencil-thin tread across steep slopes of loose sand or snow
58. Get over fear of naked hippies in hot springs
59. Learn how fun being knocked over by a wind gust can be when choreographed correctly
60. Learn how to sleep in all situations without chemical help
61. Have time to think about what the hell you're doing with your life
62. Have opportunity to forget about what the hell you're doing with your life
63. Possibly get your money's worth out of your health insurance
64. Obtain relief from making daily abstract decisions about things
65. Fall madly in love with a puffy jacket
66. Fall madly in love with a pair of sandals
67. Fall madly in love with random beds
68. Fall madly in love with an apple
69. Meet people from all over the world
70. Meet trail angels and learn the true meaning of gratitude
71. Watch people gather around water sources like animals do
72. Remember that you're an animal

73. Be cared about by strangers
74. Have nonstop haiku material
75. *Truly* test gear
76. Learn one hundred uses for a bandanna
77. Be a single woman on a trail mostly populated by fit and happy men
78. Be a man away from the wily ways of evil women
79. Test your relationship
80. Let your kids develop a closer relationship to their other parent while you are away
81. Make your kids proud of you
82. Prove endurance and stick-to-itiveness on your resume
83. Truly feel like you've done something for yourself in your life
84. Learn how strong you can be
85. Be amazed at what the human body can endure
86. Put your feet in a cool stream after miles of desert hiking
87. Hallucinate without drugs
88. Give your parents another opportunity to compare you to some strange relative in the distant past the whole family still talks about
89. Get family members to join you for sections for quality bonding time
90. Be "in the world" and not "of the world"
91. Care nothing about politics or sports outcomes for five months
92. Become unreliable to needy people in your life for five months
93. Begin to see a forest as your home and not feel like you're an outsider exploring it
94. Learn at least fifteen ways to prepare couscous
95. See and maybe even grow some of your own super-impressive blisters
96. Learn how popular a flask of tequila can make you
97. Learn how to *not* take pictures when having an experience
98. Stand underneath hyperactive wind turbines
99. Earn every meal
100. Learn a new language
101. Mostly, have an experience of a lifetime that you will never forget!

Happy trails!

THE PLEASURE OF YOUR COMPANY

HOWARD SHAPIRO

What is a perfect day in the mountains? For Howard Shapiro it combines the majesty of a special place along the PCT with the magic of an early autumn day and the opportunity to share it with a friend. Some of our most intimate human interactions come away from the distractions of modern, urban life. And, without the rush of time, conversations can be their deepest and most satisfying. When just walking is enough, even a short trip to the mountains can create an unhindered spaciousness that lasts beyond the return home. For Howard and his friend, Dick Simpson, these were several perfect days.

I completed the PCT a few years ago after stitching together many years of section hikes. It was with great pride and relief that I reached my goal of going the distance. Most of those sections were completed with my long-time hiking partners and dear friends Rees Hughes and Jim Peacock. Those two also walked my final section with me, and that was truly a gift and pleasure. Incomparable and priceless, the bond the trail has forged between us is unbreakable.

Over the years, other friends and family have joined me in my quest to walk sections. Despite having completed the trail, I can't seem to ignore the siren call to return to the PCT and include people like my close friend Dick Simpson. The PCT has been a gift that keeps on giving.

Dick and I taught together and have known each other for over thirty years. We have always shared a love for the outdoors, but we hadn't ever shared a walk on the PCT. Even after I had completed the trail, we continued to talk about the two of us hiking some miles together. Finally our time came. I suggested one of my favorite pieces of the trail from Harts Pass north. Given our time frame, we agreed on going at least as far as Woody Pass, about twelve miles south of the border.

The weather in late summer in northwestern Washington can often be sublime. The bugs have left, the temperatures are pleasant, and the days are still plenty long. Dick was really interested in sharing my trail experience. Over the years, Jim, Rees, and I have settled on a style that is not all that unusual but is still our own. Our style is relaxed. We share everything from the food to the tent and tend to take long afternoon breaks. We share thoughts, ideas, hopes, and dreams. If we have any style, it is more Three Musketeers and less me, myself, and I. Our approach has become like slipping on a well-worn walking shoe. One that has become so much a part of me that I worry about even unconsciously imposing it upon another person. But Dick was very open to following my lead in this regard. Dick's only requirement was that we would take our time. The intent was not to crush miles but embrace them, having time together to appreciate where we were and who we were with. I had absolutely no problem with that notion. To be honest, I have never crushed the miles with much consistency.

We arrived at Harts Pass on a gorgeous day to begin our journey. Dick's deliberate pace allowed us to take in the surroundings. Here we were in the heart of the North Cascades with expansive views of peaks and valleys in nearly every direction. The trail pleasurably meanders with moderate elevation gains and losses unlike farther south near Glacier Peak. Autumn was in the air and forcing summer off the stage. We imagined these deep glacial valleys full of snow in another month. Scanning the lingering snow patches dotting the grassy hillsides, the invitation to keep walking was hard to ignore. This is the "high country" referred to in guides and other descriptions of mountain travel. I appreciated the undivided time shared with a hiking companion. Time for conversation, reflection, and simply being in each other's company.

As we walked above Windy Pass, the huckleberries were prolific, with their showy red leaves announcing the coming autumn. Without that hint, the air remained warm until after we got to camp and ate dinner. The combination of our pace and surroundings sparked shared stories of past hikes as well as recollections from our day. These conversations added to the appreciation for what we were finally getting around to after years of talking about it. We could acknowledge the joy we get from being in the mountains and being with each other. Being here in this place alone would be one experience, but being here together only heightened our gratitude to amble with each other. As we walked, I kept going back to past hikes in the North Cascades. Years before, on my first hike here, I was taken by the grandeur of the Pasayten and the company I was in. All these years later I found myself with someone who could appreciate my affection for this place, and I realized the indelible hold this trail and these mountains have had on me and continue to have.

The gift the trail can deliver can be quietly astounding whether one walks the whole thing or a short section. The added gift that comes from sharing the views, the sunsets, and the ups and downs of the tread with a close companion is extraordinary. We can seek and find these experiences in our day-to-day life. Unfortunately they are often hiding among the phone calls, email, dishes, garden weeding, or any number of other tasks, and the time left for deeper conversations and observations can get lost or at least abbreviated.

As we reached Woody Pass, my appreciation for this place and my friend Dick came together in an overwhelming wave of emotion. My love of place, shared friendship, and a perfect day. We ate our lunch realizing that this was our turn around point. We would descend through Rock Pass and make our way back to our camp on the edge of some trees surrounded by a crescendo of wildflowers that in a short time would be no more. They would give way to frosty nights and shortened days. We are like those ephemeral alpine wildflowers. We will come back to the mountains and the trail as long as we are able. This is where we will celebrate these experiences and our friendship again. It is a total pleasure. A gift.

ATTITUDES AND LAYERS: LAST ONE TO CANADA WINS

NATALIE FISHER

Most thru hikers complete their hike during the beautiful fall days of September and early October. By early November, winter is well underway in the high country of Washington's Pasayten Wilderness. If you are just leaving Stehekin then, with eighty-eight miles remaining to finish your PCT thru hike, you are rolling the dice. This is Natalie "Dances with Lizards" Fisher and Steven "Brr" Wilson's story as they make the final push north. Fisher's journal entries capture the humor, spirit, and attitude necessary to complete the journey in these difficult circumstances.

88 miles to go. We leave Stehekin with our pockets loaded with cinnamon rolls and sticky buns. We each have food for ten days—six days of good stuff, four days of boring stuff. Lots of layers. Lots of attitude (mostly positive mental attitude, with a little bit of the other kind). A whole village and the whole PCT community is now sending good thoughts our way. We aren't just two people out for a walk to see what we can do anymore. We're being watched. Bets are being made. People are being inspired.

Never thought we'd actually be the last two striving for the goal. The last to Canada wins!

Brr finally weighed his pack for the first time the whole trip. Eighty pounds. Probably always weighed that much.

"Ready to go for a walk, Dances," Brr asks.

"Ready as I'll ever be."

We're walking into a storm, and we know it. It's going to be cold, but we want to try to get as far as we can while the hiking is easy. Of course, with heavy packs, I only make it a quarter mile before I break down and eat a sticky bun.

As promised, it starts to snow by late afternoon. We cross creeks that are starting to freeze over and make camp at a place called Hideaway.

74 miles to go. Middle of the night. Wake up to a tent that's too warm. Realize we're in a snow cave. Nothing is venting anymore, and it's all dripping on Brr's down sleeping bag. He eventually musters courage to go outside and uses a snowshoe to clear off the tent. There's at least eight inches on the ground, three to five inches more than predicted.

In all the excitement, I see a cinnamon roll sticking out of my jacket pocket. We've recently had problems with mice, and the only thought in my sleepy head is *I don't want the mouse to eat my cinnamon roll!* Brr jumps back into the tent to find me chomping on the sticky treat without a care for snow or anything else.

64.5 miles to go. It's a slow day to get up to Rainy Pass and beyond. We make burritos and hiker mochas at the pass and consider how easy it would be just to hitch out to Bellingham and be warm. Instead, we march past civilization, to camp above six thousand feet and tuck in for another snowy night.

Surprised in the morning to hear voices as we're packing up camp. Flatlander and Bouncer arrive on scene. Snowshoes on, GPS in hand. Making one more attempt at the goal.

At this point in the game, joining up to hike with someone is no casual contract. That's for summer business. Brr and I have been practicing in this kind of weather for the last month. We've got a system down that works for us. We know each other's skills well. As Brr puts it "She doesn't freak out. Ever." On an expedition like this, the last week is not the time to meet someone new and try to fit them into your system. We are happy to say hello. Short conversation. Have to move to keep warm.

They continue. We finish packing and follow their tracks to the top of Cutthroat Pass (scary name, easy pass), where we sit down to have second breakfast and watch as two figures traverse the ridge and round the corner. Then we watch in surprise as one figure and then another returns.

We pack up and continue on our way. We chat again as they pass us. The ridge got steep, and the snow was icy around the corner. Too much for them.

I have the utmost respect for Bouncer and Flatlander that they recognized when something was too much. They knew when to call it. That is an important skill. One most people ignore. We continue on.

We traverse the ridge and make the steep descent in a couple feet of snow to Granite Pass. Then across the next ridge. The going is slow. We don't have snowshoes on yet. The snow is at the point where it really wouldn't be any easier in snowshoes. We'll post-hole one way or another.

55 miles to go. Setting up the tent. Exhausted. Bummed that we couldn't make it any farther. At this rate, we might not make our rendezvous.

There's a crack. We pause, stock still, and assess the damage. One of the tent poles broke. Shattered on one end due to cold. Nothing to do but wrap it with Tenacious tape and hope it holds.

48 miles to go. Get to the top of Glacier Pass. Another steep ascent just ahead of us. Time for another hiker mocha as the sun sets. Bodies are complaining. Nothing to do but tape what hurts, hope it holds, and don't look again. Pep talk to the body. Come on, just need you to get me through a few more days.

We begin the next ascent. Switchbacks across a meadow. Why couldn't they put them in the trees? Wading across snow drifts at each turn. Brr gets fed up. We're about four switchbacks from the top. Pull out the GPS to double-check our location. We can just go straight up. The trail stays on top of the mountain for a while. We'll hit it.

Switch to the microspikes. Glorious microspikes. Time for some mountain climbing. Brr pulls out his ice axe. I put my trekking poles in my pack and use his sturdy hiking sticks. Up we go on a starry night with microspikes and broomsticks.

It is icy, extremely steep, but the alternative is no easier. The only way to get out of a sketchy spot is to move. One way or another, you have to move. I choose to move up.

Hit the top. Absolutely stunning. Make another hot drink.

We are the only people out in this wilderness. Two small people on top of a snow-covered mountain gazing at the stars. One of those nights when I felt like the stars were watching us.

I get this feeling that Mother Nature has finally decided we are worthy to pass. She will never let us off the hook, but she will let us pass.

We finally don our snowshoes and cross the ridge to Grasshopper Pass and the next traverse. Our slogan becomes "When in doubt, follow kitty." We know the right direction to go, can't see the trail, but there are lynx or bobcat prints that seem to know where the trail goes.

No matter what else happens, I have this moment. This moment on top of a starry snow-covered mountaintop. Everything that has happened before is worth it. Anything that happens after doesn't matter.

I have this.

44 miles to go. Wake up to fog. White on white. Takes us most of the day to go four miles. Now we have to trust the technology of Brr's GPS. Crossing meadows or open areas with no sign of a trail. The usual dip is covered by a drift. When it gets too slick and steep, we know we're above the trail. We don't like to descend because gaining any elevation is such hard work. Maps, compass, check the GPS, look for blazes, look for lines through the mist.

38 miles out. Harts Pass. Our last exit point. My biggest mental struggle. Getting this far today was brutal. If there had been a warm car, with warm people in it, I don't think I would've had the fortitude to continue. As luck would have it, there is just a bleak campsite.

Not much discussion. Make a hot drink. Cook some food. All Brr has to say is "If we don't continue, I'll regret it."

34 miles out. On top of another snow-covered mountain. I open up the tent in the morning for the difficult process of putting trash bags on my feet so I can struggle outside into the cold to pee. "Oh my God."

"What is it?" Brr asks.

"Look outside!" The world is stunning. Bright sun. Blue sky. A small tent on the mountaintop, surrounded by stoic snow-covered ridges and peaks. This is why we're still out here.

We've got this.

22 miles out. We actually made twelve miles today! There's a celebration. I have to do a mental shift from "we'll get as far as we can" to "we're going to make it!" I can finally let myself believe that I'll get there.

Canada is now our nearest out.

16 miles out. Six miles today. I worked for every inch. All day and most of the night for six miles. Up to Rock Pass, down the other side, up to Woody Pass. We kept switching who broke trail throughout the day.

We took a break at what we thought was the last switchback up. False summit. Got dark. Fog rolled in again. Took a turn down a wrong trail that was unsigned. We knew we were on a trail. We could see the line. The going was easy, but the ridge was on the wrong side. Kept waiting for a switchback to turn us the right way. GPS again. Turned around.

Wind was whipping up. Couldn't tell if it was snowing more or just blowing everything around. Post-holing up to knees or hips with snowshoes on. Brr's foot has a bruise from the snowshoes. He switched to spikes, and we kept rolling.

We worked for every step.

Sent a prayer to Mother Nature: *Please give us a break.*

The wind died. No more ice blowing in my eyes. I could see the line of the trail. We slowly followed it across huge drifts. Exhausted. Getting frustrated with everything. Stopped for a break but didn't want to deal with the wind chill, so we didn't cook and just keep moving.

Finally to the top of Lakeview Ridge. Above seven thousand feet. Everything was downhill from here. But I couldn't go on. We cooked and tried to see if we could get some more energy. But we're done for the night. We're supposed to get out tomorrow. We've already pushed the rendezvous back one day. But sixteen miles might be impossible.

Must sleep. Hope that tomorrow is a better day.

14 miles out. We hit the valley. Took all morning to traverse the ridge, descend the Devil's Staircase, and get down to Hopkins Pass.

We can do this. It's just six more miles to the border. Make spam burritos one last time (my favorite trail food: spam, Idaho potato mix, corn chowder, and Cheez-Its!). Ready to go.

3.5 miles to the border. Castle Pass. The world is black-and-white today. Cloud-covered sky, trees a green so dark they look black. Snow-covered world. A raven overhead. We take that as a good omen. We're flying today. Nothing can stop us now. The only question: can we get to the border with a little daylight left?

November 18. 5:30 p.m. PCT mile 2660. We hit the border.

This monument that I've been waiting to see for seven months is right before me.

Not a dream anymore.

I've had this image in my head of arriving here. How we imagine it is never how it turns out. It turns out the way it was going to happen all along. It turns out better than I imagine.

Dark. Victory yells. Running and jumping around like crazy. Disbelief. I pop open a bottle of champagne that I've carried for eighty miles. I can now admit to carrying it. (Otherwise that would have been a bottle quietly drunk in a corner.)

One more hiker mocha with the last of our coffee and instant breakfast mix. Sitting staring at the monument. This is really the end. We got each other to the end.

8 miles to get out. We have family waiting for us. And we don't want to camp in the broken tent on cold snow another night. It starts to snow giant flakes.

Eight miles to let it settle in. We're getting out. We've accomplished the goal. I have to go do something other than walk now.

Eight miles to laugh about all the moments. Favorite, worst, most epic, hardest, weirdest, most random.

4 miles out. One more pass. To the end, it is not easy. Mother Nature never lets it be easy.

11:30 p.m. Manning Park. Anticipation as we arrive at the road. Then the parking lot. The resort door is locked. A security guard pulls up right as we're taking off our packs. "They were just looking for you. Weren't sure if you were gonna make it out tonight."

Into warmth. Into waiting arms. Into a shower and clean, warm bed.

Into whatever happens next.

LARCH MADNESS

Compared to the extravaganza of fall color associated with New England's deciduous forests, the visual display that occurs in the North Cascades receives little attention as summer wanes and autumn arrives. The lone conifer that tries its best to keep up with the maples, beech, ash, and hickories of New England is the larch. While its conifer cousins retain their various shades of green throughout the North Cascades, the larch turns a spectacular shining yellow.

Larches are important forest trees across the northern hemisphere. They require a cool and fairly humid climate like we have in the temperate mountains of northwestern Washington and British Columbia and the immense boreal forests of Siberia and northern Europe. Larches are not very demanding of the soil and they can live a relatively long life, spanning more than one hundred years. These trees prosper in pure or mixed forests together with other conifers and more rarely broad-leaved trees. Larches may lose much of their canopy and still regrow needles the following year. This gives western larch a competitive advantage over other conifers where they share habitat.

The tree's thick bark and deciduous nature makes western larches fire-resistant and resilient from injury. As fire becomes a more consistent threat throughout the West, the larch appears to be well positioned for the challenge posed by global warming.

In the eastern United States, larches are often referred to as tamaracks. Colonists found the trees to be virtually knot-free and excellent for boatbuilding, posts, and paneling. Native Americans chewed resinous secretions from the tree as a candy and used extractions from the needles and branches to treat a variety of ailments. The larch trees we see along the northern reaches of the PCT are often growing at high enough elevations that their biggest threat is lightning and fire, not the logger's axe.

I live close enough to experience the larch in their full autumnal glory as they provide closure to one season and anticipation for another. The air is crisp while the colors of the landscape appear to pop in the lowering angle of late September sunlight. The majority of the PCT hikers are long gone when many locals make a yearly pilgrimage toward Rainy Pass in order to catch a last glimpse of summer and the golden larch. The larch reminds us that this summer will soon be a memory. Dreams and aspirations for next summer will likely form in the ensuing darker months ahead. When we return the larches will be waiting, but it won't be until fall that they will again reveal themselves, standing out the way these trees do.

—*Howard Shapiro*

DEALING WITH THE POST-TRAIL BLUES

KATHLEEN "TOKEN" NEVES

There is a Buddhist saying, "Begin, the rest is easy." Starting the PCT can be daunting but invigorating. That spirit can keep one going for many long miles. Ultimately the time will arrive when the last filtered water is gulped down, the sleeping bag stays in its place in your pack, and you come to the realization that the final mile and final steps have come and gone.

Kathleen "Token" Neves thru-hiked the PCT in 2018 and wrote about her transition back to the life she left behind at Campo. She shares her experience and feelings in unvarnished ways. Neves returned to the trail in 2019 only to have to exit after about eight hundred miles due to injury. She relates her feelings with an openness that comes from deep reflection on her experiences and her expectations while striking a balance between the two.

As my PCT thru hike was coming closer to the end, I kept hearing more and more from other hikers about *post-trail blues*. At first I didn't think it was a thing. How could not hiking make me depressed? After spending five months of my life living on a dirt trail and hiking over eighteen hundred miles, the possibility never crossed my mind. There were plenty of times when I was on trail and daydreamed about not having to hike for a day. The thing about thru hiking, though, is that it's less about hiking and more of a lifestyle. When you spend five months of your life hiking fifteen to twenty miles a day, sleeping in a tent, eating whenever you're hungry, filtering water whenever you're thirsty, and living with everything you need on your back, the nomadic lifestyle becomes a habit. You crave living on the trail. Spending a day or night in town becomes weird, so it makes sense why the transition period from trail life to city life isn't easy.

As I walked north, anytime a day hiker would ask me where I was hiking to, I'd tell them, "To Canada!" As I hiked the PCT each day, I imagined what the northern terminus would look like and how I would feel once I got there. I pictured myself being overwhelmed with happy emotions knowing I had accomplished the biggest thing in my life I'd ever set out to do. I thought about what song I would be listening to once I got there, what I would write in the logbook, the photo I would want to take of myself with the terminus monument, and what I would eat while I was there. After the northern terminus celebration, I figured, I would skip the rest of the way to Manning Park, knowing there were only eight miles between me, a warm bed, and unlimited warm showers. Not once did I ever imagine myself being sad about finishing my hike.

The morning after I got to Manning Park, the first thing I did was grab my phone and check the Guthook app. It was one of the habits I had developed over the preceding 153 days. It took me a minute to realize I wouldn't be hiking out that day. I didn't have to worry about finding a water source for the next ten or fifteen miles. I didn't have to look for a tent site that night. I didn't have to worry about the elevation gains for the day. I didn't have to figure out how many miles I would hike that day. The trail was over. We were at the end. I lay there in my warm bunk bed, kind of confused.

There was a time, before hiking the PCT, when I took for granted always having access to a flush toilet, running water, a warm shower, and a washer and dryer to do laundry. Having access to these things on the trail was considered a luxury. I'd gotten used to digging a hole anytime I had to poop or squatting behind a tree anytime I had to pee. Anytime I needed water, I'd have to not only find a water source but also filter the water before I could drink it and carry it with me throughout the day. Now I could just turn on the faucet and take all the water I needed whenever I needed it. On the trail I went days without washing my hands. Instead, I would bathe at the end of each day in my tent using baby wipes and pack them out in ziplock bags. Warm showers and doing a load of laundry were luxuries saved for town days.

Thanks to my dad, I had an easy introduction back into off-trail life. The day we got to Manning Park, we spent the night in a cabin with all my hiker trash friends, including Grit, the French couple Pine Nut and Gourmet, and Fitty Shrimp. The next morning, the French couple got a ride into Vancouver, we dropped Grit off at the Greyhound station in

Hope, and then we dropped Fitty Shrimp near the border so he could catch his bus. My dad and I spent the rest of the day driving around, being tourists in Canada.

Later that night, we decided to go to the movies. Since the movie theater was located in an outdoor shopping center and it was a Friday night, this would be my first time being around a large group of people since I started hiking the PCT back in April. I felt a bit anxious. It was weird being around so many people and so many cars. Everyone looked so clean. Then I started thinking about clothes. Here I was, still in my hiking leggings, shorts, town shirt, and town shoes (sandals), a clean and respectable town outfit. Everyone else seemed very dressed up. It felt a bit excessive. I couldn't stop thinking about how one of the first things I wanted to do when I got home was go through all of my own clothes and get rid of all my non-trail clothes.

As we waited to buy popcorn before the movie, I watched the teenagers in front of us taking selfies of themselves while in line. Then the mother of the teenagers turned around to us and complained about having to wait fifteen minutes in line to buy popcorn. I hadn't realized how long we'd been waiting there. I didn't care. I was at the movies with my dad and not on a time schedule. Her whining made me feel really uneasy. I could see the guy behind the counter was nervous. Maybe it was his first night, working at his first job? This was my first night being back in civilization. I was probably just as nervous as he was and could relate more to him than to the whining, impatient woman.

My first time going into a grocery store after getting off the trail was really weird too. It was hard to be in a grocery store and not think about resupplying for the next section. I would have to figure out what was already in my food bag, how many days it would take me to get to the next town, how much food I would need for the section, and how much of it was I willing to carry. I had to figure out how many meals and snacks I would need and whether I would be able to find something to eat I wasn't already sick of. Now that I was in town and off the trail permanently, I had to remind myself that I could go to the store whenever I wanted, whenever I was hungry, and I no longer had to worry about carrying the food I would need throughout the day.

I have missed hiking the PCT every single day since I've been back home. I miss the freedom of going wherever I wanted, whenever I wanted. I enjoyed not knowing what day of the week it was. I loved not having to worry about anything other than feeding myself, making sure I had enough water, and getting camp set up before it got dark. Since I've been back, I'm much more aware of myself, things around me, and other people's energy. I'm way more emotional than I've ever been in my life. All it takes is a small trigger or a certain song to bring up a trail memory, and I start crying.

There have been some cool perks with coming back to off-trail life. I enjoy and appreciate food so much more now. I learned on the trail you never say no to food or water. Whenever I meet up with friends now, I'm fully present with them and not distracted by technology. I no longer have a half-hour debate with myself at two in the morning trying to decide if I really need to get out of my cozy sleeping bag and tent to go pee in the cold and dark. I can just walk a few steps to a warm bathroom.

I've been back in civilization a little over a week now and know that post-trail blues is a thing, and it's been hitting me hard. It's hard to focus. I'm constantly overwhelmed by the amount of choices I have to make throughout the day. Life was simple when I only had to choose between pork or "oriental"-flavored ramen. I have yet to put away my pack and hiking gear. I still feel anxious around large groups of people. Driving makes me nervous. Even though I'm sleeping on a warm bed, I'm still sleeping in my sleeping bag. This must be a comforting mechanism. There is a certain level of sadness that follows me around throughout the day now. I miss hiking the PCT, not only physically but also mentally. I was the best version of myself out there. I had never been so dirty, tired, and happy in all my life.

As hard as this might be, I know this transition will soon pass. I have to keep myself busy, continue to share my trail stories with anyone who wants to listen, keep in touch with my hiker trash friends, and start planning the next adventure.

EPILOGUE

A CALL FOR ACTION

All of the prose and poetry found in this collection reflects shared membership in the Pacific Crest Trail community and a deep caring for this beloved trail. Each contributor describes an experience or appreciation derived from time on or near the PCT. Their intentions in sharing their story are both the same and different. Some tell of experiences that are harrowing, others humorous, informative, challenging, or celebratory. Some are told from the perspective of a thru hiker, others as section hikers or even day hikers. They vary in motivation. They vary by age, gender, and background. Those are the differences. The sameness is a theme that runs like the trail itself, curving here, dipping there, and exposing a view that takes one's breath away but still remains on the path we call the trail. Each contributor has been profoundly touched by their experience of the trail. The impact has often been life-changing and always life-affirming. Authors share their full-throated appreciation, their enduring love for the PCT. We hope that you, the reader, will share that love for the trail.

How do we find a place in our hearts and minds for the Pacific Crest Trail? One may develop an affinity for the Pacific Crest Trail through the stories found in this anthology and stop there. Others may read this book and find further inspiration to explore the natural world in their own area. Still others will find that getting out on the PCT for a day or a week or months becomes positively necessary for their well-being. For these people, nothing but hiking the trail will suffice in clarifying how they feel the way they do about this national treasure. However we develop our passion for the trail, it comes with responsibility.

For the Pacific Crest Trail to endure, we all must be stewards. As stewards for the PCT, we have an important charge. If we want the Pacific Crest Trail to last, we must do what we can to make that happen. For some that means volunteering to be on a trail maintenance crew. For others it means writing letters to decision makers. For still others it means sending money to organizations like the Pacific Crest Trail Association. There are myriad ways to be a steward of the trail, and efforts both large and small make a difference.

Through our stewardship we are creating a legacy. We are doing our best to ensure that the Pacific Crest Trail will be around for the next generation and the one after that and the one after that. As we face the encroachments of development and the challenges of overuse, wildfires, and other effects of climate change, the importance of effective stewardship could not be clearer.

Without thoughtful care the trail will certainly deteriorate, and the stories in this collection will become mere memories of a past that no longer exists. For now, though, these stories are seeds of hope, and it is our desire that reading them also sparks action.

A decade ago, in the first two volumes of *The Pacific Crest Trailside Reader*, our appeal for stewardship lacked the urgency we feel today. Now we join the calls to action made in this anthology by Mark Larabee and Alice Tulloch, who challenge us to tweak not only our approach to the trail but also our approach to the planet. Caring for the trail is more than leaving no trace while we are walking. That is a minimum. We must all adopt a life course that will help preserve the planet, otherwise the Pacific Crest Trail will be just one more casualty in a massive environmental crisis. Say good-bye to the glorious ribbon stretching from the arid landscape of Southern California, through the dramatic Range of Light and Klamath Mountains, to the peaks of the North Cascades.

Finally, we encourage you to consider one more action: tell your own story. Every story you tell, every story you write, and every story you share can be an act of stewardship. Stories will keep the magic and importance of the Pacific Crest Trail alive in our hearts and minds, recruit new lovers of the trail, and help to guarantee that it will live on.

ACKNOWLEDGMENTS

My relationship with the Pacific Crest Trail began more than four decades ago and has been a thread through my adult life. I will forever be indebted to Howard Shapiro and Jim Peacock who have been a constant throughout those many years. We have shared the trail and life's journey across countless miles with laughter, support, encouragement, and awe. I am a much better person because of our friendship. Thank you to Howard for being willing to co-edit this volume with me, tolerating my nitpicking tendencies and adding his touch to the final product which is far better because of his participation.

I am no less indebted to my wife and life partner, Amy Uyeki, who has supported my obsession with the PCT from the beginning. In addition to periodically joining me on the trail, she has parented in my absence, willingly contributed her wonderful art to each of the three PCT anthologies that I have been a part of, and patiently understood my commitment to walking and working on trails. I thank my parents, Mary and Pete Hughes, my daughters, Chisa and Mei Lan, and the extended Hughes and Uyeki clans for so many years of support and encouragement on all my endeavors. I am a very lucky man.

There are many who have joined me for sections of the PCT, provided generous logistical support, and many others, often nameless, who have demonstrated the kindness that I associate with PCT culture. Although Howard and I have singled out the PCTA as the beneficiary of all of our royalties, there are so many individuals past and present who have contributed to the creation, maintenance, and preservation of this national treasure. I honor them.

I am very grateful for the assistance and support we received from the staff of the Pacific Crest Trail Association including Liz Bergeron, Mark Larabee, Jack Haskel, and Megan Wargo who wrote pieces for the collection and facilitated contacts with a number of key contributors. Thank you, too, to the many hiker-writers who contributed their stories to this project.

And lastly, but very significantly, thank you once to again to Kate Rogers, Mary Metz, Chris Dodge, and the staff at Mountaineers Books for making this anthology possible. Thank you for believing in this project and recognizing the value and importance of stories as part of the legacy of the PCT.

—*Rees Hughes*

The Pacific Crest Trail stretches from one border to another in one continuous thread. I discovered that thread and my journey along its reach has stretched for more than half my lifetime. The trail has allowed me to discover some of my greatest strengths while also reminding me of my weaknesses. I never would have stitched all of the many sections together without the help and encouragement of many.

First and foremost, my unwavering hiking partners, brothers, and friends, Jim "Pierre" Peacock and Rees "Boris" Hughes. We started and finished together and now the trail extends onward. You two have literally picked me up when I have fallen, heard me, and helped me shape my ever-changing goals. You continue to provide the blazes I need to find my way.

I also want to acknowledge many others who have been integral to my journey both on and off the trail. Their efforts ultimately led me to this project. Jim Peacock reminded me of the "guardian angels" that come in and out of our lives. For me, they include my parents, my wife, Kathy, and daughters, Emily Shapiro and Jenny Riffle. Another is Amy Uyeki whose art has graced every edition of this work. Her vision is a gift and always speaks to me. Other angels include Billie Robinson, Doug Robinson, and Brad Furlong—all willing listeners, supporters, and hikers. Angel Tracy Dabbs created a system for us to track our progress with the authors and stories. That was magic! Kate Rogers, Mary Metz, and Chris Dodge at Mountaineers Books never hesitated in their belief in us and the importance of these stories while honoring the author's voices . . . angelic. The authors whose work lives in these pages: To a person, they joined us in contributing their work and ultimately the profits of the sale of these books to the Pacific Crest Trail Association. Real Trail Angels. Over time there have been numerous other angels I am indebted to for pickups, drop-offs, and even opening their homes and hearts to me, thereby lending me the insight to comprehend the many important PCT stories that exist out there.

Lastly, I want to acknowledge my co-editor Rees Hughes. He invited me to join in our first PCT hike and to this joint project. Your belief in me, then and now, that I had something to contribute lifted me to new heights. Thank you.

—Howard Shapiro

CONTRIBUTING WRITERS

Heather Anderson is a National Geographic Adventurer of the Year, three-time Triple Crown thru hiker, and professional speaker whose mission is to inspire others to "Dream Big, Be Courageous." Heather is the author of *Thirst: 2600 Miles to Home* and *Mud, Rocks, Blazes: Letting Go on the Appalachian Trail* and co-author of *Adventure Ready: A Hiker's Guide to Planning, Training, and Resiliency.*

Tami Asars is the author of four hiking guides, including *Hiking the Pacific Crest Trail: Washington.* An avid thru hiker, Tami has hiked the Pacific Crest Trail, the Continental Divide Trail, the Arizona Trail, the Colorado Trail, Wonderland Trail, and the West Coast Trail among others. She can be found at www.tamiasars.com.

In 2015, former management consultant, **Kathryn Barnes**, overcame her natural aversion to camping and the outdoors to take on the Pacific Crest Trail. A self-confessed daydreamer—"the one vocation I've successfully nailed"—Kathryn is a born-and-bred Londoner with a lust for travel who lives with her hiking partner Conrad.

David H. Baugher, a.k.a. "Chief," lives in the small town of Arnold, California, near Ebbetts Pass. After retiring in 2014 from his position as fire chief of the Ebbetts Pass Fire District, Dave began his Multi-Year Through-Hike (MYTH) of the PCT.

Matt Berger is an avid botanist and long-distance hiker who tries to document all the plant species he comes across on his hikes. He enjoys sharing what he finds with the world through photos and descriptions on Instagram (@sheriff_woody_pct) and other social media to get people interested in the world around them.

Liz Bergeron is executive director and CEO of the nonprofit Pacific Crest Trail Association. She lives in Sacramento, California.

Robert Birkby is an internationally recognized expert in trail design, outdoor education, and adventure travel. His books include *Lightly on the Land*, *Mountain Madness* (a biography of Everest climber Scott Fischer), and three editions of *The Boy Scout Handbook*.

Born in Whittier, California, **Rosemary L. Broome** discovered Northern California at the age of ten. After veterinary school at UC Davis, she moved to the Santa Cruz mountains. Rosemary shares her love of western landscapes with her husband, Guy, and two children, Chloe and Geoffrey. She is completing a memoir, *A Horse Runs Through It*.

Dorothy "Bacon Bit" Brown-Kwaiser is an interpretive park ranger who periodically decamps for long walks. Her essays—typed by thumb in a sleeping bag—have appeared in the PCTA's *Communicator*, on PCTA.org, and on trailsidereader.com. Dorothy lives in Oregon with her husband and their two future park ranger/firefighter thru hikers.

Heather "Mama Bear" Burror thru-hiked the Pacific Crest Trail with her then nine-year-old daughter, Sierra "Monkey," in 2012. Since then the pair have shared thousands of miles in the mountains, completing the Colorado Trail, Continental Divide Trail, and countless other hikes near their eastern Sierra home.

Mark "Flyboxer" Collins currently lives in Maryland and walked the PCT in 2010.

Ben Dake has enjoyed leading climbs in the Cascade Range and along the Pacific Crest Trail for the past fifty years.

Kimberlie Dame is an oncology nurse residing in Portland, Oregon. In her free time, she likes to escape as deep into the wilderness as possible for as long as possible. Kimberlie completed a thru hike of the PCT in 2013 after her 2012 attempt nearly killed her.

Mary E. Davison completed the Appalachian Trail, the Pacific Crest Trail, and, at the age of 76, the Continental Divide Trail. She wrote *Old Lady on the Trail* based on those journeys. Her latest book, *Aren't You Afraid?*, details her experiences walking the American Discovery Trail from the Atlantic Ocean to Nebraska.

Backpacking is hard because you have to stop at some point and make camp. **Andy Dischekenyan** doesn't like camping very much: camp chores are a hassle and the sleep is never great. But Andy finds the peace, sense of accomplishment, and rejuvenation are worth the sacrifice.

Natalie Fisher hiked the PCT in 2012 when she was twenty-two. Her adventures eventually led her to Cottage Grove, Oregon, where she now owns a small farm with her husband. Natalie raises sheep and ducks and sells homemade croissants at the local farmers market. She and Brr still marvel at their adventure together.

With over 25,000 miles of outdoor experience, **Shawn Forry** has continued to refine the limitations of ultralight travel. In collaboration with Justin Lichter, he has pioneered routes across the world including the spine of the Himalaya and the Southern Alps of New Zealand. The author of *Ultralight Winter Travel*, Shawn was inducted into the California Outdoors Hall of Fame in 2017.

Keith Foskett is the author of several books on the subject of long-distance thru-hiking, including *The Last Englishman: Thru-Hiking the Pacific Crest Trail*. In addition to the PCT, Keith has hiked the Camino de Santiago and the Applachian Trail logging more than 15,000 miles in recent years. Learn more at keithfoskett.com.

San Diego native **Karen Friedrichs** has hiked more than 1,000 miles on the PCT, completed the Appalachian Trail, and reached the summit of thirty of Colorado's fourteeners as well as forty-five of the US high points. Internationally, she has hiked the Great Walks in New Zealand, to the top of Australia, the West Coast and Juan de Fuca trails on Vancouver Island, and Chilkoot Trail from the ghost town of Dyea, Alaska, to Lake Bennett, British Columbia.

Steve Ghan has dreamed of completing the PCT ever since he walked across Washington State as a sixteen-year-old in 1973. After retiring from a career as a climate scientist, he sauntered the southernmost 1,500 miles in 2018, and hopes to savor the rest in the near future.

Scott Gnile has loved wilderness his entire life. After years of hiking and practice he set out to hike the PCT in 2016. He journaled every day in order to be able to share the experience with his twelve (thus far) grandkids. He lives in Northern California with his wife.

Peggy Goshgarian has lived beside the PCT for more than forty-five years and has worked clearing trails and packing mules and horses alongside Bill Roberts. Peggy has traveled solo with her horse and pack animal on the PCT from Seiad Valley north through Oregon and Washington and into Canada.

A Frenchman with a passion for outdoor activities, **Philippe Gouvet** used to teach American Studies at a university. He caught the PCT bug from Charlie Jones on the John Muir Trail in 1996, and attempted to thru-hike it in 2012 after retiring. It was a poor attempt, as his knees strongly disagreed with his desires.

As the trail information manager for the Pacific Crest Trail Association, **Jack Haskel** works to connect people to the PCT. He is involved with a variety of projects that benefit the trail, the trail's users, and the community that surrounds the experience. Jack has thru-hiked the Pacific Crest Trail, the Continental Divide Trail, and the Colorado Trail, and he is an obsessed weekend warrior.

Greg "Strider" Hummel (1956–2014) is past president of ALDHA-West and co-founded the Annual Day Zero PCT Kick Off in 1999 serving many years as president. Known for his tireless commitment to the PCT and his distinctive stature (6' 9" tall), Greg died following a battle with ALS. He is survived by his wife, Laurie, and five grown children.

Born in 1942 in Southern California, **Glenn William Jolley** took to the mountains early in life and continues to find time and places to revisit. Now in his late seventies, Glenn hikes the Olympics, Cascades, and trails on Mount Rainier. He lives on an island in the Puget Sound, Washington, with his wife and their two cats.

Sue Kettles has been married to Alex for forty-three years; she is the mother of four adult kids and has five grandchildren. Since her first hikes in 1991, she has done most PCT sections numerous times and California's Section A ten times. One of her best memories is hiking from Stevens Pass to Snoqualmie Pass with two daughters and a granddaughter . . . just passing on the love.

Megan Kirkpatrick studied Pacific Northwest forest ecology at Oregon State University. When she's not abandoning everything to be in the mountains or working in the field, she can be found among her chickens and plants on her homestead in the Skagit Valley. Megan's favorite place to view whitebark pine on the PCT is along the Glacier Peak section.

Kasey Koopmans was born in Seattle and raised in its suburbs but now lives in Oakland, California. As a kid, Kasey remembers her mom referring to her as "My Good Little Hiker." Behold, the power of suggestion! Kasey ran with the moniker, hiking the PCT in 2015 and the CDT in 2018.

Laurie Kramer was four months old when she first went backpacking. It took her mother two trips to the car to pack in all their gear. When Laurie was a child, her mom encouraged her to keep hiking by placing candy on the trail. To this day, Laurie looks down in search of gummies!

Nicholas Kristof is a Pulitzer Prize winner who writes columns for *The New York Times*, when he's not dragging his kids out on backpacking trips. Nick is happy that Caroline, his youngest, survived these trips; she is now running the family farm in Oregon.

Doug Laher is the father to perished PCT Class of 2020 thru hiker Trevor "Microsoft" Laher. Trevor died on March 27, 2020, on Apache Peak while attempting to thru-hike the PCT. He was only eleven days into his trek. Doug, his wife, Karen, and daughter, Olivia, live in Fort Worth, Texas.

After completing the PCT in 2015, **Chloe Lalonde** thru-hiked the Arizona Trail in 2016. She then moved to Atlanta, Georgia, to attend Emory University School of Medicine, where she is now a resident physician in internal medicine. She is an avid runner and hikes in the North Georgia mountains.

Mark Larabee is the advocacy director for the Pacific Crest Trail Association. He co-authored the book, *The Pacific Crest Trail: Exploring America's Wilderness Trail*, and was on a team of reporters awarded the 2007 Pulitzer Prize for Breaking News. He lives in Portland, Oregon.

Barney "Scout" Mann is an author, long-distance hiker, and outdoor advocate with articles appearing in *Backpacker, The New York Times,* and the Portland *Oregonian.* His recent book, *Journeys North: The Pacific Crest Trail,* was a 2021 Banff Book Festival finalist.

Anna Marston is a high schooler who loves running and reading. When she goes hiking she takes lots of photos, mostly of sunsets.

Brad Marston, Anna's father, is a climate and quantum physicist at Brown University who has been section hiking the PCT since 2013. He can be followed on Twitter @Brad_Marston. Anna, Brad, and Steve Ghan thank Mark Larabee and Heidi-Lynn Mitchell for their careful reading of their text.

Christine Martens lives in Asheville, North Carolina, with her husband, John Haffner. She has hiked more than 10,000 miles including completing the Appalachian Trail and the Pacific Crest Trail. She does not own a TV, so for entertainment she lets foster kittens destroy her house.

Aspen Matis is the bestselling author of the backpacking memoirs *Your Blue Is Not My Blue* and *Girl in the Woods.* A contributor to *The New York Times* and *The Atlantic,* she serves as a contributing editor of *The Best American Poetry.* She is currently working on a novel.

After retiring, **Patti McCarthy** lived in a van for three years. In 2019, she was the PCTA Terminus Host, finishing the PCT herself later that season. Patti currently shares a house in California with her husband and their puppy, Juno. She frequently questions if she was right to give up her nomadic lifestyle for a hot shower and comfy bed.

Chuck McKeever is a community college instructor, author, and union organizer. He lives in Seattle, Washington, with his wife.

Russ Mease is a recent escapee from the financial and software industries. His earliest memories are of exploring the mountains of the Pacific Northwest, experiences that drew him back to the wilderness as a thru hiker. Currently living in Portland, Oregon, Russ has completed solo thru hikes of the PCT (2012), CDT (2014), Sierra High Route (2015), and the Arizona Trail (2021) with his partner, Quyen.

Michael Meyer, a former *Newsweek* editor and senior UN official, is author of *1989: The Year That Changed The World* and founding dean of the graduate media school at Aga Khan University in Nairobi, Kenya.

Claire Henley Miller is the author of *Mile 445* and *Letters to Levi*. She currently lives in Chattanooga, Tennessee, with her husband, "Big Spoon," and their two children. Follow Claire on Instagram @clairehenleymiller.

Kit Mitchell lives with her partner, Jacob Gallagher, on the flanks of the Wind River Range in Wyoming. Kit is a storyteller and bird biologist, while Jacob ("Pyrite") is a programmer by day and adventurer at heart. They both continue to try to experience and learn from the world as much as is possible.

Kathleen "Token" Neves, known on YouTube as the "Hungry Hiker," is currently a Salomon and Osprey Packs ambassador who is passionate about hiking, backpacking, and spending time in the Great Outdoors. Her goal is to inspire others to get outside and plan their next adventure— whether that's a day hike, an overnight backpacking trip, or thru-hiking a long distance trail.

Rachel Newkirk is an artist and lover of nature with an infectious spirit for helpfulness and gratitude. She, her husband, Ian, and their four children have been "trail angels" for PCT hikers in the Tehachapi, California, area for almost a decade, opening both heart and home to weary travelers.

Writer **Aer Parris** ("Pine Nut," PCT 2015) finds solace in long self-powered journeys through the outdoors.

Carrot Quinn is the author of the books *Thru-Hiking Will Break Your Heart* and *The Sunset Route*. When not on the trail, Carrot lives in Alaska and the western United States.

Mama and Papa Raven have backpacked nearly 16,000 miles together, including a thru hike of the PCT in 1996. They have completed the JMT ten times, the Sierra High Route, Theodore Solomon, Wonderland Trail, and numerous other hikes throughout the Sierra and Cascades. Hiking the PCT in 2015, the CDT in 2017, and the AT in 2019, Mama, Papa, and their two children, Will and Juniper, earned hiking's Triple Crown.

Bill Roberts has been packing mules and building trails and bridges in Northern California since the early 1970s. He is also a "cowboy poet," writing poems that, like his trail work, have a lasting impact. The Crest Trail is part of him and he is a vital part of the Crest Trail.

Hailing from Louisiana, **Will "Akuna" Robinson** is an army veteran who discovered hiking while looking for ways to treat his post traumatic stress disorder. In 2016 he embarked on his first PCT trek. On September 15, 2019, Akuna completed the Continental Divide Trail, becoming the first Black man to achieve hiking's Triple Crown.

Shawnté Salabert is a Los Angeles–based freelance writer interested in the connections between humans and the natural world. Her work has appeared in *Adventure Journal, AFAR, Alpinist, Backpacker, The California Sunday Magazine, Outside,* and *Sierra,* among other outlets. Shawnté is the author of *Hiking The Pacific Crest Trail: Southern California.*

Ian Sarmento was born and raised in Chester County, Pennsylvania. He thru-hiked the Appalachian Trail northbound in 2008 and then completed his Pacific Crest Trail thru hike in 2012.

David Smart is a student of life and author of *The Trail Provides.* Every once in a while he updates his blog, podcast, and social media presence with insights and stories, which can be found at thinkingwithdavid.com. He would love to hear from you and connect if you feel called.

Hiking the PCT in 2018 was the culmination of a thirty-eight-year dream for **Eric Smith**, the ultimate expression of a life spent exploring and appreciating the natural world. He continues to enjoy the outdoors, working as a guide in order to share the infinite and varied wonders of the Colorado Plateau with others.

Gwynneth "Gizmo" Smith walked the Pacific Crest Trail (at least the parts that weren't actively burning) in 2014 with her partner, Dirt Trap. She went on to walk the Arizona Trail in 2016 and looks forward to continuing to do a lot of walking—hard and otherwise—for as long as she can.

Gail D. Storey meditates, jumps out of cakes, and writes a blog (GailStorey. com). Her book *I Promise Not to Suffer: A Fool for Love Hikes the Pacific*

Crest Trail won the National Outdoor Book Award as well as the Barbara Savage Award from Mountaineers Books.

Cheryl Strayed is the author of the *New York Times* bestseller *Wild*, as well as three other popular titles, *Tiny Beautiful Things*; *Torch*; and *Brave Enough*. She lives in Portland, Oregon.

Alice "Stone Dancer" Tulloch (PCT Class of 2006) is an environmental engineer and climate activist. In addition to hiking on the PCT, Alice has hiked the JMT, CDT, and elsewhere.

With a love of the outdoors instilled by his father, **Michael Tyler** has been hiking and backpacking since he was a young child. After completing the PCT in 2018, and hiking most of it again in 2020, he has set his sights on the Appalachian Trail.

Amy Uyeki is a mixed media artist whose work focuses on narrative. Her art has explored her cultural background as well as social issues. She has lived in Northern California for the past thirty-five years and often draws inspiration from the natural beauty and wildness of the landscape. Learn more at amyuyeki.com.

Mark Votapek is a professional cellist, specializing in solo, chamber, orchestra, and pedagogy. He has held title positions in orchestras such as the Saint Louis Symphony and schools such as Interlochen Arts Academy. Mark is the proud father of a happy toddler daughter, and calls San Francisco home, partly because it's near the PCT.

Megan Wargo is the director of land protection for the Pacific Crest Trail Association where she works on landscape-scale conservation. She lives in the San Francisco Bay Area and enjoys spending time outside with her husband, Dan, and son, Jacob.

Barbara Wiedemann, professor emerita at Auburn University Montgomery, is the author of four chapbooks: *Half-Life of Love* (2008), *Sometime in October* (2010), *Death of a Pope and Other Poems* (2013), and *Desert Meditations* (2018). She spent five months on the PCT in 2015, completing much of it with her dog Angel.

Bob Welch is a longtime columnist for the *Register-Guard* in Eugene, Oregon. He is the author of more than two dozen books, including *Cascade Summer: My Adventure on Oregon's Pacific Crest Trail*. He hopes to publish a sequel, *Seven Summers (And a Few Bummers)*, soon after he completes the PCT.

Crystal Gail Welcome is an experiential educator, public speaker, author, storyteller, activist, and Black outdoor leader. She chooses to speak out against racial injustice in the United States by hiking and giving voice to her experiences. Crystal is the founder of the non-profit youth organization Only Footprints.

ABOUT THE EDITORS

Growing up in the wilds of Kansas, **Rees Hughes** found the lure of the mountains so irresistible that he traded the flatlands for Seattle, the Cascades, and finally Northern California's Klamath Knot. Although he has hiked all over the world, the Pacific Crest Trail has been his true love for more than forty years. He applied his knowledge of and interest in the PCT to co-editing *The Pacific Crest Trailside Reader: California* and *The Pacific Crest Trailside Reader: Oregon & Washington*, a two-volume anthology of stories published by Mountaineers Books. He is also the author of a popular hiking guide, *Hiking Humboldt*; serves on the Board of the Bigfoot Trail Alliance; and coordinates a local Volunteer Trail Stewards program.

After a forty-year teaching career that included a focus on students with special needs, **Howard Shapiro** retired from full time teaching in 2016. He has spent more than four decades hiking the Pacific Crest Trail and recently completed all sections. He has spent countless hours in the North Cascades near his home, as well as hiked extensively in Europe, Nepal, Canada, and elsewhere. He joined the editorial team for The Pacific Crest Trailside Reader website in 2017.

The Pacific Trailside Reader: California

—Rees Hughes and Corey Lee Lewis, editors

The Pacific Trailside Reader: Oregon & Washington

—Rees Hughes and Corey Lee Lewis, editors

Find more historical stories of the people, places, and adventures of the Pacific Crest Trail! These two original volumes of *The Pacific Crest Trailside Reader*, published by Mountaineers Books (2011), together showcase short excerpts from classic works about and boot-tested stories from the trail.

Mary Austin, Barry Lopez, Ursula LeGuin, Cindy Ross, William O. Douglas, Jeffrey Schaffer, John Muir, Mark Twain, and so many others tell compelling trail tales, including historical accounts, American Indian myths and legends, environmental perspectives, encounters with wildlife and wild weather, and plenty of trail magic.

Sales of each of *The Pacific Crest Trailside Readers* benefit the Pacific Crest Trail Association (PCTA). Learn more online at https://pcttrailsidereader.com.

OTHER TITLES YOU MIGHT ENJOY FROM MOUNTAINEERS BOOKS

A BLISTERED KIND OF LOVE
Angela and Duffy Ballard

"This book was such a page-turner that the co-authors would have been hard-pressed to write anything more exciting even if it had been a fiction thriller." –Foreword Reviews

WALKING TOWARD PEACE
Cindy Ross

". . . an ode to those who serve, an accounting of the true costs of that service, and the stories of healing that only the natural world can bring." –Shannon Huffman Polson

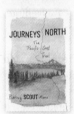

JOURNEYS NORTH: THE PACIFIC CREST TRAIL
Barney Scout Mann

"Here's the next best thing to being on the Pacific Crest Trail yourself!" —Richard Louv

THIRST: 2600 MILES TO HOME
Heather "Anish" Anderson

"Beautifully and deftly written and intimate and searing in its honesty, Anish's is a quest to conquer the trail and her own inner darkness." —Foreword Reviews

I PROMISE NOT TO SUFFER
Gail D. Storey

"Witty, wise and full of heart . . . as inspiring as it is hilarious, as poignant as it is smart." —Cheryl Strayed

JOURNEY ON THE CREST
Cindy Ross

A colorful cast of characters is sharply drawn in both words and pictures in this account of a young woman's 1982 thru hike of the PCT.